S0-BEJ-002

LEGENDS *of* ROCK

Dalmatian
P·R·E·S·S
an imprint of dalmatian publishing group

LEGENDS OF ROCK

Published by Dalmatian Press, an imprint of Dalmatian Publishing Group.

Produced by Hylas Publishing, 129 Main Street, Irvington, NY 10533.

Publisher: Sean Moore
Publishing Director: Karen Prince
Art Directors: Gus Yoo, Brian MacMullen
Editorial Director: Aaron Murray
Senior Editor: Ward Calhoun
Editors: Suzanne Lander, Rachael Lanicci, Lisa Purcell
Designer: Gus Yoo
Proofreader: Ed Sczesnak

ISBN: 1-40373-719-3
16563-0607

07 08 09 10 SFO 10 9 8 7 6 5 4 3 2 1

LEGENDS *of* ROCK

MARJORIE GALEN and GORDON MATTHEWS

CONTENTS

INTRODUCTION

Rock and roll music is now over half a century old. It's mutated in many different directions, some that its founding fathers could never have foreseen. The sound seemed to spring full blown in the '50s, when rhythm and blues collided with country and gospel music in the form of Elvis Aaron Presley. It was a sound young America had been waiting for. But long before Elvis shook his hips on national television, rock and roll was being built in backwoods shacks and boogie-woogie bars up and down Highway 61 from Chicago to New Orleans, through Memphis, Tennessee.

Experts continue to argue about what song should be considered the earliest rock and roll record. Some say Sister Rosetta Tharpe's rollicking gospel music, including her 1938 song "Rock Me," shared much with '50s rock and roll. Others point to the powerful blues guitar work of Big Bill Broonzy. Sam Phillips, owner of the famed Sun Records, insisted that Jackie Brenston and his Delta Cats' 1951 recording of "Rocket 88" (actually Ike Turner and his Kings of Rhythm under a different name) was the first rock and roll record, with its distorted guitar, upbeat groove, and lyrics appreciating a modern automobile. Others, like *Rolling Stone* magazine, point to the Elvis Presley 1954 song, "That's All Right (Mama)," originally written and recorded by Arthur "Big Boy" Crudup. The following year Bill Haley's "Rock around the Clock" topped the *Billboard* charts, and teenage culture and rock and roll music were forever fused.

Of course, no one can imagine rock and roll without such innovators as Bo Diddley, Chuck Berry, and Little Richard. It seems that everyone does agree that Cleveland disc jockey Alan Freed first popularized the phrase "rock and roll"—which was African-American slang for the proverbial roll in the hay—to describe the R&B music he was playing for the first time for a mixed black and white audience. Although rocking may have originally had sexual connotations, it ended up becoming more of a transcendental experience in which pleasure and power chords, shared with a gathering of like-minded friends, feels heroic, historic, and just plain fun.

From the screams of Beatlemaniacs to the mosh pits of Green Day fans, rock and roll is continually being rediscovered and passed down from generation to generation. Young bands today may use a rockabilly rhythm mixed with a vocal style courtesy of Talking Heads' David Byrne, while combining the experimental textures of David Bowie and Brian Eno's collaborations with Beach Boys production values. The great thing about rock and roll is that with a minimal amount of effort and skill, a group of folks can get on the same page musically and bang out a raucous racket of their own design. Three chords, some amplification, and a backbeat and you are suddenly ready to put on a show.

Legends of Rock gathers together pioneering artists from the '50s to today's indie-rock garage punks—and everything in between. Every teenager with a guitar builds on what came before, but the legends of rock were chosen for their innovation. Sometimes these breakthrough artists didn't even sell very many records, but they changed the course of music and affected the culture that followed. Captain Beefheart and Iggy and the Stooges come to mind. Other legendary rockers gathered up elements that were around and exploded them into the stratosphere, building on less-focused ideas and taking them multiplatinum. Think Metallica and Pearl Jam.

This rock and roll stew is made up of rockabilly, surf music, girl groups, British invasion, folk, soul, psychedelia, funk, heavy metal, punk, new wave, hardcore, and more—all cross-pollinating and, in the end, all part of the legendary status of rock and roll. Some of the legends of rock burned brightly and then were gone, but they left solid—if small—bodies of work behind. Others, like Neil Young, have continued to innovate through the decades, constantly reinventing themselves and figuring out ways to keep it interesting. (With more than 30 albums to his name, Neil is defying his own lyric, "it's better to burn out than to fade away.")

Technology has changed a lot in the years since rock and roll took over the popular music scene. Forty-fives—for those who don't know, small 7-inch records with one song on each side, played at a speed of 45 revolutions per minute—have given way to a succession of new music delivery systems. Remember 8-track tapes? It's now possible to wake up in the middle of the night with a song on your mind, walk over to your computer, and download it in less than a minute for only 99¢. We have come full circle and are now in an era where every song is a single in cyberspace. It's hard to imagine it was ever any other way.

Times, they are really changing, and rock and roll, once considered at worst a dangerous corrupting influence or at best a passing fancy, is clearly here to stay. From sold-out stadium shows to claustrophobic clubs, people around the world are drawn to this music and its undeniable energy. It may only be rock and roll, but we like it.

Elvis Presley's telegenic good looks helped him spread the gospel of rock and roll faster and farther than anyone before or since.

AC/DC

1973–

The ferocious young rockers who busted out of Australia in 1973 were cocked and loaded for their shot on the world stage. Punk rock was raising its angry head, and AC/DC's balls-to-the-wall music redefined the harder side of rock with a grittier approach relying on big brash power chords, simple beats, and vocals that sounded like they'd been on a highway to hell and back. Their message was simple: There will be no dancing gnomes or fairy kings in our songs, no elaborate progressive time signatures, no fancy harmonies or glittery stage costumes. We are here to rock you hard and help you connect with the hedonistic pleasure zone in your head that imagines the night has much to offer . . . even if all it really adds up to is spilled bong water on the back seat of Dad's new car.

Brian Johnson sings and Angus Young plays lead guitar as they rock the house (or in this case, Wembley Arena) during a stop on their 2000 *Stiff Upper Lip* tour.

Malcolm Young and younger brother Angus, age 15, came from a down-under rock dynasty. Their older brother was part of The Easybeats, who scored a huge international hit with "Friday on My Mind." Angus helped forge AC/DC's bad-boy image by playing lead guitar in his old school uniform, complete with short pants and cap. Lead singer Bon Scott, of the party 'til you puke and spit blood school of singing, had a voice that roared over Angus' beefy power chords—schoolboy meets devil!

"I'm sick and tired of people saying that we put out 11 albums that sound exactly the same. In fact, we've put out 12 albums that sound exactly the same." —Angus Young

In 1979, the band busted out with *Highway to Hell*, their first million seller. This initial success, however, was nearly derailed by the drunken death-by-misadventure of Scott. The band picked up the pieces with Scott sound-alike Brian Johnson on vocals, and produced their masterpiece *Back in Black*, a tribute to Scott. *Back in Black* became one of the best-selling albums of all time, and catapulted AC/DC to the top of the rock and roll heap.

AC/DC have kept touring and releasing albums at a regular pace over the ensuing decades. Their song, "It's a Long Way to the Top (If You Wanna Rock 'n' Roll)," was part of a quintessential rock 101 lesson taught by Jack Black in the 2003 film *School of Rock*—that pretty much says it all.

AC/DC's Secret Weapon

The real secret weapon of AC/DC was their producer Robert John "Mutt" Lange, the reclusive musical mastermind who isn't afraid of any genre. Lange, born in 1948 in what is now Zambia, understood better than anyone at the end of the last century how to turn sonic ear candy into platinum goodies. Lange's first major hit album was AC/DC's *Highway to Hell*, which followed the massively successful *Back in Black*. Since then Lange has been all over the rock, pop, and country charts producing, and sometimes co-writing songs, with successful artists like Def Leppard, Bryan Adams, The Cars, and his wife, Shania Twain. Lange, enamored of her first album, arranged to meet Twain, and has since helped her to cross over from country to the pop charts.

GREATEST HITS

Year	Song
1975	"It's a Long Way to the Top (If You Wanna Rock 'n' Roll)"
1979	"Highway to Hell"
1980	"Back in Black"
	"You Shook Me All Night Long"
	"Hells Bells"
1981	"Let's Get It Up"
	"For Those About to Rock"

AEROSMITH

1970–

Since he was barely in long pants, Steven Tyler was a wild kid kicking around the music scene, looking for a way in. Joe Perry was more laid back, the kind of guy who would sit around all day watching TV, playing his guitar until he was an absolute virtuoso. The two saw themselves as the new Jagger/Richards, with an injection of Led Zeppelin's power. Tyler, originally a drummer, soon became the full-time lead singer. By 1972, Aerosmith signed a deal with Columbia Records; they soon released their eponymous first album, and had a minor hit with the song "Dream On." Their third album, *Toys in the Attic,* was a major breakthrough, spawning hits like "Sweet Emotion" and "Walk This Way," and reviving "Dream On" as a hit single.

STEVE TYLER AND HIS AEROSMITH BRETHREN (AMAZINGLY ALL ALIVE AND STILL KICKING) WERE INDUCTED INTO THE ROCK AND ROLL HALL OF FAME IN 2001.

Tyler and Perry were famous for more than their string of hits in the '70s. The pair were known as the Toxic Twins, for indulging in large quantities of drugs and alcohol. By the time Perry left the band for a solo career in 1979, Tyler was an out-of-control, drug-addled narcissist who'd let his energetic Dionysian side get the best of him. Aerosmith was virtually dysfunctional, relying on repackaged greatest hits, until Tyler and Perry reunited in 1984. Over the next couple of years, both finally kicked their old habits and focused on the music.

In 1986, Aerosmith scored a remarkable hit that was the first real rap/rock crossover, with Run-DMC's cover of "Walk This Way." This collaboration revitalized Aerosmith's flagging career. Reborn and rededicated, Aerosmith's new-found mainstream appeal helped them crank out a string of platinum albums with many hits, often co-authored by song doctor Desmond Child.

"We just wanted to be the biggest thing that ever walked the planet." —Steven Tyler

If there were any remaining doubt about their superstar status, Aerosmith appeared in an episode of *The Simpsons* in 1991 and played the Super Bowl halftime show 10 years later. It is clear Tyler, Perry, and company are back in the saddle to stay.

Run-DMC

It's been said that producer Rick Rubin encouraged Run-DMC to cover the classic rock hit from his childhood, Aerosmith's "Walk This Way," on their 1986 album *Raising Hell*. Rubin was a co-founder of Def Jam Records with Russell Simmons, whose brother, Joseph "DJ Run" Simmons, was in the band. The single went to the top of the rock charts, becoming the first hip-hop record to have major mainstream success. Tyler and Perry guested on vocals and guitar and appeared in the video, which showed Aerosmith in one room and Run-DMC in another—the wall between the rooms is eventually broken down. The video itself was a breakthrough for hip-hop artists on MTV and the album was the first rap album to go platinum.

GREATEST HITS

Year	Song
1975	"Sweet Emotion"
1976	"Dream On" (reissue)
1977	"Walk This Way"
1987	"Dude (Looks Like a Lady)"
1990	"Janie's Got a Gun"
1993	"Cryin'"
1994	"Crazy"
1998	"I Don't Want to Miss a Thing"

THE ALLMAN BROTHERS BAND

1969–

After giving music a try in L.A., Duane Allman got work as a session guitarist at Fame Studios in Muscle Shoals, Alabama—check out his playing on Wilson Pickett's take on "Hey Jude." The young longhaired freak was in contrast to the older, white session cats who had backed Aretha Franklin and Little Richard. But his crazy sound brought something new to the proceedings in a time when American studios were grappling with the new music: psychedelia and British heavy blues.

Gregg and Cher

Hard-living white blues singer from the South met—and married—L.A. pop princess with a variety show. In 1975, Cher married Gregg on the rebound, exactly three days after her divorce from Sonny Bono became final. Cher knew she'd made a mistake and filed for divorce 10 days after the wedding, but she was already pregnant with son Elijah Blue Allman. So Cher and Gregg spent the next few years in a state of on-again, off-again marriage. They collaborated on an album—*Allman and Woman: Two the Hard Way*—that was skewered by critics and a flop with fans. In 1979 they finally divorced. Elijah Blue went on to become a goth rocker with a band called Deadsy.

In 1969, Duane parlayed an offer from Capricorn Records into a deal for The Allman Brothers Band, featuring dual lead guitars, Duane (focusing on slide) and Dickey Betts—the two playing twin lead harmonic runs for a sound that defined Southern rock—Berry Oakley on bass, Duane's little brother Gregg on lead vocals and Hammond organ, and the twin drums of Butch Trucks and Jaimoe Johanson. Their first two albums didn't make a big splash, but word of mouth about their great live shows led them to release *At Fillmore East*, which exploded on FM underground radio and caught on with the suburban youth of the day. The album was an invitation to a remarkable live event that the kids wanted to be a part of. The Allmans became famous for long jams, both live and on records, and set the stage for the Southern rock explosion to follow.

In 1971, in the middle of recording *Eat a Peach*, Duane died in a motorcycle crash in Macon, Georgia. Less than a year later, bassist Oakley died as a result of injuries from his own crash only a few blocks away from Duane's. As Gregg fought his demons, the band became a vehicle for Betts, who took their incredible following into the Top 40 with the smash hit "Ramblin' Man." The band has gone through its share of break-ups and make-ups along the way but they continue to play to sold-out houses, taking the mantle left behind by the Grateful Dead for the '70s band that has jammed on longer than anybody.

NUGGET: *Eat a Peach*, their 4th album—half studio, half live—solidified their place in the rock pantheon. It was rumored that "eat a peach" referred to the erroneous story that Duane, who died during the recording, had plowed into the back of a peach truck.

GREATEST HITS

Year	Song
1971	"Whipping Post"
	"In Memory of Elizabeth Reed"
1972	"Blue Sky"
	"Melissa"
1973	"Ramblin' Man"
	"Jessica"

Despite its longevity, the Allman Brothers Band (previously the Allman Joys) went through a lot of turnover. This 1980–82 lineup (with Gregg and Dickey standing in front) is the only one without Jaimoe.

THE BAND

1967–1999

The Band was a mythic rock and roll act that America almost dreamed up out of the folklore of folk songs, moonshine, and juke joints. Once the members manifested themselves, they were welcomed into our consciousness with open arms, even if they were almost all Canadian!

After the Band (from left: Richard Manuel, Rick Danko, Robbie Robertson, Levon Helm, and Garth Hudson) broke up in 1976, the surviving members of the original group (Manuel died in 1986) didn't get back together to record another album until their 1993 *Jericho*.

The Band came together in Toronto—Robbie Robertson, Garth Hudson, Richard Manuel, Levon Helm, and Rick Danko—as the Hawks, the back-up band for American blues belter Ronnie Hawkins. Eventually they caught the ear of Bob Dylan. Dylan was a folkie who'd seen the power of The Beatles and was looking for a rock and roll band to back him up on a world tour. The Hawks fit the bill. During the notorious 1965–66 tour, they were often met with indignation by folk music purists who didn't care for Dylan's new electric sound. Afterwards, the Hawks returned to Woodstock, New York, and gathered in a pink house down the street from their boss. It was in this house where the group collaborated with Dylan and developed their unique backwoods rock sound. Their sessions in the basement of the pink house gave birth to their impressive debut album *Music from Big Pink* (1968). The album contained several Dylan compositions as well as the Robertson-penned classic "The Weight," which was featured in the film *Easy Rider*.

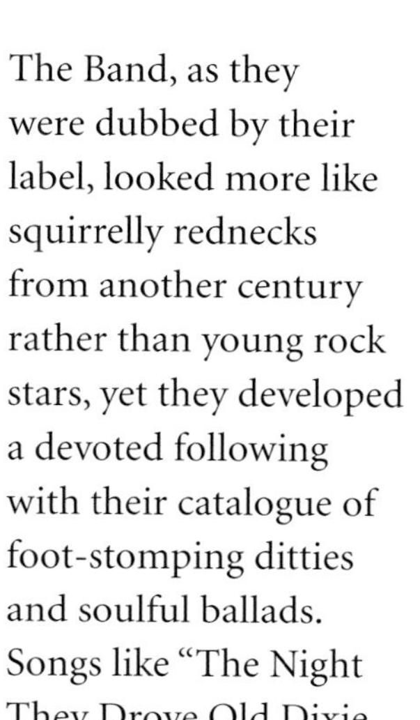

The Band, as they were dubbed by their label, looked more like squirrelly rednecks from another century rather than young rock stars, yet they developed a devoted following with their catalogue of foot-stomping ditties and soulful ballads. Songs like "The Night They Drove Old Dixie Down," with Helm's raspy, mournful vocals remain as powerful today as they were in 1969. The Band's final concert with the original line-up, preserved on film and album as *The Last Waltz* , was a larger-than-life take on a rock concert event and has kept the dream of this talented group alive all these years later. If you weren't lucky enough to see the Band in person, the film is the next best thing.

"That's really the way to do a recording—in a peaceful, relaxed setting, in somebody's basement, with the windows open and a dog lying on the floor."

—Bob Dylan, on recording with The Band in the basement of Big Pink

NUGGET: Levon Helm and Garth Hudson got a chance to work with their hero, blues legend Muddy Waters, when the pair recorded the critically acclaimed *Muddy Waters Woodstock Album* at Helm's studio in Woodstock, New York, in 1975.

The Last Waltz

Finally tired of touring, The Band arranged for director Martin Scorcese, a long-time fan, to film their final show at the Winterland Ballroom in San Francisco on November 25, 1976. Interspersed with interviews with band members, *The Last Waltz* brought the whole mythic history of the Band together on one stage. Joining the group in their farewell performance were luminaries such as Dylan, Muddy Waters, Van Morrison, Joni Mitchell, Neil Young and many others. The result was arguably the greatest concert film ever made.

GREATEST HITS

Year	Song
1968	"The Weight"
1969	"Up on Cripple Creek"
	"The Night They Drove Old Dixie Down"
1970	"Rag Mama Rag"
	"The Shape I'm In"
	"Life is a Carnival"
1971	"Strawberry Wine"

THE BEACH BOYS

1961–

In the beginning, the Beach Boys were brothers Brian, Dennis, and Carl Wilson, along with cousin Mike Love and good friend Al Jardine. Murry, the Wilson boys' father, was a frustrated songwriter and dysfunctional family man who managed the band. The one place where everyone seemed to get along was around the family piano.

Brian, the eldest son, had a natural gift for harmony and composition. When his brother Dennis (the cute one) took up the surfing craze, the muse first struck. Brian, who'd never been on a board, wrote "Surfin.'" The song featured Mike Love's signature nasal lead and was eventually picked up by Capitol Records. The Beach Boys sound blended Chuck Berry and Doo Wop with the harmonies of the Four Freshman for a sound that put them on the charts over and over. Before the Beatles reached these shores the Beach Boys ruled the airwaves with hits like "Surfin' Safari" and "Surfer Girl."

From there came a slew of car songs, songs about being true to one's school, and stealing Daddy's Thunderbird. Some suggest that *All Summer Long* was the first rock and roll concept album. Wilson's odes to teendom culminated in the ultimate cruising anthem, "I Get Around," and the West Coast fantasy opus, "California Girls." The opening chords of that song hinted at just how musically deep Brian Wilson was becoming.

While head Beach Boy Brian Wilson (center) crafted multipart vocal harmony and R&B rhythms, the singing of (from right to left) Carl, Dennis, Al, and Mike really gave the group its distinctive "California sound."

GREATEST HITS

Year	Song
1962	"Surfin'"
1963	"Surfin' USA"
	"Little Deuce Coupe"
1964	"I Get Around"
	"Fun, Fun, Fun"
1965	"Help Me Rhonda"
	"California Girls"
1966	"Wouldn't It Be Nice"
1967	"Good Vibrations"
	"Heroes and Villains"
1969	"Do It Again"
1973	"Sail On Sailor"
1988	"Kokomo"

The Beach Boys kept up a frantic pace of touring and recording. It was finally too much for Brian, who had a nervous breakdown in 1966 as they were about to leave for a European tour. Brian stayed home to work in the studio and Glen Campbell took his place on the road. After Campbell left to pursue his solo career, Bruce Johnston (who later wrote the Barry Manilow hit, "I Write the Songs," as a tribute to Brian) took his place.

NUGGET: The first thing people heard from the ill-fated *SMiLE* project was the revolutionary single "Good Vibrations," a song that completely raised the bar in pop music. Brian described it as "a pocket symphony" based around the idea of all the good vibrations one could pick up when inspired by the sight of a beautiful girl.

Inspired by the Beatles' *Rubber Soul*, Brian, working with lyricist/adman Tony Asher, made the landmark album *Pet Sounds*. Painstakingly assembled in the studio with the Wrecking Crew, a well-known group of L.A. session musicians, Brian created a sonic masterpiece much more introspective than anything he had yet recorded. When the band returned from the road, they didn't know what to make of the new direction, but recorded their vocals anyway. Foolishly, the record company released a greatest hits album at the same time and *Pet Sounds* languished, despite classics like "God Only Knows" and "Wouldn't It be Nice."

"I've often played Pet Sounds and cried. It's that kind of an album for me." —Paul McCartney

Brian put up a tent in his living room and built a sandbox around his piano so he could feel like he was living at the beach. He surrounded himself with a bunch of young creative types and a sycophant or two and began recording his major work, a song cycle called *SMiLE*, which he considered a "teenage symphony to God." Unfortunately, Brian couldn't figure out how to finish *SMiLE*. Summer turned into fall and the Beatles released *Sgt. Pepper's Lonely Hearts Club Band*, their answer to *Pet Sounds*. Brian, the ultra-competitive maestro, had dropped the ball. Suddenly the Beach Boys were seen as passé, belonging to a much more innocent time.

As the '70s began, Brian's involvement was more marginal. *Surf's Up* got its title from a lost *Smile* song by Brian and Van Dyke Parks. He also contributed "'Til I Die," wherein he describes himself as a cork bobbing in a raging sea. It was a long way from "Fun Fun Fun." When his father died, Brian retreated to bed and indulged in drugs and junk food.

In the mid-'70s a new generation discovered the Beach Boys with the release of *Endless Summer*, a double album of all their early hits, which sent them to the top of the charts again. They struck again in 1988 with the song "Kokomo," their first #1 in two decades, which proved without a doubt that the Beach Boys still knew how to surf those airwaves.

THE BEACH BOYS WERE AT THE TOP OF THE CHARTS AND THE DARLINGS OF BOTH FANS AND CRITICS WHEN THEY PERFORMED FOR THIS YMCA BENEFIT AT THE HOLLYWOOD BOWL IN NOVEMBER 1963.

THE BEACH BOYS INITIALLY PERFORMED AS THE PENDLETONS, AFTER THE POPULAR SURFER SHIRT. THE NAME WAS CHANGED TO THE MORE OBVIOUS BEACH BOYS FOR THEIR FIRST SINGLE, "SURFIN.'"

SMiLE

SMiLE was an ambitious album that was never finished by the Beach Boys. In 1966, Brian Wilson set out to make what he believed would be the greatest album of all time. He wanted to create a new kind of positive pop music. He was feeling his way through the process, recording songs in sections, and then attempting to make sense of all the pieces later. A song like "Good Vibrations" had hours of tape attached to it as Brian moved the sounds around in his head, trying to pull fantastic new arrangements from the ether.

Themes were introduced and would reappear later in the album. Many of the songs were part of an elements suite, representing earth, air, fire, and water. There were the concrete noises of hammering, vegetables being chewed, and fire engine sirens. The brilliant young composer Van Dyke Parks became Brian's partner in crime, penning surreal lyrics like "over and over the crow cries uncover the cornfield," for the song "Cabinessence." "Poetic, beautiful even in its obscurity," said Leonard Bernstein about the song "Surf's Up." *SMiLE* was supposed to be the first album on the Beach Boys Brother Records label, and album jackets were even printed. Internal band squabbles, drug experimentation, and the massive scope of the project all contributed to *Smile* being shelved. In 2004, 38 years after it was abandoned, Brian would finally re-record and release *Smile* as a solo artist. It is a wonderful piece of American music for the ages. One wonders what effect it would have had on popular culture had it been released as planned in 1966.

THE BEATLES

1962–1970

On a subway platform recently, a 2-year-old child in a stroller began to sing. He sang a simple song about a yellow submarine that echoed through the tunnel bringing a smile to the face of everyone there. People of all races, ages, and walks of life recognized the music that had touched them at some point in their lives, and there on that platform, for a brief moment, they were all connected.

Virtually no band has ever had as much impact on the citizens of this Earth as the Beatles—the Fab Four: John Lennon, Paul McCartney, George Harrison, and Ringo Starr. It is amazing to think they only recorded properly as a group for a little over eight years, and toured for less than half of that (if you don't include their early years before Ringo was a member of the group). The stories of the albums are like chapters in a book, with the power of their personalities running through the narrative. But beyond each individual was the collective spirit that they created together.

"At the beginning I was annoyed with John, jealous because of Yoko, and afraid about the breakup of a great musical partnership. It took me a year to realize they were in love." —Paul McCartney

In their career, the Beatles probably wrote every kind of song you could imagine, from ballads, to folk rock, heavy metal and blues, lullabies, dance hall, big band, swing, and psychedelia. At the end of their time together they had never written a comedy song so they came up with the B Side to "Let It Be" entitled "You Know My Name," which is a brilliant collective giggle.

Meet the Beatles

The Beatles were truly a case where the sum was greater than the parts. There was John Lennon, the early leader of the group and a contradictory personality: the angry man of peace, the social activist who would rather stay in bed, and the brilliant songwriter who didn't always complete the task. Paul McCartney was the cute one with the boundless energy, the consummate musician whose own songwriting could get a little silly unless slapped into line by his rival. If John was the leader in the early years, it was Paul who tried to keep the machine rolling at the end. George was the lead guitarist who had to learn at the feet of one of the greatest songwriting duos in history. When they ran out of steam, he was the one with a stockpile of great songs to head into the solo years. All things must pass, indeed. Ringo Starr, always the new kid, was considered the best drummer on the Liverpool scene and the parts he came up with are some of the most distinctive in rock and roll (think "Daytripper" or "Strawberry Fields Forever").

LOVE THEM DO! AFTER GRUELING, MARATHON-PLAYING STINTS IN HAMBURG, PAUL, GEORGE, RINGO, AND JOHN CAME BACK WITH MOP-TOP HAIRDOS AND AN EXPANDED REPERTOIRE, BECOMING THE HOTTEST BAND IN LIVERPOOL—THEN ENGLAND, THEN THE WORLD.

THIS IMAGE OF THE FAB FOUR BECAME THE COVER OF THE EP *TWIST AND SHOUT*, WHICH CONTAINED FOUR TRACKS FROM THEIR *PLEASE PLEASE ME* LP AND SOLD MORE COPIES THAN ANY EXTENDED-PLAY ALBUM IN BRITISH POP HISTORY.

The excitement the Beatles generated when they first arrived in America can best be described as pandemonium. It was a black-and-white world of AM radio and clean-cut youth, and along with the Twist dance craze and the Kennedy clan in the White House, the Beatles music saturating the airwaves was a bright, shiny new thing that signaled the true end of the '50s. The exuberant pop of those early albums was something that sounded wholly new, and was sweet and fun at the same time. A lot of it can be attributed to John learning banjo before guitar and coming up with a lot of interesting chords that most songwriters were not using in popular music at that time. The Tin Pan Alley crowd started re-writing fast. In no time a wave of bands known as the British Invasion followed in their wake: Herman's Hermits, the Dave Clark Five, and the Animals, to name a few. Some, like the Rolling Stones, the Who, and the Kinks would make it into the rock pantheon.

With the film *A Hard Day's Night*, the mania was captured on celluloid. And with *Help!* the Beatles were finally in living color and the psychedelic '60s were on their way. Dylan met the Beatles and their music changed. Listen to "Norwegian Wood (This Bird Has Flown)" by Lennon and "4th Time Around" by Dylan. Listen to how The Byrds re-worked "Mr. Tambourine Man" into a Beatlish number, or how Lennon's "You've Got to Hide Your Love Away" spoke of love in heavier psychological terms, much like a Dylan lyric. The Beatles were no longer singing "I Want to Hold Your Hand."

Rubber Soul was the Beatles folk-rock record and the album where they got off the road, leaving screaming fans behind for the confines of the recording studio. Many considered *Revolver* their finest moment as it stretched their experimental side, but it also had the widest range of moods and song styles of any album up to that point. *Sgt. Pepper's Lonely Hearts Club Band* was the album that made people think about "albums" rather than singles. They deliberately didn't

John & Yoko

At John and Yoko's first encounter she handed him a card with one word on it: "Breathe." The historic meeting was in 1966 at a preview of Yoko's art exhibit in London. By the time three years had passed, John had divorced his wife Cynthia and married Yoko, and the two were sitting in bed in their pajamas holding a press conference about peace. Their famous bed-ins for peace led to the pair recording their hit single, "Give Peace A Chance." Beatles fans were suspicious of Yoko, and blamed her for the break up of their favorite band. John and Yoko both denied this: The Beatles had simply run their course. In 1975, five years before John was murdered, Yoko gave birth to their son, Sean.

The Beginning of the Story

Let's whirl through their history. John and Paul were childhood friends from Liverpool playing in skiffle groups (a kind of British folk music made popular by Lonnie Donnegan). They added a young fellow named George who knew more chords than they did, and Pete Best, a drummer whose parents owned a club. John's art school buddy Stu Stutcliffe looked cool and was their first bass player but died early of a brain hemorrhage shortly after they began to gig regularly in Germany. Manager Brian Epstein, whose parents owned department stores, grew enamored with the group and added them to his stable of local stars. They broke with a version of "My Bonnie," and got signed by EMI. Soon after, they fired Pete, hired Ringo, and worked under the tutelage of producer George Martin, who was mainly known for making comedy records!

release any songs as singles, to make it an intact listening experience (although George Martin has bemoaned that they didn't put "Penny Lane" and "Strawberry Fields Forever" on the disc since they were the first two songs cut for those sessions).

The Beatles continued to morph and surprise with each new season, broadcasting those changes on television starting with *The Ed Sullivan Show*. There were the strange psychedelics of "I Am the Walrus" from the ill-fated *Magical Mystery Tour* TV show, the glorious, in the moment (although partially pre-recorded) "All You Need Is Love" beamed out all over the world, and the rousing group sing-along of "Hey Jude." By the time they made *The White Album* they had been to India and had various experiences with the Maharishi and transcendental meditation. George got deeply into it. John, at his cynical best, wrote, "Baby You're a Rich Man" and "Sexy Sadie" about the experience. Brian Epstein, their manager, died mysteriously of a drug overdose while the Beatles were in India.

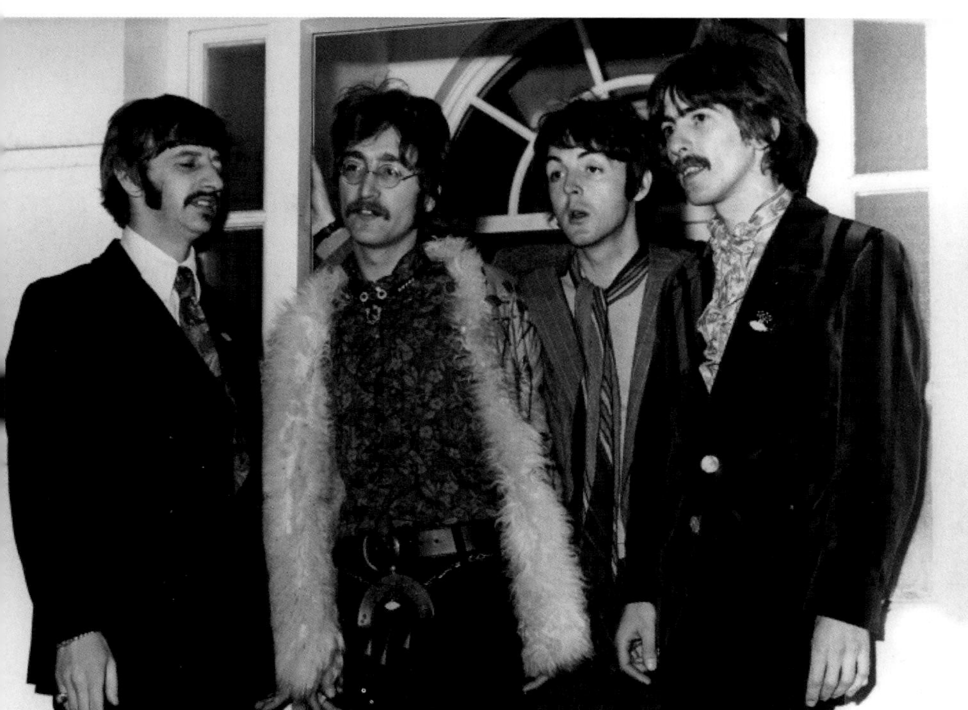

THE BAND AT A PRESS CONFERENCE FOR THE 1967 RELEASE OF THEIR EIGHTH ALBUM, *SGT. PEPPER'S LONELY HEARTS CLUB BAND*. GONE WERE THE DAYS OF MATCHING SUITS.

The White Album showed the group moving into separate corners. *Let it Be* might have been the end, an album and a painstaking documentary about the process, but they all agreed it wasn't the best way to go out, so they gathered with George Martin and recorded the satisfying *Abbey Road*. Listen to George, John, and Paul duel on guitar during "The Weight" and listen to their beautiful group harmonies on "The End" and you know they took the nobler path. Even if *Let It Be* was released later, *Abbey Road* was the grand finale.

John is gone, George is gone, Paul still tours stadiums, Ringo tours concert halls, and we will still love them when we turn 64; and when we have all left Earth and only the music remains, they will continue to shine on.

GREATEST HITS

YEAR	SONG
1963	"Please Please Me"
	"She Loves You"
	"I Want To Hold Your Hand"
1964	"Can't Buy Me Love"
	"Love Me Do"
	"A Hard Day's Night"
1965	"Eight Days a Week"
	"Help!"
	"Yesterday"
1966	"Yellow Submarine"
1967	"Strawberry Fields Forever"
1968	"Hey Jude"
1969	"The Ballad of John and Yoko"
	"Something"
1970	"Let It Be"

BECK

July 8, 1970–

Battling for the same record bin space as '70s guitar god and Yardbirds member Jeff Beck must have been a challenge at first for the artist called Beck. He seemed to come from nowhere in particular, when an independently released 12-inch single,"Loser," was picked up and started getting airplay on L.A. radio.

"Loser" incorporated some scratchy blues guitar, a Dr. John sample, and re-mixed drum beats; seemingly sloppy and casual, "Loser" was a song for the times. The grunge/slacker culture was in full bloom and a generation of kids were wondering if there was a way into the American dream, or if were they destined to live with their parents well into their 30s while trying to get jobs at the new coffee-house chain popping up everywhere. Behind the slacker façade was an ambitious young man who had been watching and waiting for the moment when he could do his thing his way and get noticed. Beck landed himself an interesting contract with Geffen Records that allowed him to record albums for different independent labels if he felt Geffen wasn't the right home for a particular project.

Beck solidified his career with the release of *Odelay*, produced by the Dust Brothers, which garnered stellar reviews and spawned hit singles—"Where It's At," "Devils Haircut," and "The New Pollution."

GREATEST HITS	
Year	Song
1994	"Loser"
1996	"Where It's At"
	"Devils Haircut"
	"The New Pollution"
2002	"Lost Cause"
2005	"E-Pro"
	"Girl"
	"Hell Yes"
2006	"Nausea"
	"Think I'm in Love"

Beck has reinvented himself many times since his first hit, "Loser."

"I think my whole generation's mission is to kill the cliché."—Beck

Beck has continued to innovate and make different kinds of albums over the years. *Sea Change* is a melancholy concept album about a breakup, and *The Information*, which made the most of modern digital technology, came with a sheet of stickers so listeners could make their own CD cover.

Beck put the idea across that you could make art that was not slick and formulaic, that lo-fi homemade art of your own design was okay. You may never make it into the mainstream but you might have some fun along the way, cutting and pasting to your heart's content.

NUGGET: On stage, Beck often delivers with an encyclopedic knowledge of rock star moves—dancing like James Brown one moment, making grand Bowie gestures the next.

CHUCK BERRY

OCTOBER 18, 1926–

There is arguably no one in the history of music who had more to do with creating rock and roll than Chuck Berry. Even if others like Roy Brown had already written songs such as "Good Rocking Tonight," it was Berry who solidified the blueprint with a series of riffs, licks, and runs that would define the style. He also added lyrics celebrating life in the U.S. of A. that spoke straight to the youth who were looking for something different from what their parents' big band swing had to offer.

> **NUGGET:** In 1977, Chuck Berry's "Johnny B. Goode" was among the cultural artifacts sent out into space on the *Voyager* space probe chosen to explain to creatures from alien planets just what we are about here on Earth.

To simple 1-4-5 patterns that were the foundation of much of blues and R&B, Chuck added his unique searing guitar that put the instrument front and center. Some of the licks came from Johnnie Johnson, a piano player he met up at the Chess Records studios in Chicago where all the blues greats were recording, including Howlin' Wolf, Muddy Waters, and Bo Diddley. Johnson was considered by many to be Chuck Berry's right-hand man.

Chuck loved the American dream, and while rock and roll was still a euphemism for sexual relations, it became something more in his hands. It was "hamburgers sizzling on an open griddle night and day," it was the freedom of movement, of "riding along in an automobile," it was the escape from a "cabin made of earth and wood," and the adulation that a poor boy could discover if he learned to play guitar "like ringing a bell." This was a modern man, using modern technology, singing about the modern world. It was immediate, specific, and to the point—and you could dance to it.

> *"If you tried to give rock and roll another name, you might call it 'Chuck Berry.'"* —John Lennon

Chuck shocked the powers that be in the '50s, and they were always gunning for him. He was detested, arrested, but ultimately ingested right into the heartland of the U.S.A. Berry's songs were recorded by the Beatles and the Rolling Stones, and the cover versions just keep coming. You can't call yourself a rock guitarist if you don't know your Chuck Berry, the brown-eyed, handsome man who changed the world.

CHUCK BERRY HAD GREATER SUCCESS WITH HIS 1957 SONG "MY TAMBOURINE" WHEN HE RERECORDED IT FIVE YEARS LATER AS THE RISQUÉ "MY DING-A-LING," WHICH WENT TO #1.

GREATEST HITS

YEAR	SONG
1955	"Maybellene"
1957	"Rock and Roll Music"
1958	"Sweet Little Sixteen"
	"Johnny B. Goode"
1960	"Too Pooped to Pop (Casey)"
	"Let it Rock"
1972	"My Ding-A-Ling" (Live)
	"Reelin' and Rockin'" (Live)

Rock and Roll 101

In some ways Chuck's music was best played on the fly by anyone who had studied the formula. Berry was notorious for waiting in his car at a gig until he had been paid in cash, then hitting the stage with a local pickup band (carrying musicians along on the road cut into one's profit margin) without rehearsal, and letting the other musicians fly by the seat of their pants trying to catch the key and tempo.

BLACK SABBATH

1969–

In the fall of 1970, two albums defined the polar spheres of the teenage mind: James Taylor's heartbreakingly sensitive *Sweet Baby James* and the ultra-heavy first album by Black Sabbath. Lead singer Ozzy Osbourne sounded like he'd been to the crossroads; and if he hadn't struck a deal with the devil, the two at least had reached an understanding. The slow syrupy rhythms were a tar pit of aural goo. This was the prototype. Black Sabbath had forged the new ore: heavy metal.

> **NUGGET:** The band name came from an occult-themed song, entitled "Black Sabbath," written by bassist Geezer Butler. The inspiration for the song was a dream: One night Butler saw a black figure standing at the end of his bed, and the next day, he noticed that an occult book he'd received from Osbourne was missing.

The band was formed in Birmingham, England, by kids who didn't want their fathers' factory lives. Ozzy was ultra-confident that they had the talent to get out of town. He loved the Beatles, but the band couldn't master all those fancy chords. Black Sabbath kept it simple, pummeling you deftly with their songs. Their first album, and in fact all their albums, were slammed by the rock critics but the kids ate it up. The band racked up million-selling albums through most off the '70s (over 70 million to date) and got radio airplay with songs like "War Pigs," "Paranoid," and "Iron Man." People came to see Sabbath for the vicarious thrill of seeing someone live out their darker fantasies on stage. In 1979 Ozzy quit over creative differences with guitarist Tony Iommi and went on to form Blizzard of Ozz with guitarist Randy Rhodes, and the hits just kept coming. Rumors of hidden satanic suicide messages in LP grooves and biting the head off a real bat (though by mistake) fueled the Ozzy image—the ultimate wildman. Rhodes' death in a plane crash in 1982 slammed the brakes on the "Crazy Train" and sent Ozzy into a deep depression.

Black Sabbath still had its original lineup (from bottom left, clockwise: Bill Ward, Geezer Butler, Tony Iommi, and Ozzy Osbourne) in 1979, when Ozzy left. While band members have come and gone, their 2007 release features all four of the founders.

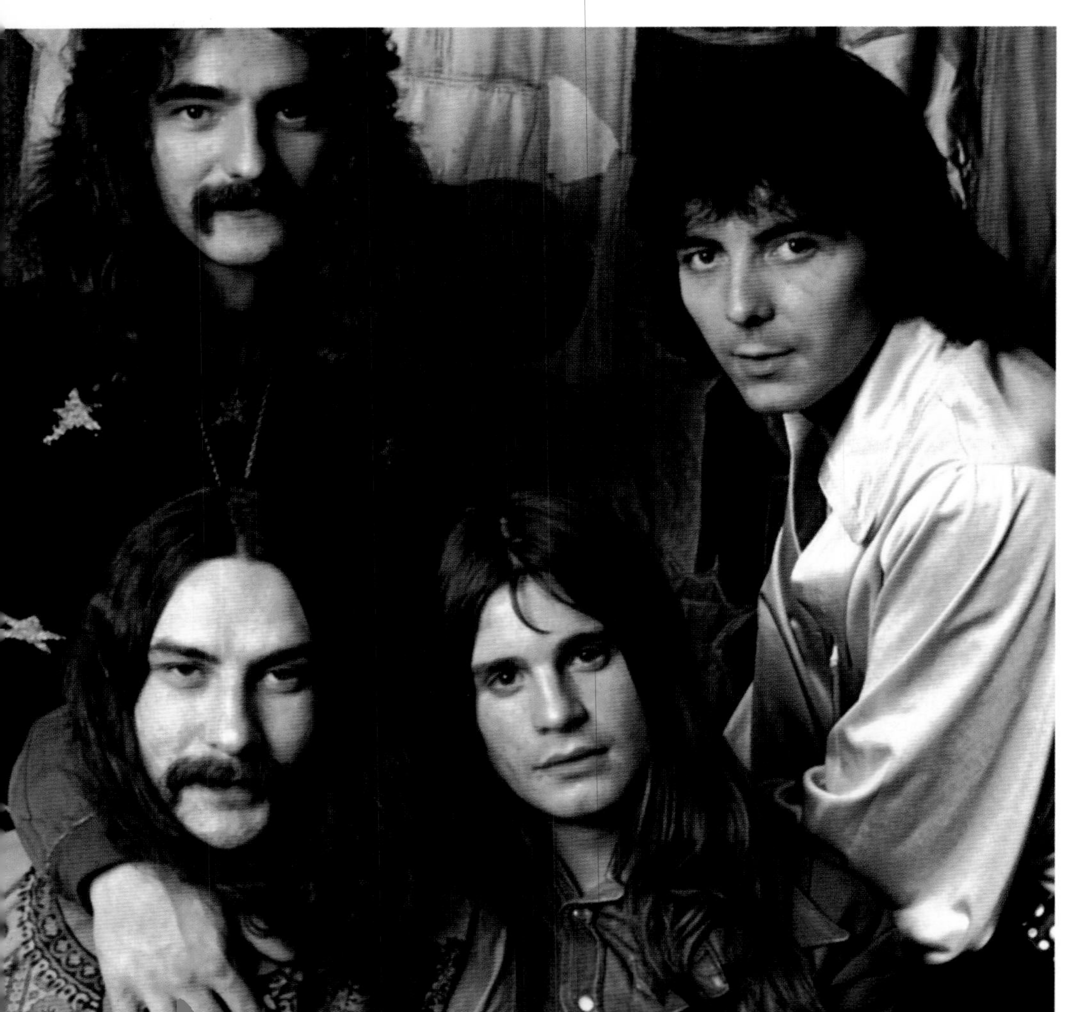

"I got rabies shots for biting the head off a bat but that's OK—the bat had to get Ozzy shots." —Ozzy Osbourne

As Black Sabbath kept rolling with various lineups Ozzy bounced back, too. In 1996, he created Ozzfest, the summer concert institution that became a breeding ground for many young metal bands. He later reunited with the original members of Black Sabbath: Iommi, Geezer Butler on bass, and Bill Ward on drums. Just when Ozzy had accomplished it all, he was piped into America's living rooms and became everyone's favorite madman on MTV's *The Osbournes*. Long may he rave.

GREATEST HITS

Year	Song
1970	"Iron Man"
	"Paranoid"
	"War Pigs"
	"Behind the Wall of Sleep"
	"Black Sabbath"
	"N.I.B."
	"The Wizard"
1971	"Sweet Leaf"
	"Children of the Grave"

BLONDIE

1974–

"Blondie is a group!" the band kept reminding people; even printing the slogan on buttons to differentiate the band from Debbie Harry the blonde who led Blondie. Nonetheless, catcalls of "Hey Blondie" inspired Harry and then boyfriend Chris Stein to start the band; and let's face it, there would be no Blondie without Deborah Harry.

Deborah Harry was a new kind of rock icon when she appeared on the late '70s CBGB (rock club) scene in New York. She borrowed from movie bombshells like Marilyn Monroe, with a strong nod to early '60s girl groups like the Shangri-Las. But in Blondie, she held her own with talented male musicians, and led the charge with tough-girl vocals, a unique fashion sense, and songs she co-wrote with the band. Perhaps because Harry was so photogenic, it took Blondie a long time to be taken seriously. But with guitarist Chris Stein, keyboard player Jimmy Destri, bassist Gary Valentine, and drummer Clem Burke; Debbie had some co-workers ready to break out of the local scene. Eventually a small deal came with Private Stock Records and a single, "X-Offender," held its own on the CBGB jukebox against the Ramones early releases. But it wasn't until their third album that they put it all together and left club land behind. On *Parallel Lines* they mixed elements of rock, new wave, and disco beats to bang out a series of giant radio hits including "Heart of Glass" which hit #1 in the U.S.

GREATEST HITS	
YEAR	SONG
1976	"X Offender"
1977	"I'm Always Touched By Your Presence Dear"
1978	"One Way or Another"
	"Hanging on the Telephone"
	"Heart of Glass"
1980	"Call Me"
	"The Tide Is High"
	"Rapture"

Eat to the Beat era Blondie, featuring (from left) Jimmy Destri, Frank Infante, Debbie Harry, Nigel Harrison, Chris Stein, and Clement Burke. Infante had taken over for Gary Valentine.

"Chris really loved the Stones, Clem was originally a Deadhead, Jimmy was into Procol Harum and I was into girl singers." —Debbie Harry

Blondie tried it all in their career: reggae with "The Tide Is High," synth dance pop with "Atomic, " and even a touch of hip-hop with the aptly titled "Rapture," which also became a chart-topping single. When CBGB finally closed in October 2006, Debbie and Chris played an acoustic set on one of the final nights. Today, Deborah Harrys can be seen all over the world stage in the likes of Madonna, Gwen Stefani, Shirley Manson, and Courtney Love.

Pre-Blondie

While she seemed like the complete package, it took New Jersey's Deborah Harry awhile to find her way. Debbie was originally in a hippie band called Wind in the Willows in the late '60s; and she put in long hours as a waitress at Max's Kansas City, the Warholian hot spot that ushered in the glam era, and stayed active through the punk years. She was even a Playboy bunny for a short stint. During that time she was in a group, *The Stilettos*, that was right out of *West Side Story*. The group's backup singers, Tish and Snooky, were the two sisters responsible for the punk hair dye Manic Panic, and their guitarist was Chris Stein.

Born in Miami, Harry was adopted and grew up in New Jersey.

DAVID BOWIE

January 8, 1947–

David Bowie performs one of his many hits during the Live Aid Benefit Concert at Wembley Stadium in July of 1985.

If one David Bowie song could reveal the man himself, or at least describe his modus operandi, it would be "Changes." The lyric describes a man who refuses to be defined by others, who will not be nailed down, or led to the slaughter. Just when they see he's a faker he's moving on to something new and he's going to bring all the misunderstood kids along for the ride.

Most of Bowie's early recordings were somewhat dismissed until he hit upon "Space Oddity," a song that resembled the Bee Gees "New York Mining Disaster 1941." It was the first glimmer of a persona for David Bowie: Major Tom, the slightly removed spaceman lost in a void of his own isolation as great as the universe. The song was not readily followed up with a quality album, though the single would be repackaged many times. Things came together with Bowie's *Hunky Dory* album; a beautiful valentine to all the musical strains he loved, including the Velvet Underground and Andy Warhol, Dylan, and singer Anthony Newley. Mainly an acoustic affair, it featured excellent songwriting; on the back cover, Bowie sported a dress, putting him at the forefront of the early '70s glam movement, where androgyny and a fluid approach to defining one's sexuality were the flavors of the day.

With his next album, which many consider his greatest, Bowie became the ambisexual space alien Ziggy Stardust, with his band the Spiders from Mars. With Mick Ronson delivering unique melodic guitar runs in a heavy setting, this was Bowie as rock god and all the young dudes got it. He was suddenly an international success. Bowie claimed he was retiring from live shows but kept the characters coming: *Aladdin Sane* featured Bowie looking like a futuristic mime, and singing teenage drama on an

GREATEST HITS

Year	Song
1969	"Space Oddity"
1972	"Changes"
	"Starman"
	"Suffragette City"
	"The Jean Genie"
1974	"Rebel Rebel"
1975	"Young Americans"
	"Fame"
	"Golden Years"
1977	"Heroes"
1979	"DJ"
1983	"China Girl"
	"Let's Dance"
	"Modern Love"

Bowie as Producer

Bowie used the power of his stardom to work at a breakneck clip producing albums for some of his heroes: Lou Reed had a hit, and a resurrected career thanks to Bowie's production of *Transformer* and the classic single "Walk on the Wild Side." He also produced The Stooges finale *Raw Power*. For Mott the Hoople, he wrote the classic glam tribal anthem "All the Young Dudes," sung from the perspective of the new young glam fan who didn't feel connected to the social revolution of the '60s—"Who needs TV when I got T. Rex."

epic scale with songs like "The Jean Genie" and "Drive-In Saturday." In 1974, he roared back in the *Diamond Dogs* album with the classic rocker "Rebel Rebel." "This ain't rock' n' roll—this is genocide!" he screams before launching into the album's title track. The music that followed created a surreal sci-fi wasteland of the future.

"I always had a repulsive need to be something more than human." —David Bowie

Bowie would continue to evolve and stay one step ahead of his fans. He ditched the rock and roll for something he called "plastic soul" which owed a lot to Philadelphia R&B of the time. The title song, "Young Americans," was one of Bowie's finest and seemed to nod to a young fairly unknown singer named Bruce Springsteen. Indeed, years later bonus tracks appeared with Bowie performing cover versions of the Springsteen songs "Growin' Up" and "It's Hard To Be a Saint in the City." The album also included "Fame," a huge hit he cowrote with John Lennon and Carlos Alomar. Bowie was in the pantheon. From the young American he became the thin white duke, rock and roll royalty pumping out very muscular disco funk of the Kraftwerk variety with a return to that Newley croon for *Station to Station*.

Collapsing from exhaustion from all this activity, Bowie left behind a failed marriage and tales of great drug-addled excess. He retreated to Berlin, Germany, and simplified his life. His music took a turn away from the swaggering commercial pomp and polish of *Station to Station*, becoming more insular and experimental with the help of Brian Eno, who wrote and produced a remarkable trilogy of albums along with Bowie and Toni Visconti: *Low*, *Heroes*, and *Lodger*. They also found time to resurrect Iggy Pop one more time as a solo artist on the classic albums *The Idiot* and *Lust for Life*.

There were more hits in the years to come. The Nile Rogers-produced album *Let's Dance* was Bowie's biggest selling album, and had two Top-10 hits. His duet with Queen, "Under Pressure," was another huge international hit. Add to that all the film work, a successful marriage to the super model Iman, and the coup of turning his career and catalog into Bowie Bonds sold on Wall Street, and you have an artist who has won at a game he loves to play and delivered some great pop art along the way.

Bowie performs his "final concert" in the guise of Ziggy Stardust, in 1973 at the Hammersmith Odeon.

Bowie's Beginnings

Bowie started his career as a mime and an actor but gravitated to music with the heat of the swinging London/Carnaby street scene. His album *Pinups* is a tribute to that time and to the performers the young singer idolized: The Who, Them, Pink Floyd, and the Yardbirds. There was also an acoustic-based UK underground psychedelic folk scene and the band Tyrannosaurus Rex was at its center. Bowie watched Marc Bolan's every move, and even toured with T. Rex as a mime for a number of shows. Add to this a fascination for the high octane croon of Anthony Newley and you had a performer who was reaching for the stars even if early on he more often saw the glitter in the gutter.

JAMES BROWN

May 3, 1933–December 25, 2006

James Brown was the self-ordained Godfather of Soul. He cut such a powerful figure in the '60s that he met with presidents and was a spokesman for the African-American community. He was a physically impressive man and a true athlete, developing a repertoire of stage moves imitated by many of the greatest following in his wake, from Mick Jagger, to Michael Jackson, to Prince.

Brown always stayed out of sight before a performance, not wanting the audience to see him in less than full pompadour glory. He wore three-piece, tight-fitting suits that would be removed as the night wore on, with James delivering hit after hit, backbeat after breakdown, always taking it to the bridge one more time. His band had to hit it on cue, lest they get a hefty fine after the show. When he had seemingly given it his all, he would collapse on stage and be escorted under a cape to the wings. But then the cape would be flung off and he would be back to give the audience more than they could have imagined—one more time.

> *"I've outdone anyone you can name—Mozart, Beethoven, Bach, Strauss. Irving Berlin, he wrote 1,001 tunes. I wrote 5,500."*
>
> —James Brown

James had trouble with the law as a young man and also late in life—jail time bookended his career. But he also spoke out to calm rioters after Martin Luther King's assassination, urged kids to stay in school, and gave African-Americans a music they could call their own with anthems like "Say It Loud—I'm Black and I'm Proud." His funky grooves were like Cubist paintings, utterly original and leaping full blown from an unseen creative well deep within the man.

The lines at his funeral at Harlem's Apollo Theater in 2006 said it all. He had touched many; from entertainers, to dignitaries and politicians, to the common man. The hardest-working man in show business will never shake off his cape and rise again, but the man's music lives on, vibrating on every continent.

The Godfather of Soul performing in 2005 at a concert in Amsterdam. Though more than 70 years old, he could still deliver to the enthralled crowd.

James Brown helped to evolve gospel music and rhythm and blues into soul and funk.

The Greatest Show on Earth

James Brown always started his shows with a role call of his many names and accomplishments. While the band vamped on a muscular groove, Mr. Brown's valet of the moment (Al Sharpton once filled this role) would call out, "Ladies and gentlemen, Mr. Please Please Please, The Hardest Working Man in Show Business, The Godfather of Soul, Mr. Dynamite, Jaaaaaaames Brown!"

GREATEST HITS

Year	Song
1956	"Please, Please, Please"
1965	"I Got You (I Feel Good)"
	"Papa's Got A Brand New Bag"
1966	"It's a Man's Man's Man's World"
1967	"Cold Sweat"
	"Mother Popcorn"
1968	"Say It Loud–I'm Black and I'm Proud"
1970	"Get Up (I Feel Like Being A) Sex Machine"
1985	"Living in America"

THE BYRDS

1964–1973

Sometimes when you try to imitate one thing, you miss the mark and come up with something new. This was true of The Byrds, a bunch of young American folkies who saw The Beatles in *A Hard Day's Night* and quickly re-thought their options.

From the band's name (another improperly spelled animal name) to their Beatle boots and mop-top haircuts (drummer Michael Clarke was asked to join for his looks, not his drumming), they were designing a band with the look and sound of the Fab Four. Songs of young love, three-part harmony, and pop-idol good looks were all there, but the Byrds also brought their own spin to the Beatles formula.

Roger McGuinn, David Crosby, Gene Clark, and Chris Hillman came together on the folk-club circuit, and hence were familiar with the songs shared by the artists. Two of their earliest hits were

The Story of "Mr. Tambourine Man"

Bob Dylan's "Mr. Tambourine Man" was not a likely hit single, but the Byrds' electric reworking of his long mysterious acoustic ballad would become one of the most memorable songs of the '60s. The Byrds were initially unimpressed with the song given to them by their manager, who had an unreleased demo. Most of the members of the band didn't even play on the original session, except to sing. Only Roger McGuinn joined L.A.'s elite musicians the Wrecking Crew, a hit machine who cut sides for Phil Spector, Elvis Presley, Simon & Garfunkel, and many others. The band had just cut a track for the Beach Boys, "Don't Worry Baby"—the signature uptick guitar part was used on the Byrds' "Mr. Tambourine Man" track, with McGuinn improvising a variation on a Bach theme over the top of the intro and outro of the song. Dylan's original version had four verses and five choruses. The Byrds used only the second verse and a couple of choruses. The song is considered the beginning of folk rock, and would inspire Dylan to "go electric."

"Folk-rock hasn't changed much over the decades since the Byrds started it."—Steve Forbert

THE MEMBERS OF THE BYRDS—(FROM LEFT) ROGER MCGUINN, CHRIS HILLMAN, DAVID CROSBY, MICHAEL CLARKE, AND GENE CLARK—APPEARED ON NEW-FANGLED *TOP OF THE POPS* TELEVISION PROGRAMS ON BOTH SIDES OF THE ATLANTIC.

THE BYRDS PERFORMING ON THE POPULAR U.K. TELEVISION SHOW *READY STEADY GO!* IN 1965.

radical reworkings of Bob Dylan's "Mr. Tambourine Man" and Pete Seeger's "Turn Turn Turn." The band's secret weapon was Roger McGuinn's electric Rickenbacher guitar, which jangled and rang with a sound never before heard. It was transcendent music that seemed steeped in ancient tones, and fused all the folk elements of the moment with the driving beat of rock and roll.

The Byrds scored a number of big records very quickly. One of the first was "I'll Feel A Whole Lot Better" by Gene Clark, who was the prime writer on the first two albums. When the publishing checks started pouring in and Gene got a fancy new sports car, the other band members decided they were not only jealous, but needed to get some copyrights of their own. A fear of flying and the comfort of all that new-found cash sent Clark off on a solo career. His parting gift was a song he wrote with McGuinn and Crosby, "8 Miles High," which would put the band at the middle of the psychedelic hippie culture. They claimed the raga-rock number was just about an airplane ride, because drug references could get a song banned from radio.

By 1967, the band was fracturing: Crosby and McGuinn were at each other's throats. At the Monterey Pop Festival in 1967, Crosby sat in with the Buffalo Springfield to help out Stephen Stills in Neil Young's temporary absence. This did not endear Crosby to the other members of the Byrds, and when their next album, *The Notorious Byrd Brothers*, came out, Crosby's songs were left off the album; on the album cover, his head was replaced by that of a horse!

When Chris Hillman brought a young Southerner named Gram Parsons into the fold the group moved into a distinctive countrified direction. Where they had helped pioneer folk-rock a few years earlier they were now creating the first strains of country-rock with *Sweetheart of the Rodeo*. But before that album could be properly promoted, Hillman, Parsons, and Clarke all took off to start a band without McGuinn: The Flying Burrito Brothers.

McGuinn soldiered on with a new lineup and kept the Byrds flying for many years. The addition of Clarence White, one of the great country-rock guitarists of his generation, found McGuinn's 12-string guitar taking a back seat to White's pyrotechnics. Eventually McGuinn went solo himself.

The Byrds' sound lives on in the generations of jangle rockers, from R.E.M. to U2, who've borrowed from their sound. Imitation in the end turned into innovation.

The Hardest-Working Byrd in Show Business

The names of Crosby, McGuinn, and Parsons are more well-known to the record-buying public, but Chris Hillman, one of the architects of country-rock, may be the hardest working Byrd in show business. After the Byrds, Hillman joined Parsons in the the Flying Burrito Brothers, and after they disbanded moved on to Stephen Stills' Manassas. His next project—the Souther-Hillman-Furay Band—was with Eagles songwriter J.D. Souther and ex-Poco singer Richie Furay, then back to fellow Byrds-men in the band McGuinn, Clark & Hillman. He's still working to this day, making bluegrass records.

NUGGET: The Byrds' last big hit of their early years was a song called "So You Want to Be a Rock 'n' Roll Star," on the 1967 album *Younger Than Yesterday*. Cowritten by McGuinn and Hillman, it was about the artist's bargain with the devil—"for your riches and fame you're a little insane," and was rumored to be poking fun at the success of bands like the Monkees.

GREATEST HITS

YEAR	SONG
1965	"Mr. Tambourine Man"
	"Turn, Turn, Turn"
	"I'll Feel a Whole Lot Better"
1966	"Eight Miles High "
1967	"So You Want to Be a Rock 'n' Roll Star"

CAPTAIN BEEFHEART

JANUARY 15, 1941–

Captain Beefheart and his Magic Band have probably sold fewer records than any other artist in this book. With the exception of the Bo Diddley cover "Diddy Wah Diddy" early in his career, there was no real chart success; but in the departments of inspiration and innovation the Captain has few equals. Captain Beefheart, aka Don Van Vliet, made music that almost seemed to spring from another dimension. Perhaps because he was originally trained as a sculptor, his songs were like three-dimensional Cubist paintings, full of gears and bubbling motor oil belching the blues, free jazz, and rock and roll.

NUGGET: Tom Waits acknowledged that he has Beefheart to thank for the change in his musical direction that began with his 1983 album, *Swordfishtrombones*. Waits' wife, Kathleen Brennan, was a big fan of the Captain and her enthusiasm was contagious.

The Magic Band got its start in the Mojave Desert in California where they played in hard-driving blues bands. One can hear some influence of Howlin' Wolf in Beefheart's growl. Added to that were the strange Dada lyrics that seemed like nonsense on one level, but also had an inner heartfelt logic. The first album, *Safe as Milk*, was misconstrued to be about LSD. Beefheart claims that he had enough wild imagery stored up in his head that he never really needed to be chemically enhanced. Adding insult to injury, it's been said that his next album, *Strictly Personal*, was remixed and "psychedelicized" with sound effects. Beefheart was supposedly horrified and moved to a label started by high school friend, Frank Zappa. Frank promised him complete control and the Magic Band rehearsed Beefheart's songs for months on end. Beefheart could hear all the music in his head, but couldn't write music charts and had to whistle all the parts to the other players.

The Musician as Artist

While he has cited Stravinsky as an inspiration, the Captain always saw himself as an innovator. He had very little interest in popular culture. In reality, he was an artist who worked in many mediums. All through his days as a musician, he carried with him sketchpads and notebooks and would often sit in the back of nightclubs sketching and smoking the night away. Beefheart always hated the music business and, after his recording days were over, retreated to Northern California where he's rarely heard from. His painting career took off in the last decade, and he has found real commercial success at last; without musicians as middlemen to convey his meaning, his visual art could go straight from the heart to brush to canvas.

The songs came quickly, but getting them out into the world was a painstaking process. The double album, *Trout Mask Replica,* is considered the finest moment of his career: intricate, otherworldly, and surreal with song titles like "The Dust Blows Forward 'n' the Dust Blows Back," "Neon Meate Dream of a Octafish," and "Sweet Sweet Bulbs."

Some albums that followed *Trout Mask* would be disavowed by the Captain, but there were highpoints like *Clear Spot* produced by Ted Templemen (who would later produce Van Halen), and his final two albums, *Shiny Beast (Bat Chain Puller)* and *Ice Cream for Crow,* were considered great returns to form.

WHO CAN ARGUE WITH "A SQUID EATING DOUGH IN A POLYETHYLENE BAG IS FAST AND BULBOUS, GOT ME?" FROM BEEFHEART'S *TROUT MASK REPLICA*?

GREATEST HITS

YEAR	SONG
1966	"Diddy Wah Diddy"
	"Moonchild"
1967	"Yellow Brick Road"
	"Sure 'Nuff 'n Yes I Do"
1970	"Pachuco Cadaver"
1972	"Click Clack"
1973	"Too Much Time"
1974	"Upon the My-O-My"
1982	"Ice Cream for Crow"

ERIC CLAPTON

MARCH 30, 1945–

Eric Clapton has managed to stay at the top end of his game for over 40 years—sometimes as an innovator, sometimes paying tribute to the past, but always as a consummate player, and always playing the blues. He is a loner who knows how and when to collaborate, and he does play nice with others.

Blues was almost a religion for Clapton, or at least an obsession of the highest order. From the moment he heard the electric blues of B.B. King, Buddy Guy, Muddy Waters, and others he was hooked. At 13, he was already writing blues compositions that hold up as original innovative work. He has a feel and a power in his playing that is impeccable and truly his own.

Layla

The story of "Layla"—Clapton's most famous song released by his group Derek and the Dominoes in 1970—is the story of unrequited love. The title comes from Persian poet Nezami's "Layla and Majnun," a classic story in the Middle East. Layla was a moon-princess whose father wouldn't let her marry the man who loved her, causing him to go insane. Majnun means madman, and Clapton's love for close friend George Harrison's wife, Pattie Boyd-Harrison, was making him insane. Pattie divorced George years later, and finally married Clapton in 1979, and she became his muse. He wrote the love song "Wonderful Tonight" about Pattie, but unfortunately even great love doesn't always last, and the two divorced in 1988.

CLAPTON IS THE ONLY THREE-TIME INDUCTEE TO THE ROCK AND ROLL HALL OF FAME, AS A MEMBER OF BOTH THE YARDBIRDS AND CREAM AND AS A SOLO ARTIST.

Clapton got his start in The Yardbirds in 1963, the first of three major figures in British blues-rock to man that position. He was followed by Jeff Beck and Jimmy Page. The Yardbirds were a traditional electric blues band in need of a hit when they developed some pop material including "For Your Love." Clapton left the band, not wanting to be part of a pop act, and moved on to John Mayall & the Bluesbreakers, a more traditional blues outfit.

For many years, Clapton was the ultimate team player, lending his guitar-playing chops (and songwriting) to powerhouse bands like Cream and Blind Faith. By the mid '60s, Clapton was considered a guitar god, and in fact, the slogan "Clapton is God" was spray painted by a fan on a wall in a London Underground station in 1967, and famously preserved in a photograph. Clapton, embarrassed by the slogan, repeatedly denied that he considered himself the greatest guitar player in the world.

In the late '60s, Clapton met a band of American musicians he grew to admire for their authentic approach. Delaney Bramlett and his wife, Bonnie, were making music that drew on delta blues, soul, and rock and roll, and Clapton signed up as a sideman, where he could learn and grow outside the center spotlight. Eric brought his star power on tour with Delaney and Bonnie.

As the group played Europe and the U.S., famous friends like George Harrison and Dave Mason joined the proceedings. Later, when Clapton was ready to make a solo statement, he took the group's rhythm section and worked with them on a number of recordings, including his first solo album.

CLAPTON TOURED WITH DELANEY & BONNIE AS A SIDEMAN BEFORE DEVELOPING WHAT BECAME THE PSEUDONYMOUS DEREK AND THE DOMINOES, WHOSE SOLE ALBUM HAS BEEN REVERED IN HINDSIGHT BUT WENT LARGELY UNNOTICED UPON ITS RELEASE.

Eventually this group became Derek and the Dominos, and Clapton cut what many feel is his finest achievement, *Layla and Other Assorted Love Songs*. For the classic "Layla," and several other cuts, Duane Allman sat in on electric slide guitar.

A heroin problem had gotten the better of Clapton by the early '70s, but his back catalog kept him in the spotlight. When he returned with *Ocean Boulevard* in 1974 he was a much more subdued performer, confusing his fans. Much like Bob Dylan after his famous motorcycle accident, he delivered a laid-back, low-key sound inspired by J. J. Cale's work, earning him the nickname "Slowhand." Over the years Clapton has continued to release retrospectives, collaborations with the likes of B. B. King and Cale, and even a reunion with Cream. Occasionally incendiary, but always tasteful, Clapton has kept playing the blues, filling stadiums, and keeping his legacy alive.

GREATEST HITS

YEAR	SONG
1965	"For Your Love" (The Yardbirds)
1968	"Sunshine of Your Love" (Cream)
	"White Room" (Cream)
1969	"Crossroads" (Cream)
	"Can't Find My Way Home" (Blind Faith)
1970	"Layla" (Derek and the Dominos)
	"After Midnight"
	"Let It Rain"
1974	"I Shot the Sheriff"
1977	"Wonderful Tonight"
	"Slowhand"
	"Lay Down Sally"
	"Cocaine"
1992	"Tears in Heaven"
1998	"My Father's Eyes"

A HENDRIX-HAIRED CLAPTON WITH CREAM BANDMATES JACK BRUCE AND THE REDHEADED GINGER BAKER. CREAM WAS THE FIRST BAND TO BE MARKETED AS A "SUPER GROUP."

Clapton's Super Groups

After seeing the Jimi Hendrix Experience, Clapton suddenly saw that there might be other ways to explore the blues. Not only did he pump up his hair to resemble Jimi's but he put together a power trio that aped the Experience. With the excellent vocalist Jack Bruce and the deft jazz drummer Ginger Baker, Cream was born. They were considered the first "super group" laying down the framework for much heavy, so-called British blooze. They gave blues standards like "Crossroads" a thorough reworking, but also managed a number of radio hits like "Sunshine of Your Love"—a song learned by every garage band at the time—as well as "White Room" and "Badge," the latter cowritten by George Harrison.

Cream was one of the most popular groups of the late '60s, but eventually the overblown musical pretensions of the group and infighting between Baker and Bruce led Clapton to call it a day. An interest in working with Steve Winwood, who'd just broken up his group Traffic for the first time, led to the much-anticipated new super group Blind Faith: Clapton, Winwood, Ric Grech, and Ginger Baker. Blind Faith was short-lived but made a lot of money on a world tour and left behind a controversial album cover—a topless girl holding a silver space ship—and some great songs.

THE CLASH

1976–1986

While the Sex Pistols fired the first shot across the ocean and created the prototype of the British punk rocker, it was the Clash who kept the albums coming, leaving behind a solid body of work and knowing that it was time to break up when their hardcore hearts weren't in it anymore.

They influenced a whole bunch of bands, especially young talent in the San Francisco Bay area who embraced the Brit-punk lifestyle emanating from the Clash's early work. Bands like Green Day and Rancid would not exist without The Clash.

"What I like about playing America is you can be pretty sure you're not going to get hit with a full can of beer when you're singing and I really enjoy that!"—Joe Strummer

Joe Strummer, who had a pub rock band in England, heard the Ramones, understood their power, and formed the Clash with guitarist Mick Jones to bring punk rock to his own turf. The Clash's self-titled first album was a fiery, revved up, manic affair with two-minute songs that roared by with the passion, anger, and ideas of the times. Strummer's voice spat out lyrics in an endless series of cockney guttural growls, singing of the frustrations of English youth in the age of Prime Minister Thatcher. The first single, "White Riot," was embraced by a new movement—one that came from the streets and gave the English brand of punk a social consciousness, unlike the art-rock posing of the New York scene.

New York was calling as t he Clash did their first tour to support their first U.S.-released album, *Give 'Em Enough Rope*, in 1979. Jones (left) and Strummer had met more than three years earlier in line at their local unemployment office.

They hit the U.S. with their second album, *Give 'Em Enough Rope*. The album seemed downright polished in comparison to their debut, but holds up as a powerful blast of raw power with Blue Oyster Cult's producer Sandy Pearlman twiddling the knobs.

London Calling, their third effort, was a sprawling double LP that found the band expanding beyond the limited formula of punk to embrace ska, reggae, rockabilly, and many other forms. The title track is perhaps their signature song; it's a brooding, pulsing, pirate anthem sung by someone in the heart of it—"I live by the river," squawks Strummer. The Clash released three more albums before calling it quits, including the politically charged *Sandinista!* in 1980 and the commercially successful *Combat Rock* in 1982. If not for the untimely death of Joe Strummer in 2002, one wonders if the band would have re-formed and railed once again.

The Clash in America

From their first visit, the Clash immediately fell in love with America, and especially embraced a lot of music made by the African-American community. Like the Rolling Stones had done years earlier with Chicago bluesmen, the Clash had artists like Bo Diddley and James "Blood" Ulmer open for them. When they retuned with their epic statement *London Calling*, their opening act were hip-hop pioneers Grandmaster Flash and the Furious Five, a band that seemed to confuse their fans as much as their new album did.

GREATEST HITS

Year	Song
1977	"White Riot"
1978	"I Fought The Law"
1979	"London Calling"
	"Train in Vain"
1982	"Rock the Casbah"
	"Should I Stay or Should I Go"

ALICE COOPER

February 4, 1948–

Alice was not the prettiest girl in the Detroit music scene of the late '60s. Heck, he wasn't even a girl. But he did work harder than his compatriots in the Motor City and it paid off in platinum. Iggy was certainly better looking and the MC5 rocked harder, but Alice Cooper and his band went out and worked. With Bob Ezrin as a long-time producer, they crafted many hits; and when the promoters called with bookings, they stayed on the road until everyone owned all the fine homes and cars they could ever want. While Iggy crashed and burned in a heroin haze, and the MC5 struggled to find a sound that could lead them out of the political quagmire they had gotten into with the White Panthers, Alice sipped his beer and watched TV after the show and made a fortune.

"Reaction's applauding, passing out or throwing up, and all of that is a reaction, and as much of that we can get, the better. I don't care how they react, as long as they react."—Alice Cooper

GREATEST HITS	
Year	Song
1971	"I'm Eighteen"
1972	"Under My Wheels"
	"Be My Lover"
	"School's Out"
	"Elected"
1973	"No More Mr. Nice Guy"
1975	"Only Women Bleed"
1976	"You and Me"
1978	"How You Gonna See Me Now"

There were great songs that the kids could relate to: "I'm Eighteen" the anthem of a desperate man on the edge between childhood and responsibility, and "School's Out" the sneer of throwing away your schoolbooks because summer is here. He even had a heartfelt ode to the menstrual cycle, his last big hit—"Only Women Bleed." Alice filled the entertainment slot originally created by Screamin' Jay Hawkins, who would arrive at shows in a coffin and sing "I Put a Spell on You," and later to be taken up by the likes of Marilyn Manson and Rob Zombie. He was the ghoul who came to life for the pleasure of your company.

Alice upped the ante with every album and every tour, adding a full-size guillotine and boa constrictors to the stage show. There were albums with Liza Minelli and the Pointer Sisters singing backup. Going solo, he picked up the band that had made Lou Reed's *Rock 'n' Roll Animal* such a success. He has been recording and touring since 1969, when he worked with Frank Zappa recording for his Straight Records label, and has put out more than 25 albums. Sure beats grave digging.

NUGGET: When his perennial beer-sipping got out of hand, Alice checked himself into a hospital and wrote a recovery album with the help of Elton John's lyricist, Bernie Taupin—entitled *From the Inside*.

Though theories abound as to the origins of the name, an oft-repeated one is that manager Dick Christian's mother got out her Ouija board, which soon spelled out A-L-I-C-E C-O-O-P-E-R.

A Boy Called Alice

Alice Cooper, born Vincent Damon Furnier, pioneered the drag queen glam look that David Bowie and the New York Dolls popularized. His particular look was ugly and a little scary, like Norman Bates in his mother's dress in *Psycho*. Alice Cooper was a freak show, and everyone wanted into the sideshow tent to watch the geek. Something weird and otherworldly was going to happen if you asked Alice for a good time.

ELVIS COSTELLO

August 25, 1954–

Known at various times for playing rock, pop, punk, new wave, jazz, and country, Elvis Costello is a man of many musical genres.

He came in a strange package that somehow felt right. Elvis Costello, aka Declan McManus, the geeky, angry young man from the UK whose impassioned vitriol and clever wordplay were a little more user friendly than his compatriots the Sex Pistols. Elvis as in Presley, Costello as in Abbott and . . . (actually his mother's maiden name), he was the crooner and the clown combined into a new iconic package.

Coming out of the pub-rock world and Stiff Records camp, Elvis' first album, released in 1977, was a tour de force on which he was backed up by Clover, an American band that included Huey Lewis blowing harmonica. The album, *My Aim Is True*, had the immediacy of an early Beatles album. Every song sounded like a single with classics including "Alison," "(The Angels Want to Wear My) Red Shoes," and "Less Than Zero." The list goes on.

"Elvis Costello writes novels in three minutes."—Liz Phair

When he showed up in America, before his second album had been released, he had an edgier combo called the Attractions that took no prisoners with their punky '60s garage-rock style. On what was supposed to be the *Saturday Night Live* performance of "Alison," Elvis and the Attractions instead slipped into a new number called "Radio Radio," a scathing attack on the state of commercial radio.

Knock-kneed with thick glasses and bad teeth, Elvis contorted his way into our hearts and was a major influence on a generation of would-be bar bands with songs like "Pump It Up." Costello, with and without the Attractions, was loved by the rock critics but scorned by the likes of David Lee Roth, who sneered, "Rock critics like him because he looks like them." But rock critics really liked him because he sounded like them. He turned a phrase like no one before or after, and in fact has mockingly referred to himself in interviews as "rock and roll's Scrabble champion."

After the growing success of *Armed Forces*, which featured such radio faves as "Oliver's Army" and his enduring classic cover of producer Nick Lowe's "(What's So Funny 'Bout) Peace, Love, and Understanding," Costello

Nick Lowe

Nick Lowe was the first artist on Stiff Records, and soon became house producer for the label, which was started by Jake Riviera and Dave Robinson, manager of Lowe's band, Brinsley Schwarz. As house producer for the label, Lowe recorded albums by the Damned, the Pretenders, and many albums by Elvis Costello, including the first five. He's a pop guy—writer of songs like "Cruel to Be Kind" and "(What's So Funny 'Bout) Peace, Love, and Understanding"—but his rough-and-ready production style was a major influence on punk rock, and earned him the nickname "Basher." "(What's So Funny 'Bout) Peace, Love, and Understanding" has quite a history: First recorded by Brinsley Schwarz, it was a hit for Elvis Costello on *Armed Forces*, recorded by Curtis Stigers to appear on the soundtrack for the Whitney Houston film *The Bodyguard* (the soundtrack was a massive seller and the royalties made Lowe a millionaire), and sung by actor Bill Murray in a karaoke scene in the film *Lost in Translation*.

In 2004, Costello was still going strong; he was nominated for an Academy Award, he completed an orchestral work for an Italian Dance Troupe, and he wrote songs for new wife Diana Krall's album.

pulled back a bit, especially after some bad press he got after a bar fight with Bonnie Bramlett, of the group Delaney & Bonnie.

Elvis the provocateur became Elvis the song craftsmen with an ear to the entire history of popular music. There was the soul-tinged *Get Happy* and the straight-up country of *Almost Blue*. On *King of America*, he used Elvis Presley's backing musicians, and he went on to score more MTV-charged hits with "Everyday I Write the Book" and "Veronica" (co-written with Paul McCartney). Other high profile collaborations include Roger McGuinn of the Byrds, Burt Bacharach, and most recently Allen Toussaint. His most high-profile association is with his wife, the highly regarded jazz singer and pianist Diana Krall.

He has done big band, jazz albums, classical recordings, and every once in a while the elder statesman gathers with members of the Attractions (now renamed the Imposters) to deliver some rock and roll with the wail of the angry young man.

The Attractions

By the time Elvis' first album was released, he'd assembled the perfect band for his ever-changing sound—the Attractions. With Steve Nieve on keyboards, Bruce Thomas on bass, and drummer Peter Thomas (no relation to Bruce), the Attractions helped Elvis get a rawer sound on his successful second album, *This Year's Model*. Elvis Costello and the Attractions, now renamed The Imposters, were inducted into the Rock and Roll Hall of Fame in 2003.

GREATEST HITS

Year	Song
1977	"Watching the Detectives"
	"Alison"
1978	"Pump It Up"
1979	"(What's So Funny 'Bout) Peace, Love, and Understanding"
	"Oliver's Army"
1980	"I Can't Stand Up for Falling Down"
1983	"Everyday I Write the Book"
1989	"Veronica"

Some of Jake Riviera and Dave Robinson's early Stiff stable (from left), Elvis Costello, Nick Lowe, Larry Wallis, Wreckless Eric, and Ian Dury.

Stiff Records

Elvis was working as a computer programmer in the '70s, performing in folk clubs under the name D.P. Costello, and recording demo tapes in hopes of getting a record deal. One of these tapes found its way to Jake Riviera, who signed him to Stiff Records, one of the earliest "indie" labels; Riviera suggested he adopt the Elvis part of his stage name and became his manager. Stiff Records had attitude and was known for irreverent slogans like "We came. We saw. We left." The label was home to innovative artists such as Nick Lowe, Richard Hell, Ian Dury and the Blockheads, the Pogues, and Madness.

CREEDENCE CLEARWATER REVIVAL

1967–1972

Creedence Clearwater Revival was a band that had the unique distinction of being a triple threat: They were great live, had lots of hit radio singles, and were seen as an album group accepted by both AM Top 40 and FM underground radio. They ushered in a return-to-roots rock simplicity. The Beatles probably wouldn't have written "Get Back" if it wasn't for Creedence showing the way to stripped-down rock and roll inflected with Southern soul, blues roots, and rockabilly.

"I had gotten screwed, stolen from, and cheated so many times, I just couldn't seem to separate the songs from the memories."—John Fogerty

CCR music evoked the rural South of bayous and biways and green rivers leading into the mighty Mississippi. John Fogerty's guitar work was both melodic and gritty. He kept it simple and growled over the proceedings like he truly lived and breathed the bluesy swamp juju he sang about, even though he was from Berkeley, California. This was a case of a great dreamer listening to the radio, and to the mysterious music that came from another place and time: Bo Diddley, Little Richard, and Carl Perkins. Much like Robbie Robertson and the Band, he was imagining the kind of America that he wanted to be part of, and he created something that seemed much more authentic than what was happening around him.

John, along with his brother, Tom Fogerty, and childhood friends, Doug Clifford and Stu Cook, were originally called the Golliwogs, with Tom singing a lot of the material. After seven failed singles they changed their name to Creedence Clearwater Revival, and John took control. After testing CCR out with a couple of cover songs for singles, they released the double A side of "Proud Mary" and "Born On the Bayou," which went to #2. Solomon Burke, a great soul singer from the South, recently cited "Proud Mary" as one of the greatest songs ever written—the kind of praise Fogerty never would have imagined when they were starting out. That song, cemented in rock history by the Ike and Tina Turner hit version, is about a giant riverboat heading for New Orleans. Once they established the CCR blueprint they rarely veered from it, creating a classic set of songs that became the building blocks of a genre that would later become known as Americana.

The fortunate sons of Creedence (from left), Tom Fogerty, Stu Cook, Doug Clifford, and John Fogerty. The band's name allegedly came from Tom's friend Credence and a beer label (Clearwater), and the band's reenvisioning itself after ten years together (Revival).

Legal problems

John Fogerty split from Creedence amid much acrimony with both his bandmates and the Fantasy record label that controls their albums to this day. For many years Fogerty refused to play Creedence songs as he had given up his artist royalties in order to get out of his contract and start a solo career. He scored a big hit with the song "Centerfield," which can be heard at baseball stadiums every season. In recent years the original owners of Fantasy sold the company and Fogerty made a better deal with the new owners on the music from his past.

GREATEST HITS

Year	Song
1968	"Proud Mary"
1969	"Fortunate Son"
	"Bad Moon Rising"
	"Down on the Corner"
1970	"Who'll Stop the Rain"
	"Travelin' Band"
	"Lookin' Out My Back Door"

CROSBY STILLS AND NASH

1968–

Like an egg sandwich with cheese and sausage, Crosby Stills and Nash were a rich hippie delight, a little decadent but oh so pleasurable. Graham Nash was a transplanted Englishman with a voice that was otherworldly when butted up against the pipes of David Crosby. The former Byrd was considered by many to be the hippest cat on the scene, though some found him a bit of a blowhard. But all agreed he was fearless, egging the others on to be more creative. He was the idea guy who came up with the concept for the group as folk-rock, counterculture royalty, penning songs like the anti-war "Wooden Ships" and "Almost Cut My Hair," a song that drew a line in the sand outside the barbershop.

While Crosby was the de facto leader by sheer force of personality, Stephen Stills was the meat of the band: an excellent musician and a guitarist who could hold his own against anyone. He fleshed out Crosby's vision with long days and nights in the studio. Perhaps his greatest achievement was the monolithic "Suite: Judy Blue Eyes," an ode to girlfriend Judy Collins that used a wide variety of techniques and rhythms and clocked in at over seven minutes.

The group first sang together at a backyard barbecue at Mama Cass Elliott's house. Cass was always hosting English pop stars in Laurel Canyon, and she brought Graham Nash of the Hollies into the mix. Nash contributed the catchiest, most lightweight material—perfect for radio play. "Teach Your Children" and "Our House" (an ode to his domestic life with Joni Mitchell) were a couple of his sweet-natured group sing-alongs.

Beating the odds, all members of Crosby, Stills and Nash (from left: David Crosby, Stephen Stills, and Graham Nash) are still alive and kicking—and touring.

As influential as their work was, for their die-hard fans there wasn't near enough of it. The important albums as a group can be boiled down to their debut, their follow-up with Neil Young called *Déjà Vu*, and a double live album, *Four Way Street*. In May of 1970, they recorded "Ohio" as a response to the shootings of four students at Kent State University, and showed that their fierce, brave vision and unified harmonies could voice the collective outrage.

GREATEST HITS

Year	Song
1969	"Marrakesh Express"
	"Suite: Judy Blue Eyes"
	"Wooden Ships"
	"Helplessly Hoping"
1970	"Teach Your Children"
	"Helpless"
	"Our House"
	"Ohio"
	"Woodstock"
1977	"Just a Song Before I Go"

Fred Neil: Mentor

It's rumored that the band was almost called the Neils, after Fred Neil, an influential folkie who had mentored Crosby and Stills in their early years on the folk scene. Fred Neil (1936–2001) was a reclusive soul who sang in a deep baritone and had a powerful, unique way of playing his 12-string guitar. As the guy who ran New York's Café Wha?, Fred helped many musicians get their start. He was a little older and wiser than the rest. His songs have been covered by many: "Candy Man" performed by Roy Orbison and "The Dolphins" cut by Linda Rondstadt, Tim Buckley, and more recently Beth Orton. His most famous song was "Everybody's Talkin'," a big hit for Harry Nilsson.

THE CURE

1976–

Just as punk seized the imagination of the U.K. with bands like the Sex Pistols and the Clash hitting the top of the charts, a number of musicians began to deconstruct the power chords and politics of the genre. Post-punk rock was born. One of the first bands into the fray was the Cure. Their first album, *Three Imaginary Boys* (reconfigured for the U.S. as *Boys Don't Cry*), released in 1979, was a brilliant effort, with unique guitar parts and soul-wrenching vocals that seemed to come right from the heart.

"If I didn't wear makeup I couldn't get on stage. I'd be much too self conscious."

—Robert Smith

The Cure was started by Robert Smith, as the "Easy Cure," with three school friends. Lol Tolhurst on drums and local hotshot guitarist Porl Thompson would bounce in and out of the lineup over the years. The only constant was Smith, in pancake makeup and lipstick, who was a prolific songwriter with great imagination and a seemingly tortured psyche. Over the course of 30 years, he was an unstoppable machine, always moving forward, despite bouts with depression.

GREATEST HITS	
YEAR	SONG
1979	"Boys Don't Cry"
	"Jumping Someone Else's Train"
1981	"Charlotte Sometimes"
1982	"Let's Go to Bed"
1985	"In Between Days"
1987	"Just Like Heaven"
1989	"Fascination Street"
	"Love Song"
1990	"Never Enough"
	"Pictures of You"
1992	"High"
	"Friday I'm in Love"
1996	"Mint Car"
1997	"Wrong Number"

Goth Rock

Bands like Bauhaus and Siouxsie and the Banshees might lay claim to being originators of goth rock, but the Cure stayed on the road bringing their poppier brand of darkness to the fans. The goth kids dressed in black, wore heavy layers of mascara, and were obsessed with death and depression, candles and crucifixes. Smith admitted that he could sometimes get depressed and wrote music that reflected that; he just couldn't make those happy upbeat songs sound legitimate. The odd thing was some of the albums were made while the players felt quite joyful, and they were shocked when they listened to the playback and it was all gloom and doom.

Robert Smith, the founding and only constant member of The Cure, became the lead singer of the group only after the departure of the previous lead singer and a futile quest for a suitable new one.

On the group's next three albums, the Cure moved past post-punk into their own world. *17 Seconds* was sparse and gloomy, with a surprise U.K. hit, "A Forest." *Faith* followed, filled with questions about religion with imagery of old churches. *Pornography* moved past melancholy into rage, and what seemed like madness. After the psychedelic experimentation of *The Top*, the Cure shifted into their most popular period with albums like *The Head On The Door*, *Kiss Me Kiss Me Kiss Me*, and the epic crowd pleaser *Disintegration*. That trio of albums included the big hits "In Between Days," "Just Like Heaven," and "Pictures of You."

Just as their star might have been fading, a whole new generation of bands burst onto the scene paying obvious homage to their heroes. Bands like the Killers and Franz Ferdinand had taken the Cure to heart and were all the healthier for it. Elder statesmen though they may be, the Cure continue to record new material and tour every couple of years.

BO DIDDLEY

December 30, 1928–

Bob Diddley, aka "The Originator," is one of the founding fathers of rock and roll, and has influenced . . . well, just about everybody. Like Chess Record's label mate Chuck Berry, Bo Diddley was using the electric guitar in new ways; he created a hard-driving, riff-driven music that was not the blues, not R&B, but something new—rock and roll.

Diddley was a rhythm master. He brought his own beat, the Bo Diddley beat, to the table. Hum it—shave and a haircut, two bits—and you'll hear his influence. The Bo Diddley beat can be heard in songs by Buddy Holly ("Not Fade Away"), The Who ("Magic Bus"), Bruce Springsteen ("She's the One"), and The Strangeloves ("I Want Candy"), among many, many others.

"I made 'Bo Diddley' in '55, they started playing it, and everybody freaked out. Caucasian kids threw Beethoven into the garbage can." —Bo Diddley

Inspired by African tribal rhythms, Bo Diddley not only influenced the course of rock and roll but also provided a basis for rap music, with his famous chanted call-and-answer lyrics, his larger-than-life ego, and his finely tuned braggadocio. An early rock and roll rebel, Diddley was asked to perform Tennessee Ernie Ford's hit "Sixteen Tons" on Ed Sullivan's famous TV show and instead performed his hit, "Bo Diddley." This got Sullivan mad, and Bo Diddley, the first African-American musician to appear on the show, was never asked back.

NUGGET: So strong was Diddley's affinity for rhythm that sometimes his songs—like the famous "Who Do You Love"—are literally all about the beat, and the musicians play the same chord through the whole song.

Not just famous for his original sound, Bo Diddley was known for his signature rectangular-shaped guitar, custom made for him by the Gretsch guitar company. Bo was also the first musician to have women in his band.

Bands from The Rolling Stones to the New York Dolls have covered Bo Diddley songs, and nearly everyone has ripped him off at least once. As the old expression goes, if Bo Diddley had a dollar for everyone who incorporated his sound into their music, he would be a very, very rich man.

"Love Is Strange"

You may not know that the song "Love Is Strange," first recorded by Mickey and Sylvia in 1956, was written by Bo Diddley, because it was written under a pseudonym. Sylvia Vanderpool went on to found, with husband Joe Robinson, Sugar Hill Records, an important rap label, which released the first successful rap song, "Rapper's Delight" by the Sugarhill Gang. "Love is Strange" provided the soundtrack for one of the most famous dance scenes between Patrick Swayze and Jennifer Grey in the 1987 film, *Dirty Dancing*.

Bo Diddley still tours with a supply of his handcrafted rectangular guitars, designed by him in 1958. He also was one of the first to set up a home studio.

Everybody wants to play with Bo. Here, Diddley performs at the 1985 Live Aid Concert accompanied by George Thorogood.

GREATEST HITS	
Year	Song
1955	"Bo Diddley"
	"I'm a Man"
1956	"Who Do You Love?"
1957	"Hey Bo Diddley"
1959	"Say Man"
1960	"Road Runner"
1962	"You Can't Judge a Book by Its Cover"

DONOVAN

May 10, 1946–

Donovan was an artist at the very center of rock and roll culture for a very short period of time, but while he was there he was white hot. Young Scottish folk singer Donovan Leitch learned to finger pick from a gypsy traveler and he didn't look back, learning traditional folk songs around the time Bob Dylan was doing the same thing in America. Early in Donovan's career, Dylan was to be a major influence, right down to the little Woody Guthrie cap he wore. He scored an early hit with "Catch the Wind"—was it the wind Dylan was blowing his way?

NUGGET: When Donovan first arrived in America, he was known as Britain's answer to Bob Dylan.

Along the way, Donovan reinvented himself as a medieval psychedelic troubadour and banged out hits with producer Mickie Most and backup from musicians like Jeff Beck, Jimmy Page, and Paul McCartney, who sang backup vocals and played bass on "Mellow Yellow." Donovan in turn gave Paul a line for the song "Yellow Submarine"—"sky of blue and sea of green."

When the Beatles camped off to India, Donovan was with them along with Mia Farrow, the Beach Boys' Mike Love, and many others. Donovan claims to have taught John Lennon to fingerpick during that idyll, and John composed "Dear Prudence" and "Julia" using his techniques. McCartney kept an eye on the proceedings without directly asking for a lesson and devised his own fingerpicking style for "Blackbird."

The first-ever edition of *Rolling Stone* (November 9, 1967) contained an interview with Donovan who stated: "There's only one thing in the end, and that's singing truth in a pleasant way."

The Allman Brothers Band used Donovan's "There Is a Mountain" as the basis for their famous 33-plus minute long "Mountain Jam" on *Eat A Peach*. Stephen Stills and Al Kooper scored an underground hit with his song "Season Of The Witch."

He was the sweet, loving, child-man of the '60s, sometimes inane ("I Love My Shirt"), sometimes overreaching ("Atlantis"), but when he hit a hippie groove it was magical.

GREATEST HITS

Year	Song
1965	"Catch the Wind"
	"Colours"
1966	"Sunshine Superman"
	"Mellow Yellow"
1967	"Epistle to Dippy"
	"There Is a Mountain"
	"Wear Your Love Like Heaven"
1968	"Jennifer Juniper"
	"Hurdy Gurdy Man"
	"Atlantis"

Don't Look Back

There's a scene in the D.A. Pennebaker documentary *Don't Look Back* where Dylan is holding court in his hotel room. Donovan comes to play a simple happy ditty. Dylan seemingly blows him away with the much more sophisticated "It's All Over Now Baby Blue." In reality the two were very friendly and shared much music in common, but the celluloid moment is the memory that lasts.

THE DOORS

1965–1973

The Doors took the sleazy energy of the mid-'60s L.A. Sunset Strip and broadcast it out from Hollywood's Whisky a Go Go to the world stage. Building on the psychedelic blues-based garage rock of that scene, the Doors upped the ante and soared past groups like the Electric Prunes. They boasted some excellent musicianship and a desire to expand the format, and the mind, as far as they would go. As Jim Morrison cajoled on their first single, it was time to "break on through to the other side."

Jim Morrison and keyboard player Ray Manzarek met at UCLA film school and added John Densmore on drums and Robbie Krieger on guitar. The Doors didn't have a bass player, but they did have the low, hound-dog moan of lead singer Morrison to keep things earthy.

The Poets' Corner

Depressed and overwhelmed by police reaction to his concert performances and a court case in which he was convicted of "lewd and lascivious behavior," Morrison left the U.S. for Paris to write poetry. His first collection of poems, *The Lord and the Creatures*, was published in 1970. Paris, however, was the not refuge he'd hope for, and his drug use got the better of him. He was found dead in his bathtub on July 3, 1971, apparently of a heart attack at the very young age of 27. He was buried in the Poets' Corner of the Paris cemetery, Père-Lachaise, not far from the graves of Balzac, Moliere, and Oscar Wilde.

Morrison was an army brat with a desire to follow every hedonistic impulse he could think of. It didn't hurt that he had the handsome, bad boy looks of Marlon Brando with a Lord Byron head of hair. The teen magazines found him a must-have pinup, but the solid musicianship of the group allowed Morrison a soft landing whenever his excesses became too much. Almost all of their music was collaborative, with Morrison providing the poetry and a sonorous sexy delivery that gave everything gravitas.

The Doors delivered a string of hits, while other psychedelic outfits of the period languished in the underground. Their albums featured long exploratory workouts that impressed the rock critics, but their singles were just what the teenagers ordered—catchy, hormonally-charged songs with titles that said it all: "Hello, I Love You," "Light My Fire," "Touch Me," "Love Her Madly," and "Love Me Two Times."

GREATEST HITS	
Year	Song
1967	"Break on Through (to the Other Side)"
	"Light My Fire"
	"Love Me Two Times"
1968	"Hello, I Love You"
1969	"Touch Me"
1971	"Love Her Madly"

The Doors had a five-year run with Morrison, with their best material occurring at the beginning and the end. Morrison grew tired of the demands of being a sex symbol and pop star and ran off to Paris, where he died in 1971. Since his death, the cult of Morrison has continued to grow, though one wonders what the Doors' legacy would be if he had stuck around and grown old and bald. Instead, we keep alive the mythic cliché of the beautiful young man, born to fly too close to the sun.

The Doors (from left: Robby Kreiger, John Densmore, Jim Morrison, and Ray Manzarek) derived their name from the Aldous Huxley-penned treatise "The Doors of Perception," about the mind-altering effect of drugs.

BOB DYLAN

May 24, 1941–

There is much speculation that the famous motorcycle accident, which stopped Bob Dylan mid-career, never really happened. At the time people thought Bob was lying in a coma, the voice of a generation sidelined in a body cast. Historians, however, have suggested it was merely a minor accident. Whatever the truth, Bob Dylan desperately needed to slow down and the motorcycle accident might have been a good cover to get him out of more endless tour dates. At the time of the "accident," he had just completed the most productive year and a half of his career, releasing three landmark albums: *Highway 61 Revisited*, *Bringing It All Back Home*, and *Blonde on Blonde*. The song "Like a Rolling Stone" went to #1 and made the music world reconsider what a pop song could be. Touring around the globe with the band known as the Band, Dylan was booed by folk purists who thought he had sold out when he went "electric." In reality, Dylan played in rock and roll bands as a teenager, briefly playing piano with teen idol Bobby Vee.

"I consider myself a poet first and a musician second. I live like a poet and I'll die like a poet." –Bob Dylan

Dylan on Film

As these things go, Bob Dylan's career and music are fairly well documented on film. D.A. Pennebaker's 1967 documentary *Don't Look Back* showed the world a cocky and difficult, but essentially engaging, 25-year-old Dylan touring England in 1965. The Pennebaker follow-up, the unreleased *Eat the Document*, followed Dylan's 1966 tour with the Hawks (later the Band) where audience members—screaming "Judas!"—felt betrayed by Dylan's choice to go electric. Dylan wrote the music for a 1973 Sam Peckinpah film called *Pat Garrett and Billy the Kid*; he also wrote, directed, and starred in the poorly reviewed *Renaldo and Clara*. In 2006, director Todd Haynes started work on *I'm Not There*, a film that will tell the story of Dylan's life with six different actors playing the main role over the years.

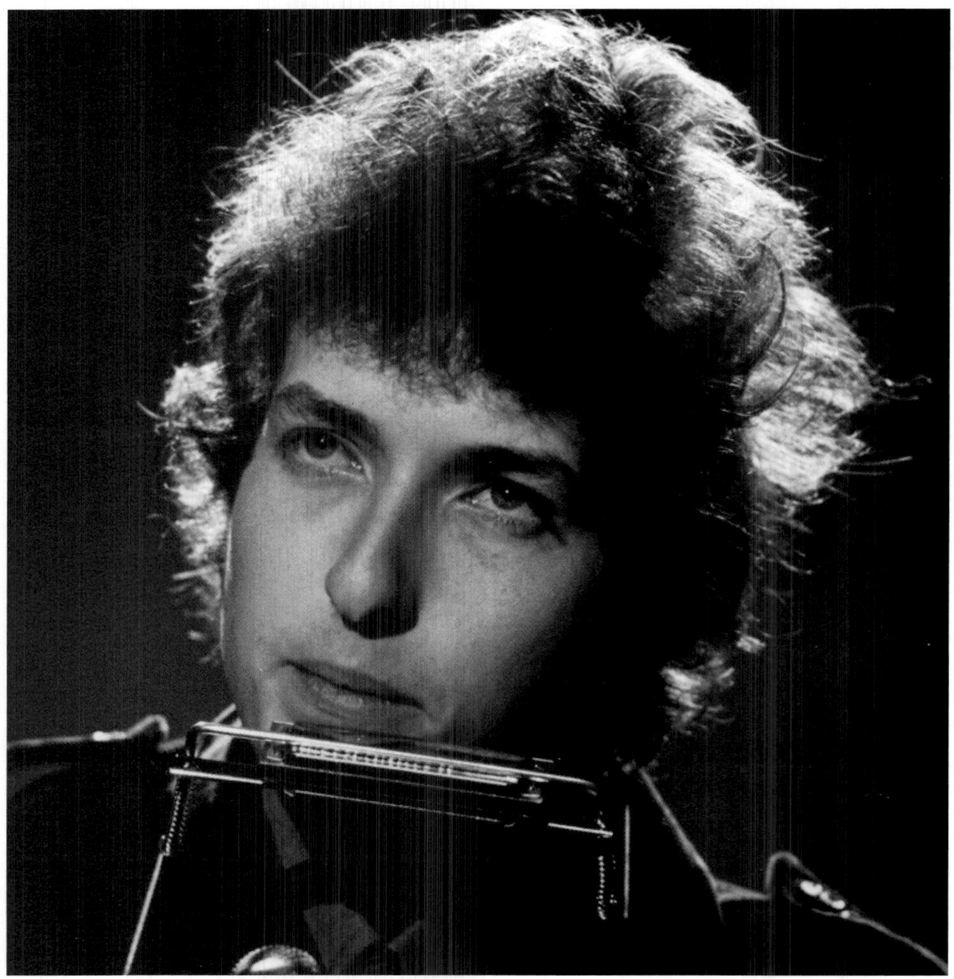

The freewheeling Dylan wanted to expand his repertoire—and go electric—much to his folk fans' consternation.

Bob Dylan was born Robert Zimmerman and raised in Hibbing, Minnesota. His father ran a hardware store, and by the standards of the town the Zimmermans were well off. Bobby was a bit of a teenage ruffian, inspired by Marlon Brando and James Dean. He left home and pretended to go to college in Minneapolis, but he mainly explored the world of folk music, sometimes borrowing others' record collections without their permission to dig deep into the American music anthologies, and especially the music of Woody Guthrie. In his memoir Dylan explains that he found the characters in these old-timey songs somehow more real to him than the people in Minnesota. He wanted to live in that other world of hobos, roustabouts, and riverboat gamblers.

When he had absorbed his influences, he went to New York City to try to find Guthrie, the folk troubadour who had written thousands of songs, including "This Land Is Your Land," and who had traveled and written about American life since the days of the Dust Bowl. When he found Woody, Guthrie was dying in a hospital from Huntington's

While Dylan guitars might become a bit worn from usage, they are usually top-of-the-line instruments—be they Gibsons, Fenders, Martins, or Washburns.

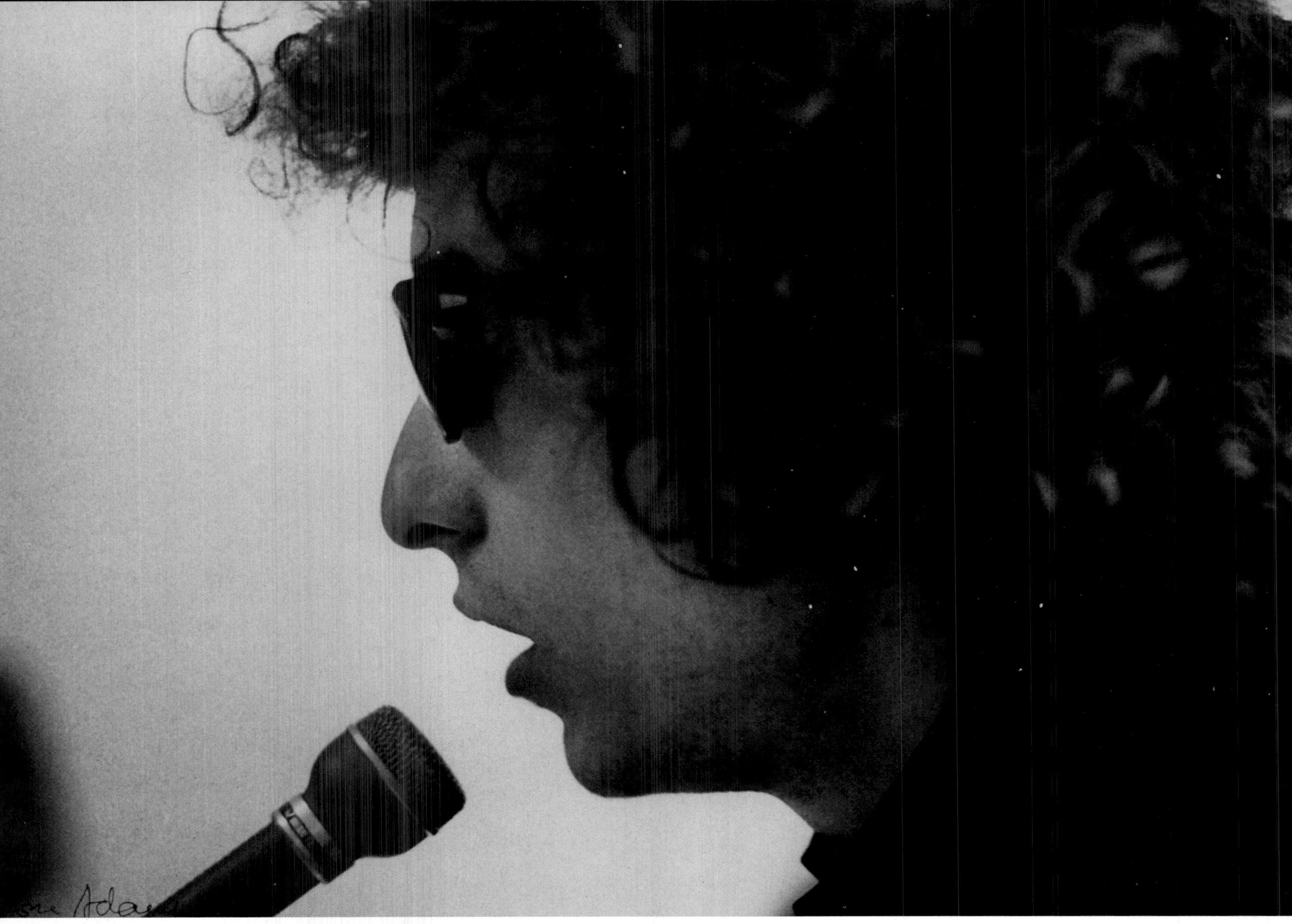

Dylan did his last all-acoustic tour (a three-week romp) in the United Kingdom in 1965.

chorea. Dylan spent time with Woody and was adopted by his compatriots, like Cisco Houston and Ramblin' Jack Elliott, and new artists like Tom Paxton and Dave Van Ronk. Dylan soon became a fixture on the Greenwich Village folk scene.

Once again he absorbed all that was around him. At that time in the Village most people played traditional folk songs from days gone by, but Dylan began writing his own folk songs. His whiny drawl and Woody-wannabe appearance kept him from being taken too seriously, until one night he delivered "A Hard Rain's A-Gonna Fall"; everyone took notice, and his stature shot up. Here was a new kind of contemporary lyric, a new kind of folk song. In short order, he had a record deal and with a cover of his "Blowin' in the Wind," by the popular folk act Peter, Paul and Mary, Dylan had suddenly blown by his contemporaries.

NUGGET: John Hammond, the renowned Columbia Records talent scout who discovered Bob Dylan playing in Greenwich Village, is the same man who discovered Billie Holiday, Aretha Franklin, and later Bruce Springsteen.

After a tentative first album that included a number of covers, Dylan delivered *The Freewheelin' Bob Dylan*. The cover showed a young man with his girlfriend striding down a Greenwich Village street like he owned the place—and he did. "Don't Think Twice It's All Right," "Blowin' in the Wind," and "Girl from the North Country," the affectionate look back to a childhood sweetheart, were all on this album. He followed with *The Times They Are A-Changin'*, a blistering set of contemporary protest songs that put him at the center of the politics of the civil rights and Vietnam War era. But just as the left-wing intelligentsia embraced him, he shifted course again, making an album that was aptly titled *Another Side of Bob Dylan*—a scathing psychological study of his character and his most personal relationships. On *Bringing It All Back Home* the surrealist poet raised his hand, splitting his personality down the middle. Back then people listened to 33⅓ vinyl LPs with two sides, and on *Bringing It All Back Home*, Dylan shape-shifted with the flip of the disc. Side one contained surreal folk songs like "Mr. Tambourine Man" and "It's All Over Now, Baby Blue," but on side two Dylan went electric with "Maggie's Farm" and "Subterranean Homesick Blues."

Dylan roared into the heavy whirlwind of 1966, now thoroughly documented by Martin Scorsese's documentary *No Direction Home*. After the motorcycle accident he came up with *The Basement Tapes* and moved on to country with

"Like a Rolling Stone"

Dylan came up with a biting lyric about a young lady from the upper class who has been taken down a peg or two. In one of his rare stand-alone choruses he took a popular Latin groove of the day, one that had already been used to great effect on songs like "Hang on Sloopy" and " La Bamba," and came up with a monster hook. When it was time to record the song, Dylan assembled a great set of players including guitarist Mike Bloomfield and had them perform live in the studio. A young guitarist named Al Kooper was there looking for a way into the game. He snuck over to the Hammond B3 organ and started playing. The producer tried to kick him out but Dylan liked the sound. Kooper had never played organ before, but the naïve approach he came up with became a signature organ sound for the 1960s. When the song went to number one Kooper became an in-demand keyboard player! Director Martin Scorsese has confessed that even though he grew up in Little Italy, a few blocks from the Greenwich Village folk scene, he had no awareness of Bob Dylan until "Like a Rolling Stone" came over his AM radio.

Nashville Skyline, sang about domestic bliss on *New Morning* and suffered genuine heartbreak on *Blood on the Tracks*. There was another album and tour with the Band, as well as the traveling road show that was the Rolling Thunder Review. He embraced Christianity, had a near death-experience, and kept rolling down the line on an endless tour. Though not quite as prolific as he once was, Dylan still puts out a new album every five years or so, alternating with excellent archival material that is always a revelation. He seems to have a solid sense of who he is and what he wants to accomplish. Every year his catalog collectively sells millions of copies, and the magic he has alchemized continues to swirl round the globe.

GREATEST HITS

Year	Song
1963	"Blowin' in the Wind"
	"Don't Think Twice, It's All Right"
1964	"The Times They Are A-Changin'"
1965	"Mr. Tambourine Man"
	"Like a Rolling Stone"
	"Positively 4th Street"
	"Subterranean Homesick Blues"
1966	"Rainy Day Women #12 & 35"
	"Just Like a Woman"
1969	"Lay Lady Lay"
1973	"Knockin' on Heaven's Door"
1975	"Hurricane"

NUGGET: Robert Zimmerman changed his last name to Dylan, after poet Dylan Thomas.

A scraggly Dylan (right) is supported by guitar wizard Charlie Sexton at the 2002 Newport Folk Festival.

THE EAGLES

1971–

THE EAGLES' LIFE IN THE FAST LANE, CIRCA 1977, WAS STARTING TO WEAR A BIT THIN. HERE (FROM LEFT) DON FELDER, DON HENLEY, JOE WALSH, GLENN FREY, AND RANDY MEISNER ARE NO LONGER THE NEW KIDS IN TOWN.

GREATEST HITS

YEAR	SONG
1972	"Take It Easy"
	"Witchy Woman"
	"Peaceful Easy Feeling"
1973	"Desperado"
	"Tequila Sunrise"
1975	"One of These Nights"
	"Lyin' Eyes"
1977	"Hotel California"
	"New Kid in Town"
	"Life in the Fast Lane"
1979	"Heartache Tonight"

In the late '60s, the L.A. pop scene had grown into a huge business with lots of television variety shows, record labels, and recording studios. There was plenty of session work to be had and musicians from all over came to break into the scene—the goldrush was on and a new kind of cowboy was in town, often living a quasi-rural life in Laurel Canyon where the city seemed far away, even if the paycheck was just over the hill.

"Sometimes I wonder if we don't take ourselves too seriously." —Don Henley

At the Troubador on the Sunset Strip, the Flying Burrito Brothers performed to less than full houses, but at the center of the drunken shambolic unit, having a kick-ass good time, was Gram Parsons. He was being watched carefully from the wings; notes were being taken on his heartbroken, laid-back, country rock sound.

Among those watching were a duo called Longbranch Pennywhistle composed of Glen Frey and J. D. Souther (who went on to co-write hits for the Eagles and Linda Ronstadt, among others). What did Gram have that they didn't, and how could they get it? Meanwhile Linda Rondstadt, the sweetheart of this particular rodeo, was recording her third solo album. She had a knack for gathering great songwriters and players around her, and after road testing a number of musicians she ended up with a backing band that included Don Henley, Glen Frey, Randy Meisner, and Bernie Leadon. Collectively they were L.A. musicians of the highest order, and had already put in time with numerous country rock outfits including Poco, the Flying Burrito Brothers, Dillard and Clark, and Rick Nelson's Stone Canyon Band. They played on her breakout third album, *Linda Ronstadt*, and were soon signed by David Geffen for his new startup label, Asylum.

They adopted the name the Eagles, and went to England where they spent two weeks recording their debut album, *Eagles*, with producer Glyn Johns. The album included the immediate hit single "Take It Easy," written by Frey with friend Jackson Browne.

The Eagles kept touring and the hits kept coming, and coming; the band eventually gravitated to a more rocking sound with the addition of new guitarist Don Felder. A massively successful greatest hits album was released in 1976. Joe Walsh, formerly of the James Gang, replaced a departing Bernie Leadon, and his virtuosic slide playing and great songcraft were a welcome addition to their next album, *Hotel California*. Most agree that *Hotel California*, an album that went platinum in just one week, was the Eagles' finest moment.

Best-selling Album

After only four albums, the band released a compilation, *Eagles: Their Greatest Hits 1971–1975* in 1976. It was a smash hit, the first platinum album (sales of more than one million copies) ever, and to date has sold over 25 million records and counting, making it the best-selling album of all time in the U.S.

THE FACES

SMALL FACES 1965–1969, FACES 1969–1975

The Faces may be best remembered as the backup band for Rod Stewart in the '70s, but they have a legacy that reaches many branches of the rock family tree. Originally they were the Small Faces with Steve Marriott, Ronnie Lane, Ian McLagan, and Kenney Jones. They were tough guys—working-class lads with an ability to crank out the songs. And that's what they did for ex-Rolling Stones' manager Andrew Loog Oldham's Immediate label.

They didn't make much of a dent in the U.S. during those years, with the exception of "Itchycoo Park" and "Tin Soldier," but in England they were constantly on the charts. After the Beatles released their *Sgt. Pepper's* album, the Small Faces put out the equally ambitious *Ogdens' Nut Gone Flake*, an album that came in a circular cover like a tin of tobacco. Side A was a conventional album, but side B featured British comedian Stanley Unwin, the ultimate eccentric Englishman who had a way with mangled words, narrating the fairy tale of Happiness Stan.

Eventually the group began to splinter, with lead singer Steve Marriott leaving to join up with a hot young guitar player named Peter Frampton to start Humble Pie. They spent a lot of time in America and broke there with a live album recorded at the Fillmore. Meanwhile, Rod Stewart and his pal Ron Wood had decided to bail out of the Jeff Beck Group after two successful albums. Rod also started recording solo albums, but he checked his ego at the door to join the newly christened Faces with Wood, Lane, Jones and McLagan. The Faces albums never sold like Rod Stewart's solo work, but they did have a big hit with "Stay With Me," and made a number of albums that were very influential to anyone who dug great rock and roll. They were musicians whose playing melded together a one-for-all woozy groove that teetered between swaggering and staggering. Perhaps the classic example of their sound is the group sing-along "Ooh La La" with its refrain of "I wish that I knew what I know now, when I was younger."

> *"What I do now is all my dad's fault, because he bought me a guitar as a boy, for no apparent reason."* —Rod Stewart

GREATEST HITS

YEAR	SONG
1965	"What'cha Gonna Do About It"
1967	"Here Comes the Nice"
	"Itchycoo Park"
	"Tin Soldier"
1968	"Lazy Sunday"
1971	"Had Me a Real Good Time"
	"Stay with Me"
1973	"Cindy Incidentally"
	"Ooh La La"

BY 1974, THE FACES WERE NEARING THE END OF THEIR COLLABORATIVE LIFE. HERE, MEMBERS (FROM LEFT) RON WOOD AND ROD STEWART SHARE A MIKE.

When They Were No Longer Faces

After Rod decided to keep more of the paycheck, the Faces moved on to other projects, sometimes regrouping with Marriott to record again as the Small Faces. Ronnie Lane recorded an excellent album with Pete Townsend called *Rough Mix*, was diagnosed with multiple sclerosis, and died of pneumonia in 1997. Kenney Jones took over the drum seat in the Who after the death of Keith Moon. Ron Wood joined up with the Rolling Stones. McLagan became a successful session musician and formed the Bump Band, which still tours to this day. After Humble Pie, Marriott had a solo career until he died in a house fire in 1991.

ARETHA FRANKLIN

March 25, 1942–

From her 1967 hit "Respect" to her 1985 duet with the Eurythmics, "Sisters Are Doin' It for Themselves," Aretha Franklin has always been about saying it loud, and saying it proud. She holds the title of Lady Soul, and while there have been plenty of ladies in waiting, virtually no one in the history of popular music has come close to Aretha in either talent or passion.

"I always felt rock and roll was very, very wholesome music."—Aretha Franklin

She grew up in Detroit, the daughter of a preacher man. Her father, the Reverend C. L. Franklin, was the well-respected pastor of the Detroit New Bethel Baptist Church, a gospel singer who raised Aretha and her sisters, Carolyn and Erma, to sing, and a friend of Martin Luther King Jr. Her mother was also a gospel singer, but left the family when Aretha was just 6. Her voice—with its legendary four-octave range—got attention, and she was soon under the wing of the great gospel singer Mahalia Jackson and Sam Cooke, who was making the crossover from gospel to secular music. It's rumored that Berry Gordy tried to sign a teenaged Aretha to his Motown label in the early days, but her father turned down the offer. In 1960 she was discovered by talent scout John Hammond and signed to Columbia Records.

Her years at Columbia were not her most productive, and it wasn't until Jerry Wexler signed Aretha to Atlantic in 1966 that she truly found her home. With a label and producers who understood her, she set out on the road to revolutionize popular music. She recorded her first single for Atlantic—"I Never Loved a Man (the Way I Love You)"—down in Muscle Shoals, Alabama, with authentic Southern R&B men whose gritty sound freed her soul. Indeed, her work on the Atlantic label was prolific, yielding memorable songs such as "A Natural Woman," "Chain of Fools," and "Think," among many others.

Aretha's a symbol of black pride and woman power. And she's done it all—she's had more million-selling records (not to mention more Grammy awards) than any other woman in history, she's the first woman inducted into the rock and roll hall of fame, and her voice was listed by the state of Michigan as a natural resource.

Newly signed to Columbia, Aretha could sing like an angel, yet it would take a few more years, until she moved to Atlantic, that her songs charted.

GREATEST HITS

Year	Song
1967	"I Never Loved a Man (the Way I Love You)"
	"Respect"
	"Baby I Love You"
	"(You Make Me Feel Like) A Natural Woman"
	"Chain of Fools"
1968	"(Sweet Sweet Baby) Since You've Been Gone"
	"Think"
	"The House That Jack Built"
	"I Say a Little Prayer"
1971	"Spanish Harlem"
	"Rock Steady"
1972	"Day Dreaming"
1973	"Until You Come Back to Me (That's What I'm Gonna Do)"
1985	"Freeway of Love"

R-E-S-P-E-C-T

Producer Jerry Wexler came up with the idea of Otis Redding's R&B hit "Respect" as a crossover song for Aretha. It worked. "Respect" became Aretha's signature song, an anthem for feminists, one of the most famous rock and roll songs of all time, and was even included in the Millennium time capsule as an example of an important cultural artifact to be preserved for future generations. How's that for respect?

GRATEFUL DEAD

1965–1995

You didn't have to take drugs to enjoy a Grateful Dead concert, but it helped. The Dead, as their throngs of hard-core fans knew them, were all about live concerts and the on-the-road lifestyle. Their loyal legion of tie-dyed partying fans, known as Deadheads, were always along for the ride, following the tour for months, even years, at a time.

Jerry Garcia and Bob Weir perform at a Dead show in Berkeley, California, in 1981. Garcia was an accomplished guitarist despite losing a portion of his right middle finger in a childhood wood-chopping accident.

The band got their start as the house band for Ken Kesey's infamous Acid Tests—public parties thrown in the San Francisco Bay Area before LSD was declared illegal. Jerry Garcia, the reluctant leader, was famous for his unique and soaring style of guitar playing, and along with bass player Phil Lesh and guitarist Bob Weir, they were the ultimate triumvirate of hippie/jam band rockers. With band mates Ron "Pigpen" McKernan on keyboards and harmonica, and both Bill Kreutzmann and Mickey Hart on drums, they could seemingly play all night long.

The Dead released three albums on Warner Brothers Records before realizing that, not only were they substantially in debt to the label, but the records hadn't captured the magic of their live show. The fans wanted a live album, so they gave them 1969's *Live/Dead*. With its 23-minute live version of "Dark Star," the essence of the band was finally captured. The Grateful Dead were the first band to approve of fans bootlegging—illegally taping—their performances, and even sold special tickets so that tapers would all sit in the same place behind the sound board.

Two classic studio albums followed in 1970: *Workingman's Dead* and *American Beauty*, featuring many of the songs that people think of when they think of the Dead—"Uncle John's Band," "Casey Jones," "Sugar Magnolia," and "Truckin'." Their records got some FM radio play, but the band was primarily a live act, and the fans liked it that way. When Jerry Garcia died of a heart attack in 1995, at the age of 53, the rest of the band decided things wouldn't be the same without him. They toured again, first as the Other Ones, and later as the Dead—with the word "grateful" retired in Jerry's honor.

NUGGET: Ben & Jerry's Cherry Garcia ice cream was named in honor of Jerry Garcia. Cherry Garcia, cherry ice cream with cherries and fudge flakes, is one of the company's best-selling flavors.

GREATEST HITS

Year	Song
1968	"Dark Star"
1970	"Uncle John's Band"
	"Casey Jones"
	"Sugar Magnolia"
	"Friend of the Devil"
	"Ripple"
	"Truckin'"
1974	"Scarlet Begonias"
1975	"The Music Never Stopped"
1987	"Touch of Grey"

On The Road

Life on the road with the Dead was a lot like being on the road with a circus. Serious Deadheads would stay on the road for as long as they could afford to be away from home. Since the show was like a traveling city, deadheads could make money selling things—tie-dyed clothing, jewelry, food, and, of course, drugs—to their fellow travelers. A group of clean and sober fans, who called themselves the Wharf Rats, would even hold AA and Narcotics Anonymous meetings between the band's sets. There were also fans called "spinners;" who would twirl around and around when Jerry was singing, and sit down to take a rest when it was Bob's turn to do a song.

GUNS N' ROSES

1985–

Guns N' Roses' sound was familiar to hard rock aficionados of the '70s, but was a fresh breath of hedonistic rock and roll to kids who'd grown up on Wham and Madonna. They were the new bad boys on the block and the girls, and boys, couldn't stay away.

Axl Rose and guitarist Tracii Guns merged to create Guns N' Roses with a bunch of guys from their L.A. music scene, including Rose's friend, guitarist Izzy Stradlin. Tracii didn't stick it out, and the band added English-born guitarist Slash. An independently released EP caused a stir among the major labels. Rumor has it Geffen A&R man Tom Zutaut saw the band at Hollywood's Troubadour, and spread the word that they sucked in order to buy himself time to sign them. Their debut album, *Appetite for Destruction*, was off to a slow start when MTV added "Welcome to the Jungle" to the overnight rotation. Music fans took notice. The album, inspired by AC/DC and Aerosmith, was the biggest-selling debut album in the history of rock and roll.

Controversy swirled around the band almost from the very beginning. They were bad boys, on stage and off. Their second album—*GN'R Lies*—contained songs with questionable lyrics. Critics wondered whether the youth of today should be listening to cuts like "Used to Love Her" where the lyrics went on ". . . but I had to kill her." Their song "One in a Million" also featured offensive terms for blacks and gays, and got the group banned from an AIDS benefit concert. Rose responded that some of his favorite rock heroes—Freddie Mercury and Elton John—were gay.

Once a choirboy by the name of Bill Bailey, Axl Rose took the surname of his natural father, who had abandoned the family when the boy was 2 years old.

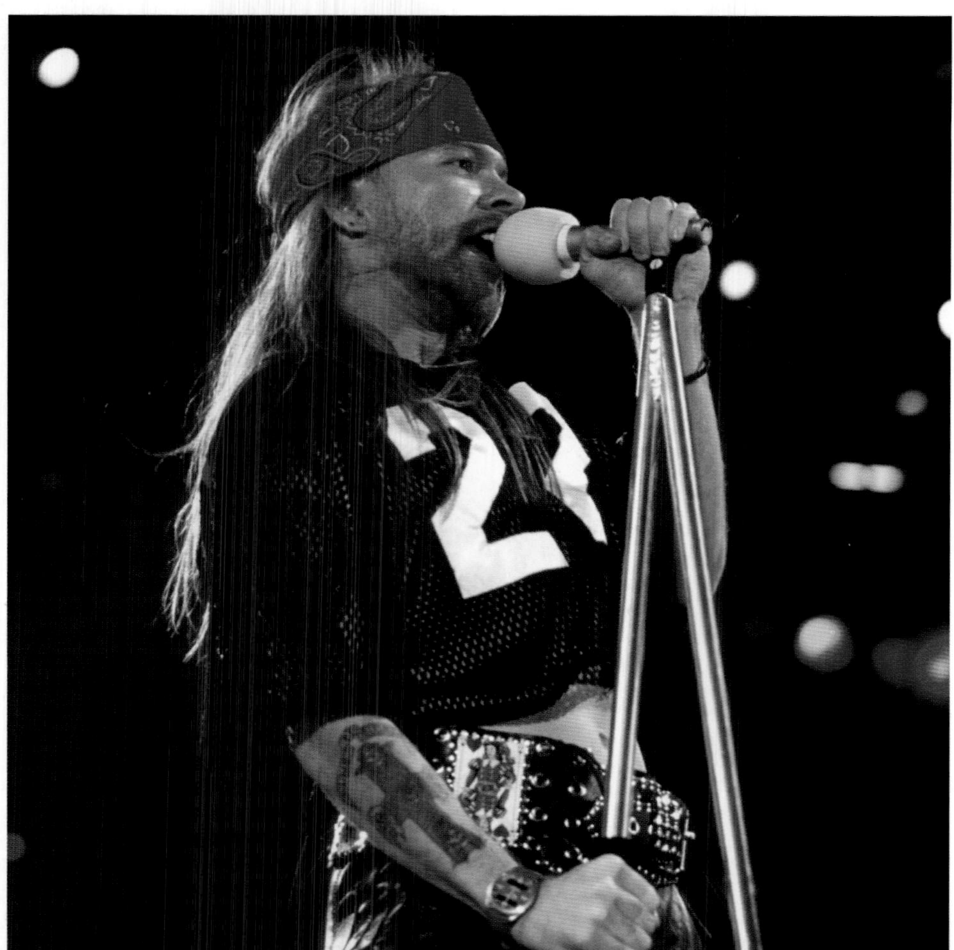

"I've really learned to control myself. It used to be that I would get mad, break everything in the room, smack somebody in the face and then leave. Now I work real hard at trying to keep things cool and together." —Axl Rose

Things started to fall apart in the early '90s, and before long Axl was the only original band member left. Slash signed the band name over to Rose, something he would later regret. A greatest hits release in 2004 caused a stir when Axl sued Geffen for not consulting him on the track listing. As of this writing, fans are still waiting for Rose to finish the next GN'R release—tentatively entitled *Chinese Democracy*—reportedly in the works for more than 10 years, at a cost of $13 million.

"Sweet Child O' Mine"

Erin Everly, daughter of Don Everly of the Everly Brothers, was the inspiration for the GN'R song "Sweet Child O' Mine." Axl met Erin in 1986 and they dated for years before Axl threatened to kill himself if she didn't marry him. The two married in 1990 but were not happy, and not long after Everly's miscarriage, the two had the marriage annulled in 1991.

GREATEST HITS

Year	Song
1987	"Welcome to the Jungle"
	"Sweet Child O' Mine"
1988	"Paradise City"
	"Used to Love Her"
	"One in a Million"
1991	"You Could Be Mine"

JIMI HENDRIX

NOVEMBER 27, 1942–SEPTEMBER 18, 1970

He was the electrified voodoo child who turned rock music upside down and backwards. Jimi Hendrix helped propel the '60s out of the innocence of the Kennedy years and into the psychedelic end of the decade. Hendrix took electric guitar playing to new places, and showed the world a different way to experience life and music: "not necessarily stoned, but beautiful."

> *"When the power of love overcomes the love of power the world will know peace."*
>
> —Jimi Hendrix

Hendrix pulled out all the stops as a showman, playing the guitar behind his back and with his teeth, and pleasing the crowd by lighting his axe on fire. Beneath the antics lay a brilliant musician and composer. He wrote killer ballads like "The Wind Cries Mary" and redefined rock music with songs that seemed to have no real antecedents, like "Foxy Lady" and "Purple Haze," riff-rock amped up and out into the stratosphere. He was also a master interpreter of others' songs, taking on Dylan and Lennon/McCartney and making their songs his own. As a blues player, he was beyond compare; and no one else has ever come close to capturing his understated hipster vocal style.

Jimi was born in Seattle in 1942. He gravitated to the guitar at an early age, and actually walked around playing a broom until his dad bought him a cheap acoustic guitar. He taught himself the blues from records by Muddy Waters and B. B. King. He learned to play a right-handed guitar upside down and backwards. After playing in local bands he did a stint in the Air Force, where he played in a band with fellow serviceman Billy Cox on bass. After being discharged, allegedly for a parachuting injury, he moved to Nashville and developed his chops on the Southern soul circuit. While the pay was often low, he backed up the likes of Sam Cooke, Ike and Tina Turner, and the Isley Brothers. He also performed with Little Richard, who some say, inspired Hendrix's flamboyant personal style.

JIMI, IN THE CROWD, AT THE FAMED 1967 MONTEREY POP FESTIVAL. ROLLING STONE BRIAN JONES WOULD LATER INTRODUCE HIM TO THE AUDIENCE AS "THE MOST EXCITING PERFORMER I'VE EVER HEARD."

Landing on the New York club scene, he performed as part of Jimmy James & the Blue Flames. He picked up on what was going on at the time, especially digging Dylan's albums from 1966, but his act wasn't taken seriously. He was seen as more of an oddity, just another poor lower East Side street musician trying to make a buck. One of Keith Richards' girlfriends befriended Jimi and introduced him to Chas Chandler, bass player of the Animals. Chandler saw his potential and took him to England, where he signed him to a management

Near the End

A peace rally at Madison Square Garden on January 28, 1970, was the place where Hendrix seemed to lose his way. He was the headliner of the concert but only performed two songs with his group the Band of Gypsys. Something was not right that night. Some have suggested Hendrix was slipped some drugs. He stopped playing, sat on the stage awhile and then left. He told *Rolling Stone* that it felt like "the end of a big long fairy tale."

Due to amplifier problems, the Experience's first show in Honolulu lasted a mere 30 minutes, so the crowd was invited back for the next day's performance.

contract, changed the spelling of his name to Jimi, hooked him up with Noel Redding on bass and Mitch Mitchell on drums, and outfitted everyone in crazy Carnaby Street clothes.

With the release of his first album, Hendrix was the toast of London. British blues-rockers, like Eric Clapton and Jeff Beck, were entranced by Hendrix. He'd learned and lived the blues firsthand, while they had merely studied it from a distance. The original African-American blues guys they'd met or played with were often much older and quite cranky. Clapton quickly formed Cream and Jeff Beck started his own foray into Hendrix-style heavy blues with the Jeff Beck Group.

Are You Experienced? went to the top of the charts in the U.K. The album beckoned listeners into a whole new world, a little darker and scarier than anything they had previously experienced. Americans had to wait almost a year to get their first taste of the Jimi Hendrix Experience. At the insistence of Paul

Because of numerous technical delays, headliner Jimi played the morning after the scheduled end of the Woodstock show. By Woodstock, Jimi had said good-bye to the Experience and hello to his new group, Gypsy Sun and Rainbows.

By the Time He Got to Woodstock

At Woodstock, Hendrix played with a large ensemble. He was supposedly also the highest paid performer at the festival. Woodstock, which was a bit of fiasco for those who attended, is remembered more fondly from the carefully edited film and soundtrack album. Hendrix was documented with a rousing interpretation of the "Star Spangled Banner" that showed how he had mastered the randomness of feedback with fuzz and wah-wah effects to forge a new kind of playing style.

The members of the Experience played together for three days before embarking as the opening act on a tour for Johnny Hallyday, "the French Elvis."

McCartney, Jimi was invited to play the Monterey Pop Festival in 1967. Monterey introduced him to the States with a blistering attack on the Troggs' "Wild Thing" and a powerful re-working of Dylan's "Like a Rolling Stone." By the time the film, *Monterey Pop*, played across the country, Hendrix was a certifiable star.

On his next album he proved to be equally adept at working in a studio, learning the soundboard and using it as an instrument in its own right. *Axis: Bold as Love* was a sonic step forward, with "If 6 Was 9" playing in the film *Easy Rider*. He would also produce bands that opened for the Experience, like Cat Mother and the All Night New Boys and Aire Apparent. From September of 1967 until his death in 1970, Hendrix was involved in almost non-stop touring, recording, and late-night jamming.

Electric Ladyland was his follow up; a sprawling affair recorded in Hendrix's own Electric Ladyland Studio, still operating on 8th Street in New York City. Al Kooper and members of Traffic contributed to the album, which featured amazing songs like "Burning of the Midnight Lamp."

The Hendrix Experience enthralled the public with its performance at Monterey, which Hendrix ended by setting his beloved Fender Stratocaster aflame.

GREATEST HITS

Year	Song
1967	"Fire"
	"Foxy Lady"
	"Hey Joe"
	"Purple Haze"
	"The Wind Cries Mary"
	"Castles Made of Sand"
	"Little Wing"
	"Wait Until Tomorrow"
1968	"Crosstown Traffic"
	"All Along the Watchtower"
	"Burning of the Midnight Lamp"
	"Voodoo Child (Slight Return)"

In 1968, with the rise of black power, Hendrix was catching some heat for playing with a couple of white guys from England. He was also sick of all the theatrics his fans expected from the Experience, so he started the Band of Gypsys, which reunited him with his Air Force pal Billy Cox and the powerful soul drummer Buddy Miles, who had played with Wilson Pickett and the Electric Flag. The band played a series of shows at the Fillmore East, but disbanded shortly afterwards.

A re-formed Experience with Cox and Mitchell returned to Europe in August of 1970 and played to 600,000 people at the Isle of Wight Festival. Hendrix was busy working on an album called the *First Ray of the New Rising Sun* in his newly built studios. A tour of Europe was supposed to help pay the building costs, but complications from an overdose of sleeping pills ended his story. Many wonder where Hendrix would have taken music if he'd lived. He was a self-taught genius who affected jazz players like Miles Davis (think *Bitches Brew*), the funk of Sly Stone and Funkadelic, as well as all the heavy blues players who came in his wake. We can only wonder and listen to the puzzle pieces he left behind.

BUDDY HOLLY

September 7, 1936–February 3, 1959

Buddy Holly and the Crickets performing in 1958 as part of Alan Freed's "Big Beat Show" tour; he would become one of the first inductees into the Rock and Roll Hall of Fame 28 years later.

GREATEST HITS	
Year	Song
1957	"That'll Be the Day"
	"Words of Love"
	"Peggy Sue"
	"Oh Boy!"
1958	"Maybe Baby"
	"Rave On"
	"It's So Easy"
1959	"It Doesn't Matter Anymore"
	"Raining in My Heart"
	"Peggy Sue Got Married"

Buddy Holly was an unlikely pioneer of rock and roll. Hailing from Lubbock, Texas, he started out as an unsuccessful country singer. When Elvis Presley came through town, Holly knew he wanted to go in a new direction, so he dusted off one of his country numbers called "That'll Be the Day" and scored a #1 hit at the end of 1957.

Buddy Holly was an innovator; using a two-guitar attack to create great rhythm tracks, he experimented in the studio with tape delay and double-tracked voice and guitar. His band style inspired groups like the Beatles, who covered "Words of Love." It's surprising how such a short career could have such a profound effect on popular culture. With his gawky physique and big framed glasses, he was the prototype of the rock and roll geek, making the music world safe for those who would follow, like Elvis Costello and Weezer's Rivers Cuomo.

Fueled by hits like "Rave On," "Maybe Baby," and "Peggy Sue," (the name of drummer Jerry Allison's girlfriend), Holly barnstormed America for a couple of years with his band, the Crickets. His quirky hiccup-style vocal approach was Holly's often-imitated signature.

American Pie

There's been much speculation as to who's who in Don McLean's metaphoric history of rock and roll, "American Pie." Written 10 years after Holly's death, the song brought Buddy Holly and his music back to the forefront. "This'll be the day that I die," sang McLean, and often the song was played on the radio back to back with Buddy Holly's "That'll Be the Day." Many rock icons are alluded to in the song, but not by name. Most agree that Bob Dylan is the court jester, mocking the King—Elvis Presley—and the Queen—Connie Francis. Satan is Mick Jagger, the "girl who sang the blues" is Janis Joplin, and the Beatles are the quartet who practiced in the park.

"He made it easy to wear glasses. I was Buddy Holly."

—John Lennon

Buddy eventually left the Crickets for a solo career. He married Maria Elena Santiago in 1958, proposing to her after just one date. Unfortunately, cash flow problems led Holly to agree to tour the Midwest with the Winter Dance Party. One night, he didn't ride on the tour bus, and instead climbed on board a small plane with the Big Bopper ("Chantilly Lace") and Ritchie Valens ("La Bamba"). The plane went down in Clear Lake, Iowa on February 3, 1959. Holly was just 22 years old.

Buddy's legacy lives on. The Rolling Stones' first chart success in the U.S. was with their 1964 cover of Holly's "Not Fade Away," and Linda Ronstadt recorded a version of "That'll Be The Day." Don McLean immortalized him forever in his epic 1971 song "American Pie"—the day Holly's plane crashed was "the day the music died."

NUGGET: John Lennon and Paul McCartney were big fans, and chose their group name, the Beatles, in homage to Holly's band the Crickets.

JEFFERSON AIRPLANE

1965–

Jefferson Airplane members Jorma Kaukonen, Grace Slick, Paul Kantner, Marty Balin, Spencer Dryden (who replaced original drummer Skip Spence when he quit to co-found Moby Grape), and Jack Casady.

With the arrival of the Beatles, most folk groups of the early '60s seemed passé, but some scrambled to update themselves. It's surprising to think of the Jefferson Airplane in this context, since they're known for being a psychedelic band from San Francisco in the Summer of Love. But when they started they were covering folk staples like "High Flying Bird" and "Get Together," and singing in a harmony style not unlike Peter, Paul and Mary.

At their peak, Jefferson Airplane was a crazy quilt of a band that played all three major U.S. rock festivals of the '60s—Monterey, Woodstock, and Altamont. The band was originally put together by Marty Balin, a visual artist with a great tenor voice; Paul Kantner, a folk strummer fascinated with science fiction; Jorma Kaukonen, a fleet-fingered blues picker; and sunglassed, head-band-wearing bass player Jack Casady. But it was Grace Slick, with her deep resonant tone, fashion model good looks, and slightly menacing demeanor who set the dark hippie tone of the band.

Starship

The Airplane remade itself as the Jefferson Starship after Kaukonen and Casady left to start Hot Tuna. Kantner had already recorded under that name on a solo project. Ironically the Jefferson Starship would turn into an MTV hit machine, making music that sold quite well but lacked social relevance. By the end, the band no longer had any original Jefferson Airplane members; Paul Kantner fought in court to have them called simply Starship. With Slick suddenly back in the fold after rehab, the rechristened Starship scored one of their biggest hits, "We Built This City," a song written by outside writers bemoaning what had happened to San Francisco after its mid-'60s heyday.

GREATEST HITS

Year	Song
1967	"Somebody to Love"
	"White Rabbit"
1969	"Volunteers"
1974	"Ride the Tiger" (Jefferson Starship)
1975	"Miracles" (Jefferson Starship)
1979	"Jane" (Jefferson Starship)
1981	"Find Your Way Back" (Jefferson Starship)
1985	"We Built This City" (Starship)
	"Sara" (Starship)
1987	"Nothing's Gonna Stop Us Now" (Starship)

NUGGET: Though listed on the album credits as spiritual advisor, Jerry Garcia was really the secret producer of the Airplane's classic album *Surrealistic Pillow*.

Grace was originally in a group called the Great Society, which frequently opened for the Jefferson Airplane. When original singer Signe Toly Anderson left to have a baby, Grace climbed on board the Airplane. She brought a couple of numbers from the Great Society with her, including "White Rabbit," her reimagining of the *Alice in Wonderland* story as a drug parable, and "Somebody to Love," which was the band's first and only major chart hit. The album *Surrealistic Pillow* was Airplane's most coherent and focused moment, and because they were the first Monterey performers with an album out, *Surrealistic Pillow* went to #3 in the Summer of Love.

Almost all of Jefferson Airplane's albums charted in the Top 20, despite little success with singles. They were making pop music at its most radical. The album *Volunteers* was a call to arms to change the world. Jefferson Airplane was the soundtrack to all the new ideas of the time: revolution, free love, and drug experimentation.

ELTON JOHN

MARCH 25, 1947–

No performing songwriter has ever had the staying power of Elton John. Currently breezing through his fourth decade on the charts, Elton has sold more albums worldwide than anyone other than Elvis Presley and the Beatles. He has worked and played hard, living life to the fullest along the way.

Born Reginald Dwight, Elton was determined from the very beginning. His first band, Bluesology, with their comprehensive knowledge of soul music, quickly became a backup band for American soul acts touring the U.K. Elton would go on to pick apart and absorb virtually every genre of popular music in his career. He is a supreme music fan, generous with his praise for his latest musical love. During his career, he befriended and collaborated with John Lennon, Cher, Queen, the Beach Boys, and many more.

NUGGET: Bluesology eventually became the backup band for the English blues shouter Long John Baldry. When Reg Dwight decided it was time to strike out on his own he took his last name from John Baldry, and his first from sax player Elton Dean for his new solo persona.

THE YEAR 1974 FOUND ELTON WOWING AUDIENCES, GETTING A RECORD-BREAKING MULTIMILLION-DOLLAR DEAL WITH MCA, AND COWRITING JOHN LENNON'S COMEBACK SINGLE "WHATEVER GETS YOU THROUGH THE NIGHT."

At an audition for a recording contract, Elton was passed a set of lyrics written by fellow Englishman Bernie Taupin. They immediately started collaborating on songs through the mail, although they wouldn't actually meet in person for some time. Meanwhile, Elton was further honing his pop vocals by rerecording popular hits of the day for budget albums. Sometimes his covers sounded better than the originals.

Empty Sky, his first album with Taupin as lyricist, was a flop, but the pair decided to raise the bar on the next album, simply titled *Elton John*. They brought on string arranger Paul Buckmaster and had a big international hit with "Your Song," one of their most enduring compositions. They followed quickly with *Tumbleweed Connection*, an epic slice of Americana from a British perspective. Some rock critics felt the album lacked authenticity, but it's stood up over the years as one of their finest efforts.

The first half of the '70s was Elton John's golden period, with *Madman Across the Water*, *Honky Château*, and *Goodbye Yellow Brick Road* spawning hits like "Rocket Man," "Levon," "Bennie and the Jets," "Crocodile Rock," and many, many more. In 1975, they released *Captain Fantastic and the Brown Dirt Cowboy*, a series of songs chronicling the friendship of Elton and Bernie and their rise to success.

Elton became known for his flamboyant shows. He wore rhinestone-studded glasses and lamé jump suits, with all manner of feather boas and capes. As the '70s rolled to a close he was struggling with burnout. The hits kept coming but

Gay Pride

In 1984 Elton married Renate Blauel, an engineer he'd worked with. They were married for four years. Concerned with what his fans would think, for a time Elton hedged his bets and professed to be bisexual. In 1991 he cleaned up his act, put in some hair plugs, and returned to writing with Taupin. He also came completely out of the closet. Now a proud gay man, he has devoted much time to fighting AIDS, setting up his own foundation, and contributing all the proceeds from his single sales to AIDS charities.

After Elton and collaborator Bernie Taupin made up, he released a number of popular albums with catchy songs that charted well, showing that he was back on top of his game.

GREATEST HITS

Year	Song
1970	"Your Song"
1971	"Levon"
	"Tiny Dancer"
1972	"Rocket Man"
	"Crocodile Rock"
1973	"Daniel"
	"Goodbye Yellow Brick Road"
1974	"Bennie and the Jets"
	"Don't Let the Sun Go Down on Me"
1975	"Philadelphia Freedom"
	"Someone Saved My Life Tonight"
1976	"Don't Go Breaking My Heart" (with Kiki Dee)
1984	"Sad Songs (Say So Much)"
1997	"Candle in the Wind '97"

"Candle in the Wind"

Elton's best-selling song is "Candle in the Wind," originally released on the *Goodbye Yellow Brick Road* album. The song was a tribute to Marilyn Monroe. It was a radio hit in its original form but then became an international smash when Elton reunited with string arranger Paul Buckmaster for "Live in Australia" in 1986. Two weeks after the concert, he went in for throat surgery. With the death of Princess Diana in 1997, Bernie Taupin re-wrote some of the lyrics to reflect the passing of England's favorite princess. Elton, a good friend of the princess, sang the song at her funeral, and a special single again went to the top of the charts around the world. Elton and Bernie donated all their royalties on sales of the single to the Diana, Princess of Wales Memorial Fund. The next year, Queen Elizabeth II knighted Elton for his charity work. He's now called Sir Elton John.

the material got thinner. There were also issues with drugs and alcohol. Elton had been a teetotaler when he started, but the grueling schedule and the desire to keep the party going led to real excess and exhaustion. After the release of the double album *Blue Moves*, Elton and Bernie had a falling out and wouldn't work together for a number of years. Critics stopped praising the music, even as Elton continued to chart singles and produce gold albums.

NUGGET: Elton John sang "Pinball Wizard" in the movie version of the Who's rock opera, *Tommy*.

Looking for new challenges, Elton wrote a pair of musicals for Disney with Tim Rice (lyricist for *Jesus Christ Superstar* and *Evita*). *The Lion King* (originally an animated film) and *Aida* were both Broadway hits. In the last decade, critics welcomed back Elton John, as he wrote a series of albums that looked back to the rootsy albums of his earliest days and were solid satisfying works of art, including *Songs From the West Coast*, *Peachtree Road*, and the sequel to *Captain Fantastic and the Brown Dirt Cowboy* titled simply *The Captain and the Kid*.

Sir Elton Hercules John (knighted by Queen Elizabeth II in 1998), more subdued in appearance, performs for an adoring throng.

JANIS JOPLIN

January 19, 1943–October 4, 1970

She wasn't the prettiest girl in the class and she knew it, but she had a power in her soul from getting kicked around the town of Port Arthur, Texas. She found salvation in the blues of the local honky-tonks and in the music of Bessie Smith and Big Mama Thornton. She was a shy child who channeled all her pain and hurt into one hell of a cathartic wail. Janis Joplin knew she had to get out of town, and in San Francisco there was a band waiting for her—Big Brother and the Holding Company.

Her voice was a once in a lifetime instrument; aged by hard living, it grew to epic proportions. It was the sound of something new, a white girl singing the blues, but with a kind of psychedelic soul power—gritty and world-weary one minute, only to rise up screaming into the skies the next, one part Mae West saloon mama, one part hippie biker queen. Janis let loose with the same audacious power heard in Jimi Hendrix's guitar.

NUGGET: Leonard Cohen's "Chelsea Hotel #2" was written about his relationship with Janis. And Janis' lover Kris Kristofferson wrote "Me and Bobby McGee," which posthumously went to #1.

The song "Buried Alive in the Blues," on her album *Pearl*, was released without vocals because Janis died early on the day she was supposed to record them.

After her Monterey Pop appearance in 1967, there was much anticipation for her major label debut, and the following year *Cheap Thrills* by Big Brother and the Holding Company quickly rose to #1. *Cheap Thrills* was a talisman of the era, with "Ball and Chain," the showpiece at Monterey, and the Top 10 hit "Piece of My Heart." Its cover, illustrated by cartoonist R. Crumb, featured a number of panels with Janis depicted in many of them sporting massive Crumbian thighs. Joplin left Big Brother and the Holding Company for her second album, *I Got Dem Ol' Kosmic Blues Again Mama!* Performed live with a horn section, the album featured "Try (Just a Little Bit Harder)."

All the while, Janis was a drug-fueled hedonist looking for affection in all the wrong places, and she toured as hard as she partied. She finally ran out of steam in a Hollywood hotel room in 1970, while recording what would be her final album, *Pearl*. An apparent heroin overdose silenced her soulful voice in 1970 at age 27.

GREATEST HITS

Year	Song
1967	"Ball and Chain"
1968	"Piece of My Heart"
1969	"Try (Just a Little Bit Harder)"
1971	"Me and Bobby McGee"
	"Mercedes Benz"
	"Get It While You Can"

Janis Discovered

Discovered at the Monterey Pop Festival, she was immediately signed up by Albert Grossman (Bob Dylan's manager), who'd been stalking the fairgrounds. Michelle Phillips of the Mamas and the Papas admitted recently that she was terrified of Janis and steered clear of her at Monterey. The Monterey film made Joplin a star, and all the young girls—at least the ones who didn't want to be Joni Mitchell—wanted to sound like Janis. No one could belt it like Janis. Robert Plant may have loved the blues from an early age, but his otherworldly vocal pyrotechnics owe as much to Janis Joplin as to any old blues shouter.

CAROLE KING

FEBRUARY 9, 1942–

AS A TEENAGER IN BROOKLYN, CAROLE KLEIN FORMED A SINGING QUARTET CALLED THE CO-SINES. SHE WOULD SOON BECOME PART OF THE STABLE WRITING FOR MR. DON KIRSHNER.

Most people don't realize that Carole King cuts across more of rock and roll history than just about anybody. Her songs written with Gerry Goffin were hits before the Beatles left Hamburg, and she continued on through the British Invasion into the folk-rock, soul, and psychedelic eras. With *Tapestry*, she also had the best-selling album of any singer-songwriter in the '70s. She continues having hits to this day, as a writer for pop divas like Mariah Carey, as well as releasing her own music in innovative ways.

NUGGET: In 1975, King wrote the music for *Really Rosie*, a TV special created by children's book author and illustrator Maurice Sendak (author of *Where the Wild Things Are*). The soundtrack, with King playing and singing, is a near perfect pop record that's engaging for kids and adults alike.

Carole Klein (King's real name) was writing and playing piano from an early age. She loved show tunes and rock and roll, and as soon as she was a teen she headed over to the Brill Building, New York City's music mecca. When her friend and fellow Brill Building writer Neil Sedaka wrote a hit song about her called "Oh Carol," she responded with the first of many "answer" songs she would write over the years, called "Oh Neil." When the Drifters had a hit with "Under the Boardwalk" she wrote "Up on the Roof." Sometimes she even answered her own songs. Her first number-one hit written with Gerry Goffin (who would later become her husband) was "Will You Love Me Tomorrow." When the Shirelles took the song to number one, Goffin and King wrote many songs mulling over the implications of a one-night stand, including "Yours Until Tomorrow."

Song Factory

With its brass façade, the Brill Building, at 1619 Broadway in New York City, was a song factory with a magical aura. There was gold to be had and hits to be written inside the walls of the many music publishing offices inside. By 1962, there were 165 music-related businesses in the Brill Building; a musician could shop for a publisher, cut a demo, and make deals with promoters just by going from office to office and floor to floor. Many of the writers were husband-and-wife teams like Goffin and King, including Barry Mann and Cynthia Weil ("We Gotta Get Out Of This Place," recorded by the Animals), and Steve Barri and Ellie Greenwich ("Be My Baby" for the Ronettes). Neil Diamond, Phil Spector and Paul Simon all started out as writers there, cranking out songs for a weekly salary. For a time, the Brill building ruled the airwaves.

The hits poured out for the team. Their babysitter became Little Eva with the smash "Locomotion," later recorded by Grand Funk Railroad. When a lot of other writers fell on hard times during the British Invasion, Goffin and King wrote songs for the Animals ("Don't Bring Me Down"), the Byrds ("Goin' Back"), and the Monkees ("Pleasant Valley Sunday"). The Beatles even covered their songs "Chains" and "Keep Your Hands Off My Baby."

Goffin and King split up as a couple but stayed on good enough terms to continue collaborating. After a couple false starts as a performer in the early '60s,

GREATEST HITS	
Year	Song
1960	"Will You Love Me Tomorrow" (The Shirelles)
1962	"Locomotion" (Little Eva)
	"Up on the Roof" (The Drifters)
1967	"Pleasant Valley Sunday" (The Monkees)
	"(You Make Me Feel Like) A Natural Woman" (Aretha Franklin)
1971	"You've Got a Friend" (James Taylor)
	"I Feel the Earth Move"
	"It's Too Late"
	"So Far Away"

Carole focused on performing at the end of that decade. She was part of a group called the City, then made a solo album called *Writer*, which contained hits for others, like Blood Sweat and Tears, but not for Carole. On her next album she got it right. Mixing her voice up front, she delivered a few Goffin-King oldies like "Will You Love Me Tomorrow" and "(You Make Me Feel Like) A Natural Woman"—The Aretha Franklin smash—and fantastic new originals of her own, including "It's Too Late" and "You've Got A Friend" (a song that was a hit at the same time for James Taylor, with Carole singing along). It seemed like everyone loved the homespun, slightly melancholy, West Coast vibe of the album, and *Tapestry* went on to sell millions of copies.

Carole King continues to write and record, while also spending time promoting environmental causes and the occasional political candidate.

"Every day we squeezed into our respective cubby holes with just enough room for a piano, a bench, and maybe a chair for the lyricist if you were lucky."—Carole King

In 1971, it was not too late for the Earth to be moved by this late-blooming singer-songwriter, who came into her own with the release of *Tapestry*.

THE KINKS

1963–

There was always something a bit of the underdog about the Kinks. While they had the talent to match anyone in the British Invasion, they always seemed to trail behind the monoliths of the Beatles/Stones/Who/Cream/Zeppelin, never quite catching their share of the breaks, yet stumbling on in their rock and roll fantasy. In the end, they left behind a great treasury of song and stories of the rivalry between lead singer and main writer Ray Davies and his younger brother Dave. Their combustible relationship created a tension that gave the band an edge, but also broke them up. Most important is the music, and the Kinks never let anything get in the way of the music.

NUGGET: Ray Davies and Pretenders singer Chrissie Hynde had a romantic relationship in the early '80s, and a daughter Natalie Rae, born in 1983.

Around the time of the British invasion of the mid-'60s, the Kinks burst onto the UK music scene. With Dave Davies playing the searing guitar hooks and manic lead parts, the Kinks in their white button-down shirts and neckties banged out glorious rockers for the screaming teenyboppers. It was often almost the same song, but what a great song it was: "You Really Got Me," "All Day and All of the Night," and "Till the End of the Day." All the early albums had names with as repetitive a formula, like *Kinda Kinks*, *Kinks Kinkdom*, and *The Kink Kontroversy*. The Kinks might have conquered the world at this time, but a fight with the United States musicians' union in 1966 kept them from touring in America and away from television shows like *Shindig*, *Hullabaloo*, and *The Ed Sullivan Show* until 1969.

THOUGH THEY SEEMED HARMLESS ENOUGH TO THE CASUAL OBSERVER, AFTER THEIR 1966 TOUR, THE KINKS (FROM LEFT: MICK AVORY, RAY DAVIES, PETE QUAIFE, AND DAVE DAVIES) WERE BANNED FROM THE UNITED STATES UNTIL 1969.

GREATEST HITS

Year	Song
1964	"You Really Got Me"
	"All Day and All of the Night"
1965	"A Well Respected Man"
	"Dedicated Follower of Fashion"
1966	"Sunny Afternoon"
1967	"Waterloo Sunset"
1968	"Days"
	"Picture Book"
1969	"Victoria"
1970	"Lola"
1978	"Rock and Roll Fantasy"
1979	"Catch Me Now I'm Falling"
1981	"Better Things"
1983	"Come Dancing"

The Kinks instead concentrated on their homeland. Ray lived in the neighborhood where he grew up, and the themes of his songs revolved around the downtrodden working man ("Shangri-la" and "Get Back in Line"), family life ("Picture Book" and "Autumn Almanac"), and the loss of pastoral old England to the modern world ("The Village Green Preservation Society" and "Waterloo Sunset"). Incorporating New Orleans rhythms and English

NUGGET: Rod Stewart grew up with the Davies boys in the Muswell Hill section of London, and was briefly lead singer of a pre-Kinks project, The Ray Davies Quartet.

After muggers stole his girlfriend's purse in New Orleans in early 2004, Ray Davies gave chase. Although he did not get the purse back, he did receive a gunshot to the leg, which broke a bone.

dancehall into their rock and roll, Davies wrote a pair of near-flawless albums in *Face to Face* and *Something Else by The Kinks*, along with one of the first rock operas, *Arthur (Or the Decline and Fall of the British Empire)*, and the boozy country rock classic *Muswell Hillbillies*.

Lola

"Lola," the 1970 hit for The Kinks, was a song about a man dancing with a man dressed as a woman and wondering all the time why she "walked like a woman and talked like a man." Ray Davies said the song was inspired by a real life event—his manager was dancing all night with a woman who, by morning, had stubble on her face. Transvestites were not all over the cultural map back then, and the fact that gay and straight people alike loved this song opened the door for performers like David Bowie and Lou Reed to take some chances. The original version contained a reference to Coca-Cola, but the BBC refused to play it until Davies rerecorded the vocals, changing it to "cherry cola."

Kink Kovers

If imitation is truly the sincerest form of flattery, then the Kinks are well-loved indeed. Van Halen (with "You Really Got Me"), the Jam (with "David Watts") and the Pretenders (with "Stop Your Sobbing") had hits with Kinks covers, but it sure seems like everyone who was anyone recorded a Kinks song at one time or other. The Fountains of Wayne and Dar Williams both recorded "Better Things." Kirsty MacColl did a version of "Days." The list goes on; Bruce Springsteen, Patti Smith, Green Day, Petula Clark, Elvis Costello, David Bowie, Sonny and Cher, Frank Black, XTC, Wilco, and Def Leppard, among others, have all recorded and/or performed versions of Kinks songs—not to mention Weird Al Yankovic with his parody of "Lola," entitled "Yoda."

In 1970 the Kinks scored a hit with the gender-confused tale of "Lola". It was their first Top 10 single in five years and it brought them back to tour the States, their ban having been lifted. The Kinks developed a reputation for spending a lot of time down at the pub; and when they fired up the touring machine, they were known for their boozy shows featuring the song "Alcohol," a tongue-in-cheek temperance classic with the refrain, "Oh demon alcohol." Their shows soon took a sophisticated turn when Davies cranked out a series of rock operas. Themes he had already worked to perfection were now puffed up into the albums *Preservation: Act One*, *Preservation: Act Two*, *Soap Opera*, and *Schoolboys In Disgrace*. The live performances were great fun, but the albums were not their best and did not yield any hits.

> *"Seeing everybody makes me realize rock 'n' roll has become respectable. What a bummer."*—Ray Davies, upon being inducted into the Rock and Roll Hall of Fame

The Kinks abandoned their theatrical pretensions and their quaint English sound and came roaring back with big guitars and a string of radio smashes. They finished their career at the top of the pop charts with songs like "Sleepwalker," "Rock and Roll Fantasy," "Father Christmas," and "Come Dancing." Best of all was "Better Things," a song equal to anything Ray Davies wrote in his golden era. Long Live the Kinks!

The Kinks performing in 1965. Because both of the Davies brothers played guitars, when Pete Quaife (center back) joined the group, he switched to the bass.

KISS

1973–

Kiss (from left: Peter Criss, Gene Simmons, Paul Stanley, and Ace Frehley) was formed by Simmons and Stanley, cofounders of their previous group Wicked Lester.

GREATEST HITS	
Year	Song
1975	"Rock and Roll All Nite"
1976	"Shout It Out Loud"
	"Beth"
	"Hard Luck Woman"
	"Calling Dr. Love"
1977	"Christine Sixteen"
	"Rocket Ride"
1979	"I Was Made for Lovin' You"

Kiss was as much about the look as they were about the music. Their crazy Kabuki makeup, wild space-age costumes and platform boots, along with their pyrotechnic antics on stage, made them look like visitors from another planet. Even if you weren't a hardcore fan, it was hard not to notice these maniacal metal monsters.

Bass player Gene Simmons, the demon with the long bloody tongue, and guitarist Paul Stanley, the star child, started the band. They found cat man Peter Criss on drums and guitarist "Space" Ace Frehley from ads in the music press. Inspired by the theatrical shows of the New York Dolls, Kiss started to experiment with makeup and costumes. The makeup was a gimmick and none of the band members were seen in public without it.

Their first few albums inspired modest success, and no critical acclaim; but their 1975 live album, *Alive!*, with their rock anthem "Rock and Roll All Nite," shot up to the top 10 and made them stars. The power ballad "Beth," sung by Criss, secured the hearts of their fans. And by 1977, a Gallup Poll named Kiss the most popular band in America.

Family Jewels

Clearly hoping for an Ozzy Osbourne-like TV experience, Gene Simmons got real on his own TV show, *Gene Simmons' Family Jewels*. The family is Gene and his girlfriend Shannon Tweed, who've been "happily unmarried" for more than 20 years, and their two children, Sophie and Nick. Along the way Sophie is starting to date, Nick learns to drive, Gene needs to lose a little weight, Shannon wants another baby—just a normal family, right? Wrong. Gene is still a demon at heart, and takes every opportunity to tell the audience all about it. It's an interesting twist when Gene and Shannon go under the knife together for very public his and her face lifts.

Kiss-mania ensued. Fans turned up at concerts wearing the elaborate, full-face makeup of their favorite band member. The Kiss Army, their fan club, grew in leaps and bounds, and there was merchandise galore: lunchboxes, a board game, even a comic book starring them in cartoon, superhero mode. The four Kiss members released solo albums on the same day in 1978, though the band didn't break up. *Dynasty*, released in 1979, contained the band's biggest selling single, "I Was Made for Lovin' You," with its disco beat.

> *"Life is too short to have anything but delusional notions about yourself."* —Gene Simmons

In the early '80s things started to slip. Criss, and then Frehley, left the band for a while. Looking for something new, Kiss decided to do away with the very thing that made them stand out in the crowd—they took off their makeup, and showed everyone their faces. It worked, and the next album, 1983's "Lick It Up," went platinum. In 1996, the original lineup reunited to rock and roll all night, and party every day.

LED ZEPPELIN

1968–1980

As the Beatles disintegrated at the beginning of the 1970s and major figures like Hendrix, Janis, and Morrison passed away, there was a void in the upper tier of the rock stratosphere. If ever there were young men willing to take on the role of rock and roll gods, it was Led Zeppelin. The name said it all: They were heavy, and yet they could soar. They made the contradictions work. They were great innovators, taking the blues and pushing its boundaries.

"I can't moan about any of it. I had a great time in the goldfish bowl."—Robert Plant

They were formed out of the remnants of the Yardbirds, and in fact on their first tour of America, they were called the New Yardbirds. Guitarist Jimmy Page was a child prodigy who'd already racked up many hit singles as a session player with the likes of Them, the Kinks, and Donovan. He brought with him another seasoned studio pro, John Paul Jones, to play bass and add to arrangements with strings and mellotron. From out in the country came John Bonham, a monstrous drummer who always came up with unique approaches that were powerful and innovative, taking songs that might have started as genre exercises into new realms. On top of it all was lead singer Robert Plant, who had an amazing range and the hair every heavy metal musician would want for decades to come.

Though Led Zeppelin (from left: Robert Plant, Jimmy Page, John Paul Jones, and John Bonham) started their 1968 tour as a supporting act on the West Coast, by the time the performers hit New York, they were headliners.

The members of The New Yardbirds (soon to be Led Zeppelin) dropped everything on Christmas Eve 1968 to fill the Jeff Beck Group's slot on a U.S. tour with Vanilla Fudge.

Extensive touring in America immediately paid off as they moved overnight from clubs like the Boston Tea Party to theaters with the rise of their first

Down Like a Lead Zeppelin

Rumor has it the name Led Zeppelin came out of a joke about a possible super group with Keith Moon, John Entwistle (both from the Who), Jimmy Page, and Jeff Beck. It's said that Keith Moon suggested the band would go down like a lead zeppelin; that is, that the band would bomb. The joke stuck around, and when the New Yardbirds needed a new name, this one seemed to tell the story. Their manager, Peter Grant, suggested they change the spelling so no one would pronounce it as *leed*.

"GET THE LED OUT!" IS A POPULAR DJ INTRO FOR THE GROUP. HERE JONES, PLANT, BONHAM, AND PAGE PERFORM IN ALL THEIR HIRSUTE GLORY.

album, *Led Zeppelin*. The band's second album, *Led Zeppelin II*, would include their first big radio hit—"Whole Lotta Love," a driving stomper of a track oozing testosterone. Rock critics viewed the band with suspicion and were slow to give them their due, but it didn't matter. Led Zeppelin was now at the arena level and they crisscrossed America taking no prisoners.

Fans were taken aback with their third album, *Led Zeppelin III*—largely an acoustic affair exploring British folk-music forms. Just to make sure the hard rockers would be on their side, they took on the guise of Viking conquerors in "Immigrant Song," a persona that fit them well as they pillaged their way to the top of the charts. Any lingering confusion was put to rest with the album known as *Zoso* because of its rune symbols on the cover. On this, one of rock's biggest-selling albums, the band took all the strains they had been experimenting with and combined them into "Stairway to Heaven," a song that was, at one point, the most played song of all time. The song starts out as an acoustic folk number with fanciful imagery about a lady in gold, and builds to a roaring, heroic crescendo. The album spawned other great songs like "Rock and Roll," a rockabilly-style number that Bonham completely transformed. Unfortunately, John Bonham drank himself to death in 1980, and Led Zeppelin decided they couldn't go on without him.

At War With *Rolling Stone*

Led Zeppelin's relationship with *Rolling Stone* magazine didn't get off to a good start. The band's first album was panned—and by a 21-year-old student who'd submitted a copy of his review from his college paper. The magazine printed it, and also let John Mendelsohn review *Led Zeppelin II*. It was war. Mendelsohn's review of *Led Zeppelin II* started out with a sarcastic, "Hey, man, I take it all back!" and ended with "Who said that white men couldn't sing blues? I mean, like, *who?*" and inbetween generally scoffed at the band. Mendelsohn stands by his words, but *Rolling Stone* strove for a kinder, gentler future with the band as time went on and it was clear they weren't going away. The band didn't care. As long as they were making music and selling records, the critics didn't matter.

The band defined classic rock, and continues to inspire new generations of teens to take up their music as a right of passage. Rock radio stations always feature blocks of Led Zeppelin so their listeners can "get the led out" in order to be motivated for the day ahead. After the Beatles, it can be argued that no one innovated as much at the platinum success level as Led Zeppelin.

GREATEST HITS

YEAR	SONG
1969	"Communication Breakdown"
	"Whole Lotta Love"
1970	"Immigrant Song"
1971	"Stairway to Heaven"
	"Rock and Roll"
	"When the Levee Breaks"
	"Black Dog"

JERRY LEE LEWIS

September 29, 1935–

There are just a few artists who can lay claim to being one of the original architects of rock and roll, and Jerry Lee Lewis is one of them. Born and raised with gospel music, he worshipped Hank Williams and Jimmie Rodgers, but saw the light when he heard Moon Mullican's boogie-woogie. After learning to play "Silent Night" at the age of 9, his parents mortgaged the family farm to get Jerry Lee a piano.

Jerry Lee had a problem with his demons, sometimes dancing with the devil, sometimes shakin' it for the Lord. He attended Bible college in Texas, but was allegedly asked to leave after adding boogie-woogie elements to a gospel number he performed in front of his screaming classmates.

Sun Records owner Sam Phillips was looking for the next Elvis Presley; he found him in Jerry Lee and the song "Whole Lotta Shakin' Goin' On." The song was loaded with sexual innuendo; delivered by the handsome young man with the wild blond hair and the shaking hips, no one was safe. His songs were great, but Jerry Lee delivered 'em live, kicking over his piano stool, playing the keyboard with his leg pounding, and splashing cascading notes in an ecstatic, frenzied performance ritual.

Teenagers everywhere were suddenly unlocking the Pandora's box of desire, and Jerry Lee had given them the keys. "Whole Lotta Shakin' Goin' On" topped the country, R&B, and pop charts—an amazing feat that he would repeat with the equally lascivious "Great Balls of Fire." There would be other hits, but those are two of the greatest rock and roll songs ever recorded. They defined his career and changed the world. In 1969, he had a comeback, reinventing himself as a country singer.

Jerry Lee Lewis, aka "the Killer," hasn't had an easy life; he's been arrested, he's been shunned for marrying his young cousin, and he's wrestled with drug addiction. But as his album released in 2006 attests, he is the *Last Man Standing*. Recorded when Jerry Lee was 71 years old, the album features duets with the likes of Bruce Springsteen, Keith Richards, and Jimmy Page, among other awestruck idols happy to work with one of the great original wild men of rock and roll.

Cousins

In 1958, Jerry Lee Lewis was flying high, buying cars and motorcycles and touring the world, when it all came crashing down. While on tour in London it was discovered by the press that he had already been married three times and his new wife was also his 13-year-old cousin, Myra Gale Brown. Suddenly shows were cancelled, he was off the radio and his asking price for gigs dropped by 90 percent. Jerry Lee has two other famous cousins and spent many hours learning songs with them as a child. One cousin, Jimmy Swaggart, grew up to be the infamous fallen preacher; the other, Mickey Gilley, is a country singer and was impresario of Gilley's Club, a famous honky-tonk in Pasadena, Texas.

GREATEST HITS

Year	Song
1957	"Whole Lotta Shakin' Goin' On"
	"Great Balls of Fire"
	"You Win Again"
1958	"Breathless"
	"High School Confidential"
1961	"What'd I Say"
1968	"Another Place, Another Time"
	"What's Made Milwaukee Famous (Has Made a Loser Out of Me)"
1969	"She Even Woke Me Up to Say Goodbye"
1973	"Drinkin' Wine Spo-Dee-O-Dee"
1979	"Rockin' My Life Away"

Jerry Lee was, at first, averse to recording what would become his second hit, "Great Balls of Fire," because the Pentecost-raised Lewis believed it the work of the devil.

LITTLE RICHARD

DECEMBER 5, 1932–

It's hard to argue with Little Richard's proclamation that he's the "architect of rock and roll." He was a major influence on the British Invasion bands, and just one listen to his "wooo" vocal styling will make it clear that Paul McCartney, for one, was never the same after hearing Little Richard wail.

"Elvis may be the King of Rock and Roll, but I am the Queen."—Little Richard

LITTLE RICHARD FELT THE PULL OF THE SECULAR AND THE CALL OF RELIGION, FOLLOWING IN THE FOOTSTEPS OF HIS FATHER, A PENTECOSTAL MINISTER WHO ALSO RAN MOONSHINE.

Born Richard Wayne Penniman in Macon, Georgia, Little Richard grew up on gospel music. He took his religious fervor, combined it with boogie-woogie piano and R&B, and came up with a rock and roll sound all his own. On his first hit, "Tutti Frutti," Little Richard appeared fully formed—electric vocals shouted out with some of his trademark nonsense lyrics, screaming saxophones, a heavy backbeat, and a six-inch pompadour that shook when he pounded the piano keys so hard they seemed to bounce.

The hits came fast in 1956–57, with classics like "Long Tall Sally," "Slippin' and Slidin'," "Good Golly Miss Molly," and "The Girl Can't Help It." He appeared in several movies, which was a good way to spread the word in the days before rock videos and MTV.

In 1957, he shocked everyone when he quit music to attend Bible college in Alabama. But by 1962, he'd returned to rock and roll. He toured Britain, where he inspired the Rolling Stones and the Beatles. In 1964, the Beatles recorded their own version of "Long Tall Sally" with McCartney on vocals.

GREATEST HITS	
YEAR	SONG
1955	"Tutti Frutti"
1956	"Long Tall Sally"
	"Slippin' and Slidin'"
	"Ready Teddy"
	"The Girl Can't Help It"
1957	"Lucille"
	"Jenny, Jenny"
1958	"Good Golly, Miss Molly"
1970	"Freedom Blues"
1986	"Great Gosh a-Mighty!"

Tutti Frutti

In early 1955, Little Richard had a day job washing dishes in Macon when New Orleans rock and roll personality Lloyd Price suggested he send his demo to his label, Specialty Records. Specialty decided to give Richard a try and booked him a recording session in New Orleans. It didn't go well at first, with Richard selecting songs that were slow and uninteresting. On a break, Little Richard hopped up to the piano and banged out a wild version of "Tutti Frutti"—the producer took notice. The song was a hit for Little Richard on the R&B chart and crossed over to the pop chart as well. Pat Boone, who covered several African-American R&B hits, had success with his own version of "Tutti Frutti," and it was also covered by Elvis Presley, Queen, and the MC5, among others.

Little Richard was popular with music fans, but he was absolutely adored by his fellow musicians. James Brown called him his idol, saying he was the one who put "the funk in the rock and roll beat." He inspired Elvis Presley to say, "you are the greatest," and Jimi Hendrix—who played in Little Richard's band when he was an unknown guitarist—to "want to do with my guitar what Little Richard does with his voice." He never repeated the success of his early years, but Little Richard could still apply his mascara, turn on the charm, and fire up the rock and roll.

THE LOVIN' SPOONFUL

1965–

There was a moment in the mid-'60s when the new strains of the counter-culture were all positive, and the pop music coming over AM radio was exciting and shiny and full of good vibes. No band was more in that moment than the Lovin' Spoonful.

Coming out of the West Village club scene in New York City, the band consisted of a couple of folk musicians—John B. Sebastian and Zal Yanofsky—who loved jug band music but believed in the power of rock and roll. Somehow they managed to mix these elements together into the good-time sounds of the Lovin' Spoonful. (The name came from an old blues song by Mississippi John Hurt.)

NUGGET: Most people haven't heard of the short-lived '60s band the Mugwumps, but their members are certainly well known. John Sebastian and Zal Yanovsky formed the Lovin' Spoonful, and Mama Cass Elliot and Denny Doherty went on to the Mamas and the Papas.

Sebastian had been much in demand as a session player for some time, adding his harmonica, guitar, and autoharp skills to albums by Bob Dylan, Crosby, Stills and Nash, The Everly Brothers, Dolly Parton, and many others. He hung around with Dylan and inspired John Lennon to wear little round glasses. The Spoonful, which also included Steve Boone and Joe Butler, was an almost immediate hit once the group emerged from their basement practice space. Songs like "Daydream," "Do You Believe In Magic," and "Summer In the City" were big hits. With lots of television appearances, they were soon touring the country playing to screaming fans.

The Lovin' Spoonful (clockwise from top left: John Sebastian, Joe Butler, Zal Yanovsky, and Steve Boone) got together about a year after Sebastian met Yanovsky at Mama Cass's apartment.

If the band had any frustration it was that they had to work incredibly hard, competing against the more sophisticated pop machine on the west coast, where many pop groups used backing bands like the Wrecking Crew to guarantee their singles' success. The Lovin' Spoonful played it all themselves. They also recorded the title song for Francis Ford Coppola's first feature *You're A Big Boy Now*, and wrote music for and appeared in Woody Allen's first film, *What's Up, Tigerlily?*

As 1968 turned into 1969, John Sebastian was getting more introspective in his approach, writing songs like "Darling Be Home Soon" that didn't quite fit the good time vibe of their early releases. Zal was the first to leave and Sebastian soon followed to go it alone.

GREATEST HITS

Year	Song
1965	"Do You Believe in Magic"
	"Did You Ever Have to Make Up Your Mind?"
1966	"Daydream"
	"You Didn't Have to Be So Nice"
	"Summer in the City"
1967	"Nashville Cats"
	"Darling Be Home Soon"

John B. Sebastian

John Sebastian was born and raised in New York's Greenwich Village in a household full of music and art. His father was a harmonica player and his mother a radio scriptwriter; family friends included Woody Guthrie and Burl Ives. One of John's first sideman sessions was on harmonica for famous folksinger Fred Neil's 1965 album, *Bleecker & MacDougal*. When Sebastian was thinking about leaving the Spoonful, he briefly considered joining his friends, and fellow Fred Neil followers, in their new undertaking—the group that would become Crosby Stills and Nash. Sebastian got dragged onto the Woodstock stage, a last-minute fill-in stalling for time between acts. He played "Darling Be Home Soon" in a tie-dyed outfit, and got his mind blown by the huge crowd. He also released an excellent solo album and went on to write and sing the theme song to the TV show *Welcome Back, Kotter*, aptly titled "Welcome Back."

LYNYRD SKYNYRD

1965–

Lynyrd Skynyrd (from left: Billy Powell, Allen Collins, Leon Wilkeson, Rickey Medlock, Ronnie Van Zant, Gary Rossington, and Ed King). Their classic "Free Bird" was inspired by Duane Allman, who had recently died.

The Allman Brothers Band's rise to success in the early '70s gave long-haired Southern men hope that they, too, could become rock and roll superstars. Southern rock was usually typified by dual or triple lead guitar solos, big oversized outlaw hats with feathers on the side, facial hair, a Confederate flag displayed somewhere, and a bottle of Jack Daniels sitting atop an amplifier. No group was more synonymous with Southern rock than Lynyrd Skynyrd. Formed by Ronnie Van Zant, they were spied at an Atlanta club by journeyman musician Al Kooper, who signed them to his Sounds of the South label.

"Free Bird," from their first album, *pronounced leh-'nerd skin-'nerd*, was a great rock and roll anthem that was immediately seized by FM radio, despite being more than nine minutes long. "Free Bird" was a song for the outsider outlaws of America who'd been beaten about by life but were free! Free to make the same

Al Kooper

Al Kooper is like rock and roll's Forrest Gump. He always seemed to be there when something was happening, and that is no coincidence. Signing and producing Skynyrd was only one of his achievements. He wrote the hit "This Diamond Ring" for Gary Lewis and the Playboys. He played the Hammond organ on Dylan's "Like a Rolling Stone" and performed on the gold-certified album *Super Session* with Mike Bloomfield and Stephen Stills. He was the founder and first lead singer of Blood Sweat and Tears. Kooper also plays keyboards and French horn on the epic Rolling Stones song "You Can't Always Get What You Want." Oh yeah, and he recorded with Jimi Hendrix. Whew!

NUGGET: It's been said that the band is named after a high school gym teacher named Leonard Skinner, who hassled some of the band members for their long hair.

mistakes again if necessary. It became an iconic rock song, so much so that hecklers at live rock shows often request the song to challenge, or show disapproval of, the band playing.

Touring behind the Kooper-produced first album, Skynyrd hit the road opening for the Who when they were debuting their mod rock opera *Quadropehenia*. When Neil Young wrote the songs "Southern Man" and "Alabama" about slavery and its lingering effects in the South, Lynyrd Skynyrd took umbrage and wrote "Sweet Home Alabama." Its percolating groove and Rebel reaffirmations helped the song become an enduring classic showing up in countless films whenever a little good-old-Southern-boy vibe is needed to move the plot along.

The tragic 1977 airplane crash that took several band members' lives, including Ronnie Van Zant's, only made their legend greater. With various incarnations continuing to fly the flag and send Bic lighters up into the air one more time for that encore, they can never change.

GREATEST HITS

Year	Song
1973	"Tuesday's Gone"
	"Gimme Three Steps"
1974	"Sweet Home Alabama"
	"Free Bird"
1975	"Saturday Night Special"
1976	"Gimme Back My Bullets"
1977	"What's Your Name?"
1978	"You Got That Right"
	"Down South Jukin'"

THE MAMAS AND THE PAPAS

1964–1972

Irving Berlin sang about being stranded beneath swaying palm trees on a beautiful day in Los Angeles wishing to be back East for a white Christmas. John Phillips flipped that sentiment around when he bemoaned "all the leaves are brown," dreaming of California "on such a winter's day." It was a song he wrote before he hit the West Coast with his group the Mamas and the Papas, and the dream became reality.

The Mamas and the Papas was based around the idea of a folk group à la Peter, Paul and Mary. There was Denny Doherty, John's old friend and a glorious tenor, and John's wife, Michelle, stunning to look at with a voice that blended well with Denny's. Added to the mix was the highly charismatic Cass Elliott, who could belt the blues or hold a harmony with equal ease. John Phillips had a voice best heard in a group setting, but oh what songs he wrote.

Besides 1965's "California Dreamin'" (their first big hit to go Top 10 in the U.S.), he wrote such classics as "Monday Monday," "I Saw Her Again," and "Words of Love." John Phillips was also a charming rogue with wicked appetites and a jealous streak.

Being the richest hipsters on the scene, everyone wanted in on the M&P's action. Their homes became the social center for the Los Angeles counterculture.

GREATEST HITS	
YEAR	SONG
1965	"California Dreamin'"
1966	"Monday, Monday"
	"I Saw Her Again"
	"Words of Love"
1967	"Dedicated to the One I Love"
	"Creeque Alley"
	"Twelve-Thirty (Young Girls Are Coming to the Canyon)"
1968	"Dream a Little Dream of Me" (Mama Cass with the Mamas and the Papas)
	"Do You Wanna Dance"

Papa John Phillips, Michelle Phillips, Mama Cass, and Denny Doherty briefly called their group The Magic Circle before changing it to the name by which it is still known today.

Musicians, actors, and artists like Dennis Hopper, Jack Nicholson, and David Crosby would come around to hang out, eat at Cass' table, and hit on Michelle. The stories of inner-band relationship dramas are rivaled only by the world of Fleetwood Mac. John was married to Michelle, who was sleeping with Denny, whom Cass loved; but Michelle loved Gene Clark of the Byrds, and John loved his drugs.

NUGGET: The story of the band is actually told in their song "Creeque Alley," with its refrain of "and everybody's getting fat 'cept Mama Cass."

Their time at the top was brief but beautiful. Most of the songs people know by the group were released in a two-year period. Michelle Phillips is the lone surviving member of the group. Cass and Denny both succumbed to heart attacks, and John's body, worn out by drug abuse, faded away.

The Next Generation

John Phillips' daughters would go on to great fame, continuing the family legacy. Mackenzie starred in the film *American Graffiti* and the TV show *One Day At A Time* with Valerie Bertinelli (who married Eddie Van Halen of the band Van Halen). She also sang in a latter-day version of the Mamas and the Papas with Spanky McFarlane of Spanky and Our Gang. Daughter Chynna was part of Wilson Phillips with Brian Wilson's daughters Carnie and Wendy. They had platinum success in their own right. Bijou, his youngest, is an actress and model who followed in her father's footsteps—she was a wild child on the New York scene and posed nude for *Playboy* magazine in 2000.

BOB MARLEY

February 6, 1945–May 11, 1981

Bob Marley spoke of his famous song, "I want to say 'I shot the police' but the government would have made a fuss so I said 'I shot the sheriff' instead ... but it's the same idea: justice."

GREATEST HITS	
Year	Song
1973	"Stir It Up"
	"Get Up, Stand Up"
	"I Shot the Sheriff"
1974	"Lively Up Yourself"
	"No Woman, No Cry"
1977	"Three Little Birds"
	"Jammin'"
	"One Love"
1980	"Redemption Song"
	"Could You Be Loved"

Bob Marley listened to a lot of Motown and American R&B music that floated over to Jamaica on the American radio airwaves. And he brought those influences along with him when he introduced reggae to the world. Reggae is more than a sound or a groove with a heavy stress on the up-tick beat. Reggae is also a philosophy. It's the music of an oppressed people yearning to be free and knowing it will be so.

Marley was born in Jamaica to a middle-aged white father and a young black mother. In 1963, he formed the singing group that became the Wailers, with Peter Tosh and Neville Livingston (later known as Bunny). Their 1964 single, "Simmer Down," was a hit in Jamaica. In 1966, Bob married singer Rita Anderson—a member of the I-Threes who sang backup for Marley for the rest of his career—and became a follower of the Rastafari movement.

Chris Blackwell, founder of Island Records, had spent much of his childhood in Jamaica and was familiar with the local music. He discovered Bob Marley and the Wailers on the Jamaican charts and signed them up. Their major label debut, 1973's *Catch a Fire*, caused quite a stir, and brought Marley's joint message of oppression and hope to the people.

NUGGET: Marley was such a powerful force in Jamaica that some felt threatened by his influence over the nation, and an assassination was attempted in 1976. He was wounded and forced to leave Jamaica for more than a year.

The follow-up, *Burnin'*, released the same year, contained the song "I Shot the Sheriff," which Eric Clapton covered and scored a hit with in 1974. After *Burnin'*, both Peter Tosh and Bunny Wailer left the Wailers for solo careers.

In 1980, Bob Marley collapsed while running in New York's Central Park. The cancer he had ignored, for religious reasons, had taken over his body. He died on May 11, 1981, at the age of 36. His music lives on, with its message of black pride, anger against oppression, and faith that all will be well in the future.

Rastafari

Bob Marley was the unofficial ambassador of the Rastafari movement. He spread the message of the Rasta way of life, equal parts religion and philosophy, which began in the '30s in Jamaica. Named for Ethiopian ruler, Haile Selassie I—"Ras" means chief and "Tafari" was his first name—the only ruler of an African nation that had escaped colonialism. Being a Rasta is not just about growing dreadlocks, though dreads do show a Rastafari's length of commitment to the faith. Many also follow an "ital" diet, which means following the dietary laws of the Old Testament, and eating no shellfish or pork. In this Afrocentric belief system, Rastafari reject modern society in favor of following a path to return to nature, a symbolic return to the African nirvana from which they were so cruelly plucked by slave hunters.

JOHN MELLENCAMP

October 7, 1951–

For years, all John Mellencamp wanted was some respect. To start he was known as Johnny Cougar, a name he claims he was saddled with by his manager, and was dismissed by critics as the poor man's Bruce Springsteen. He's not the first musician to be popular with the fans and unpopular with the critics; but, unlike some, it bothered him. Mellencamp wanted his social commentary to be taken seriously, and after spending some time paying his dues, he got his wish.

"Rock 'n' roll starts between the legs and goes through the heart, then to the head. As long as it does those three things, it's a great rock song." —John Mellencamp

When Mellencamp was 24, he left Indiana for New York and the music business. He hooked up with David Bowie's manager, Tony DeFries, who gave him his stage name. In short order, Johnny Cougar got a record deal and started to make music. He had some Top-40 success with "I Need a Lover," on his third album in 1979. But it wasn't until 1982 and *American Fool*—with "Hurts So Good" and "Jack and Diane"—that he had a major breakthrough, both commercially and musically.

The success of *American Fool* gave him the chance to add his real name to the mix on the next release, *Uh-huh* in 1983, with the hits "Crumblin' Down" and "Pink Houses." With his simple, feel-good Americana message, he had all the commercial success he could want, but he still wanted to be taken seriously. 1985's *Scarecrow*, with its empathic approach to the plight of the American farmer, brought him respect. Finally, he reached both the fans and the critics, and before he knew it, he was an advocate for the American farmer and an organizer (with Willie Nelson and Neil Young) of Farm Aid.

Mellencamp has continued to record his own brand of Midwestern roots rock, touching on the small-town life he knows so well. The 2007 release *Freedom's Road* was recorded in his recording studio near his home in Bloomington, Indiana, where he's recorded every album since *Scarecrow*.

With a career that's had its ups and downs, John Mellencamp recently noted: "I'm optimistic, but I expect the worst."

Painter

Rock and roll is his day job, but Mellencamp is also an avid painter with a book of his work published in 1998. He started painting in 1988, and was influenced early on by the French Impressionists. Along the way he's found his own style and his new work is primitive; an homage to the American folk artist, which fits right in with his love of Woody Guthrie and all things American. He donated the profits from his book to VH1's Save the Music Foundation, which keeps music programs alive in public schools across the country.

GREATEST HITS

Year	Song
1979	"I Need a Lover"
1982	"Jack and Diane"
	"Hurts So Good "
1983	"Crumblin' Down"
1984	"Pink Houses"
1985	"Lonely Ol' Night"
	"Small Town"
1986	"R.O.C.K. in the U.S.A."
1987	"Cherry Bomb"
1994	"Wild Night" (with Me'shell Ndegeocello)

METALLICA

1981–

ORIGINAL BASS PLAYER CLIFF BURTON, WHO DIED IN 1986 WHEN HE WAS THROWN FROM THE TOUR BUS, IS PICTURED HERE (FAR LEFT) WITH BAND MATES LARS ULRICH, JAMES HETFIELD, AND KIRK HAMMETT.

While mainstream heavy metal bands like Van Halen and Mötley Crüe were getting all prettified for MTV, Metallica took their cue from the underground—from the speed-soaked riffs of England's Motorhead, the ghoul punk of New Jersey's the Misfits, while always keeping lots of Black Sabbath in the queue—and formed their own seething rock and roll beast. It was a demon that was more about playing than posing; taking the speed elements from thrash punk, they added the pyrotechnics and dexterity of metal to their own complex progressive song structures.

Lars Ulrich, living in suburban Los Angeles at the time, recruited guitarist James Hetfield as much for his low, snarling vocal pipes as his guitar prowess. After a brief run with lead guitarist Dave Mustaine (who would leave to start Megadeath), they began working with virtuoso San Francisco bassist Cliff Burton and Midwestern lead guitarist Kirk Hammett. Their first proper album, *Kill 'Em All*, was a revelation to metal heads everywhere. This was street music that spoke to the hardcore fans. Their next album, *Ride the Lightning*, secured the base, but

The Morphing of Metal

Heavy metal started with the heavy blues bands of the late 1960s like Cream and Led Zeppelin. With Black Sabbath, Blue Oyster Cult, and Deep Purple, it moved into darker territory in the '70s. Pagan and satanic imagery was introduced and black leather outfits came on board. Punk brought it all back to basics, and building on the speed of hardcore, thrash metal was introduced—of which Metallica are considered the most successful practitioners. From there, heavy metal has splintered and re-splintered into many sub-genres including Hair Metal, Death Metal, Grindcore, Nu Metal, Rap Metal, and Metalcore.

GREATEST HITS

YEAR	SONG
1981	"Hit the Lights"
1983	"Seek & Destroy"
1984	"Fade to Black"
1986	"Master of Puppets"
1989	"One"
1991	"Enter Sandman"
1992	"Nothing Else Matters"
1996	"Until It Sleeps"
	"Hero of the Day"
1999	"Whiskey in the Jar"

NUGGET: *Some Kind of Monster*, the 2004 Metallica documentary, showed fans the band, and their problems, up close and personal—culminating in Ulrich screaming obscenities in co-founder and old friend Hetfield's face.

Master of Puppets is considered by most fans to be their all-time classic. It's a complex work of high-speed, pummeling grooves that are constantly veering off into interesting directions.

The band's endless touring claimed the life of bass player Burton, who was killed in a tour bus crash in 1986. For a while they thought they might throw in the towel; but they knew they had more to say, and after trying out more than 40 players, Jason Newsted was added to the team. With Newsted, Metallica had their greatest commercial success—*And Justice for All* hit #6 in the charts and received a Grammy for Best Metal/Hard Rock album. Their greatest commercial success found them hitting the #1 slot all over the world with *Metallica (The Black Album)*. Suddenly they were MTV darlings, spewing hits like "Enter Sandman" to a loving public who went out and bought up their back catalog as well. Personnel changes notwithstanding, Metallica marches on and on, working on a new album with producer Rick Rubin in 2007.

JONI MITCHELL

November 7, 1943–

Joni Mitchell was the first, the original female singer-songwriter, starting as a folkie with a strangely tuned guitar and morphing into a pop star of the highest order, comfortable performing and composing for large jazz ensembles.

Before she released her own album, other artists on the folk scene recognized her talent. She moved around the small clubs of the coffeehouse circuit and befriended the likes of Neil Young and David Crosby. Tom Rush covered "Urge for Going," and Judy Collins had a big hit with "Both Sides Now." David Crosby produced her eponymous first album. In reality, he just kept the music business suits at bay and allowed her to make a simple acoustic affair with little more than her voice and guitar, and Stephen Stills playing some bass. Her second album, *Clouds*, was a completely solo affair including such crowd pleasers as "Chelsea Morning" and her own take on "Both Sides Now." *Ladies of the Canyon*, which gave her a big hit with "Big Yellow Taxi," introduced her piano skills and her experimentation with other instrumentation. The album was written about the lives and loves of women living a quasi-rural life in the Laurel and Topanga Canyons around Los Angeles.

For *Blue*, male muses inspired her; the title track is supposedly about James Taylor, who plays guitar on the album. *Blue* seized the imagination of young girls everywhere. Joni's romantic longing became their longing; rarely was there a dorm room in America in the early 1970s that did not have a turntable spinning Joni.

Though Joni wrote the song "Woodstock," she missed the 1969 festival because of her obligation to appear on "The Dick Cavett Show."

It was obvious she could hold her own with the boys club of Los Angeles. She wrote about her friends and lovers and turned them into mythic slices of life, but these were people already living large lives. She was managed by the high-powered team of Elliott Roberts and David Geffen. Her song "Woodstock" was a big hit for her friends Crosby, Stills, Nash & Young. Jackson Browne wrote "Sing Your Songs to Me," about his brief relationship with Mitchell, and Graham Nash wrote "Our House" about their season of domestic bliss.

The Early Days

Joni Mitchell was born Roberta Joan Anderson in 1943 and raised in Saskatoon, Saskatchewan. As a young girl, she contracted polio in a Canadian epidemic, and it was during her hospital stay that she discovered she loved to sing. As well as music, she was involved with the visual arts from a very early age, and she created the artwork for many of her albums. Joni started out on the folk circuit in Toronto in the mid-'60s under her own name, but changed it to Mitchell after she married fellow folk singer Chuck Mitchell. The couple moved to Detroit, where Joni gained early notoriety as a performer in local clubs. The Mitchells soon divorced, but she kept the name. Early television broadcasts show her evolution from a mini-skirted, mod girl with cropped bangs and heavy mascara into her own earth-mama look, with long blonde hair parted in the middle.

A PROLIFIC SINGER/SONGWRITER HERSELF, JONI INSPIRED A NUMBER OF SONGS WRITTEN BY OTHER MUSICIANS, INCLUDING *ONLY LOVE CAN BREAK YOUR HEART*, *GOING TO CALIFORNIA*, AND *HEY, JONI*.

Little Green

No one but Joni knew it at the time, but the song "Little Green," on the album *Blue*, was about Joni's daughter, given up for adoption in secret as an infant. The baby was born Kelly Dale to Joni Anderson and a father, Brad MacMath, who'd already split the scene. Joni felt she had no choice but to give the baby up. She was not much more than a child herself, just 21. And as she says in the song, "So you sign all the papers in the family name/You're sad and you're sorry, but you're not ashamed/Little green, have a happy ending." Years later Kelly (like Kelly green, hence little green) and Joni were reunited. Kelly (now renamed Kilauren Gibb) searched for her birth mother for five years; the papers that arrived from the adoption agency described the mother as a folksinger from Canada who'd had polio as a child—a recognizable biography for any true Joni fan. One thing led to another, and the secret she'd kept, but hinted at, for more than 30 years was finally out.

She began to veer away from folk. She had a hit with "You Turn Me On (I'm a Radio)," which was released on her 1972 album, *For the Roses*. And on 1974's *Court and Spark*, her biggest commercial success, her pop sensibilities and jazz-tinged arrangements came together for a platinum effort, featuring the song "Help Me."

Her subsequent albums veered off in a less commercial direction as she continued to explore jazz and world music. Her loyal cult took many of her difficult discs into the top of the charts, including the wonderfully named *The Hissing Of Summer Lawns*, *Hejira*, and *Don Juan's Reckless Daughter*. In 1982 she married Larry Klein, a bassist and recording engineer, and the two collaborated on a number of albums together.

Joni's bitterness toward the music business grew, and for some years she was content just to paint. Smoking had changed her voice and it shocked many fans to hear her on *Travelogue*, a reprise of her old songs sung in a lower register. A record of new material, her first since 1998, is in the works, scheduled for a 2007 release. Joni has influenced everyone from Madonna to Elvis Costello to Prince, she was the first in a long line of confessional singer songwriters—Tori Amos, Sarah McLachlan, and Fiona Apple, among others, probably wouldn't exist without her.

A Crush on Joni

It's been said that Led Zeppelin's Jimmy Page and Robert Plant both had crushes on Joni and wrote the song "Going to California" about her. It's a song about searching for a woman, and Plant often added the name Joni after the words, "To find a queen without a king, they say she plays guitar and cries and sings" when they performed it live. On guitar, Page used an alternative tuning similar to those Joni uses.

GREATEST HITS

Year	Song
1969	"Chelsea Morning"
1970	"Big Yellow Taxi"
	"Woodstock"
1971	"A Case of You"
1972	"You Turn Me On (I'm a Radio)"
1974	"Help Me"
	"Free Man in Paris"
1982	"Chinese Café/Unchained Melody"
1988	"My Secret Place"
1991	"Come in from the Cold"
1997	"Got 'Til It's Gone" (Janet Jackson, Q-Tip and Joni)

VAN MORRISON

AUGUST 31, 1945–

HIS FATHER'S RECORD COLLECTION EXPOSED BELFAST BOY GEORGE IVAN "VAN" MORRISON TO BLUES AND JAZZ.

Van Morrison's Celtic brand of rhythm and blues was a mainstay of the early '70s, where his romantic lyricism and impassioned pipes made for a heady brew for the Woodstock generation. His songs and album covers evoked a man who had gone back to the land, a hipster mystic tilling the musical landscape. And the hits kept coming—"Tupelo Honey," "Moondance," "Jackie Wilson Said," and "Domino." Like Carole King and James Taylor, he seemed to be showing the way to the idyllic earthy lifestyle of the singer-songwriter.

"Music is spiritual. The music business is not."—Van Morrison

The story begins in Belfast where a young Van Morrison listened to pirate radio at night coming in from offshore and Luxembourg. He fell in love with Ray Charles and Solomon Burke, early influences that can be heard throughout the entirety of his career. Van was a short, red-haired, slightly chubby kid; not real rock star material, but he had a soulful voice and something to say. After playing in Irish show bands and skiffle groups, he put together an R&B outfit much like the early Rolling Stones, doing covers as well as working up their own spirited material. They were called Them, and were signed to Decca Records in 1964.

Them toured all over the States, but eventually burnout set in and Van quit the group, signing up for a solo deal with the Bang Label, home of Neil Diamond. The label was run by Bert Berns who had penned "Here Comes the Night" for Them. *Blowin' Your Mind!* was cut with New York session musicians and contained "Brown Eyed Girl," perhaps the most played of any Morrison composition. It also included the mysterious "T. B. Sheets," a long, gripping workout in which Morrison recounted the horror of visiting a friend in a sick bed. It was indicative of

NUGGET: Van's ever-popular "Brown Eyed Girl" was originally titled "Brown Skinned Girl." Initially, the suggestive line, "makin' love in the green grass," was removed and replaced with a line from the first verse to be palatable for the conservative radio airplay restrictions of the time.

ALTHOUGH THE '70S STARTED PROMISINGLY ENOUGH, WITH A MOVE TO CALIFORNIA, A GREAT DEAL OF CREATIVE FERTILITY, AND WEDDED BLISS, VAN WOULD START TO EXPERIENCE STAGE FRIGHT, GET DIVORCED, AND MOVE BACK TO BELFAST.

the direction he was heading which would be the landmark album *Astral Weeks*, a critics' favorite that is now considered a classic.

Morrison moved to Woodstock to be part of the scene that was developing there. He especially hoped to befriend the reclusive Bob Dylan; later he would uproot to Marin County, California, with members of the Band. All the while the hits kept coming and the music flowed on, with popular albums like *Moondance*, *His Band and the Street Choir*, and *Tupelo Honey*. Besides the radio hits, there were more incantatory style songs like "Into the Mystic," "Almost Independence Day," and "Listen to the Lion," where Van experimented with animal growls. *It's Too Late To Stop Now* was a remarkable live album that summed up all the work from this period. One can hear its influence on Springsteen's early E Street Band recordings.

In the mid-'70s the Morrison hit parade slowed down and his record company disparaged him to the press. Morrison's next album, the underrated and aptly titled *A Period of Transition*, was released in 1977 after an almost three-year hiatus. There would be more high points like *Into the Music*, a remarkable LP with its transcendental song cycle that ends the album. In recent years, Morrison has become a touring machine. He also manages to punch out a new disc every year or so; some lean towards the blues, some jazz, and some towards country, but at the center is always Van the man looking for a little more enlightenment in this wild world.

Them

Along with a number of singles and B-sides, there are really only two proper albums released by Them, the Belfast-based R&B outfit that put Van Morrison on the map. Those albums are incredibly solid works of art, full of fiery rave ups, blues workouts, and Morrison's distinctive howl. "Who Are Them?" and "What Are Them?" the newspaper ads read, designed to give the group an air of mystery in their early days. It's been said their 1963 performances in a Belfast club had a manic energy never captured in the studio. Despite many personnel shifts, the Them albums are solid and consistent, with Morrison delivering the goods and studio musicians like Jimmy Page adding their licks. Van was the angry young man snarling and searching for a way into the game. Them had chart hits with "Here Comes the Night," "Baby Please Don't Go," and "Mystic Eyes." Oddly, their most famous song "Gloria" was relegated to a B-Side on a single. American garage band the Shadows of Knight had a hit with "Gloria," and the Doors and Patti Smith also made it their own.

GREATEST HITS

YEAR	SONG
1967	"Brown Eyed Girl"
1970	"Moondance"
	"Into the Mystic"
	"Domino"
1971	"Wild Night"
1972	"Tupelo Honey"
	"Jackie Wilson Said (I'm in Heaven When You Smile)"
1978	"Wavelength"
1989	"Have I Told You Lately"
1990	"Real Real Gone"

NEW YORK DOLLS

1971–

The first performance of The New York Dolls, in December 1971, was as a last-minute replacement for a Christmas party at the Endicott Hotel, a seedy New York City flophouse.

The New York Dolls ruled the sweaty rock clubs of New York's early-'70s music scene. They were a trashy take on the Rolling Stones, with lead singer David Johansen growling his way through such shoulda-been hits as "Looking for a Kiss" and "Personality Crisis." Guitarists Johnny Thunders and Syl Sylvain understood what was great about a Chuck Berry riff, and the rhythm section of Arthur "Killer" Kane and Jerry Nolan knew how to keep it simple with a stupid, powerful groove.

In the glam era, they dressed like transvestites as a gimmick, and made a name for themselves at the Mercer Arts Center and Max's Kansas City in New York City. Most everyone else was embracing a back to the land aesthetic, dressing down in blue jeans and work shirts. The Dolls moved right into the decaying core of Manhattan's lower east side and celebrated its seediness. They were New York cool, taking the strut of the Jets from *West Side Story*, the sneer of *Blonde on Blonde* Dylan, and adding in a Three Stooges Bronx cheer for good measure.

Their self-titled first album is a classic; though at the time was considered tame compared to their live shows. Their second album, *Too Much Too Soon*, produced by Shadow Morton of Shangri-Las fame, was their last release until a reunion album in 2006. They ended their career in Florida dressed in Communist red leather chic, flying a hammer and sickle banner behind them. It was a look designed to shock, by manager Malcom McLaren, who helped invent British punk rock a few years later with the Sex Pistols.

"... One of the most raucous, notorious bands in musical history." —Morrissey

Johansen, who morphed into the character Buster Poindexter, and Sylvain are the only surviving Dolls. They reunited and released an album in 2006, with Iggy Pop and R.E.M.'s Michael Stipe helping out, and played for a new generation who've only heard their influences. Bands such as Kiss and the Ramones owe a small debt to the Dolls.

Todd Rundgren

Producing the New York Dolls' first album was one of many things Todd Rundgren, the self-proclaimed studio "wizard" and "true star" performer, has accomplished. He was in the Nazz, a late-'60s British Invasion-style band from Philadelphia, and Utopia, a prog-leaning outfit that carried him through the '80s. All along, he released solo albums including the landmark *Something/Anything?* and the audacious *A Wizard, a True Star*. His chart hits included "Hello It's Me," "Can We Still Be Friends," and the ballpark pleaser "Bang the Drum All Day." Rundgren is a rock and roll renaissance man in the style of Prince and Beck; but his greatest success has been as a producer, with credits including Meatloaf, Grand Funk Railroad, the Band, and XTC.

GREATEST HITS

Year	Song
1973	"Bad Girl"
	"Jet Boy"
	"Personality Crisis"
	"Trash"
1974	"Stranded in the Jungle"
	"(There's Gonna Be a) Showdown"
2006	"Dance Like a Monkey"

NINE INCH NAILS

1987–

Nine Inch Nails did for industrial music what Nirvana did for grunge—they put it in a package that the average American listener could understand. Instead of just long, noisy, grinding grooves, Nine Inch Nails was also about great hooks and song-based with lyrics you could hear. The message is one of isolation and alienation—fitting since NIN is not really a band, but a solo project with a band name. Trent Reznor, producer, singer, songwriter and sole instrumentalist for NIN, is the king of this particular underworld.

NUGGET: A then unknown Reznor played keyboards with a bar band in the 1987 Michael J. Fox/Joan Jett film *Light of Day*.

After sending demos around, Reznor signed with independent label TVT for 1989's *Pretty Hate Machine*. Reznor put together a band and opened for alternative rock bands, hoping to appeal to more than just the industrial crowd. It worked and, after two years on the album charts, *Pretty Hate Machine* went platinum. NIN's next release was through Interscope Records, where Reznor was promised autonomy and his own label. He released two EPs—*Broken*, followed later by a remix ep called *Fixed*. With the single "Wish," *Broken* won a Grammy. It was an angry record, inspired by various legal hassles, and was a big success.

Reznor claimed to have inadvertently set up a studio in the L.A. house where actress Sharon Tate was murdered by members of Charles Manson's cult family, the perfect backdrop for NIN's particular brand of pounding, angst-driven music. *The Downward Spiral*, a multiplatinum hit, is a very bleak album, though is widely considered to be Reznor's masterpiece.

Wiser, but still wild, Trent Reznor emotes to the gods of angst at a 2005 show at the Oakland Colosseum.

After *The Downward Spiral*, Reznor was not only a success, but the provocative lyrics in the hit "Closer" made him a sex symbol as well. He was a tough act to follow, even for himself; and he spent five years trying to figure out what was next. A double album, called *The Fragile*, was finally released in 1999 to initially strong sales, but not the same commercial success as *The Downward Spiral*. After another long break, *With Teeth* was released in 2005, with successful singles "The Hand That Feeds" and "Only."

GREATEST HITS

Year	Song
1989	"Down in It"
1990	"Head Like a Hole"
	"Sin"
1993	"Wish"
1994	"Closer"
	"Hurt"
	"Burn"
1999	"The Day The World Went Away"
	"We're in This Together"
2000	"Into the Void"
2001	"Deep"
2005	"The Hand That Feeds"
	"Only"
2006	"Every Day Is Exactly the Same"

"Closer"

The song "Closer" had shocking lyrics but a catchy tune, and was a big hit. The video gave the world the chance to see into the dark recesses of Reznor's head, and a surprising number of people could relate. Made to look like an old film, in sepia-tone, the "Closer" video set is a creepy old science laboratory, complete with old scientists and a crucified "research" monkey. An alternately masked and bound Reznor is screaming his plea into a breast-shaped microphone, aggressively searching for salvation. The video was seemingly on MTV all the time during 1994.

NIRVANA

1987–1994

When Nirvana appeared on the scene in the late '80s, American indie-rock was faltering. The independent labels had tried, but couldn't sell a lot of records. American major label music was fairly tame and British new wavers took any available spots on the alternative airways. Only a few American bands like R.E.M. and Talking Heads emerged from the underground scene slowly building their followings album by album. Nirvana exploded right out of the box with *Nevermind* and rock radio finally rocked again with American music. They were the ultimate rock crossover act gathering up the metal heads and the punkers and taking them to the pop charts. Suddenly the major labels were signing all the indie bands in hopes that they too would become the next big thing.

"I'm gonna be a superstar musician, kill myself and go out in a flame of glory, just like Jimi Hendrix" —Kurt Cobain

Nirvana didn't look like any pop stars anyone had ever seen. With their ripped jeans, flannel shirts, and matted, dirty hair they were anti-rock stars. They were identified with a new kind of music—called grunge. Everyone who came before them looked squeaky clean. When the "Smells Like Teen Spirit" video hit MTV, with the band thrashing in a high school gymnasium complete with a demonic janitor, tattooed cheerleaders, and a mosh pit. American youth reacted, immediately sending *Nevermind* to the top of the charts.

GREATEST HITS	
YEAR	SONG
1989	"Love Buzz"
	"About a Girl"
1991	"Smells Like Teen Spirit"
	"Come as You Are"
	"Lithium"
1993	"Heart-Shaped Box"
	"Rape Me"
1994	"Where Did You Sleep Last Night"
	"Lake of Fire"
2002	"You Know You're Right"

KURT COBAIN AT THE READING FESTIVAL IN 1991, "THE YEAR THAT PUNK BROKE."

Nirvana front man Kurt Cobain met bass player Krist Novoselic in Aberdeen, Washington, and the two bonded over their love of punk rock music and a general feeling of being outsiders. Drummer Dave Grohl, joined after the release of their first album *Bleach*. Sub Pop, the Seattle indie label who is credited with introducing grunge to the world, heard Nirvana's demo tape and signed them to a deal.

Bleach got the band some attention on college radio, and picked up a powerful fan in Kim Gordon of Sonic Youth. She suggested that David Geffen sign the band to his DGC label, and he agreed. Nirvana went into the studio with Butch Vig, who produced the Smashing Pumpkins, among others. Spending substantially more than the $606.17 it cost to record *Bleach*, they finished *Nevermind*, with a much slicker sound than *Bleach*, but with the raw rock energy still intact. The band was

Foo Fighters

One of the biggest surprises since Kurt's death and the dissolution of Nirvana was how successful drummer Dave Grohl would become fronting his new band, Foo Fighters. Grohl streamlined the Nirvana sound, emphasizing hooks and muscle over grunge and chaos. Grohl had been writing songs for years. Eventually he put together a cassette of his favorites for his friends to hear. A bidding war ensued and Grohl signed to Capitol and put together the Foo with members of Sunny Day Real Estate and Pat Smear, who played guitar with Nirvana for their *Unplugged* show. Their debut album would go platinum and all their subsequent albums have landed in the Top 10.

skittish about commercial-sounding production, and had to be talked into such studio tricks as doubling the vocals. Producer Andy Wallace was brought in to remix the album, and added—to the band's dissatisfaction—more layers of studio tricks. The record was grungy and heavy, but at the same time catchy and very listenable—just what everyone wanted to hear. *Nevermind* was released in the fall of 1991, and by February the album had sold three million copies. Everyone was surprised, including the band.

NUGGET: It's fitting that Frances Bean Cobain, Kurt and Courtney's daughter, has a couple of celebrated godparents—her godfather is Michael Stipe from R.E.M. and her godmother is actress Drew Barrymore.

Nirvana went into the studio with producer Steve Albini, known for his uncompromising aggressive production style to record *In Utero*, their third and final album. Steve Litt, R.E.M.'s producer, was brought in to remix. *In Utero* was rougher around the edges with a less-commercial sound in general, but contained hit singles "Heart Shaped Box" and the controversial "Rape Me." The album, released in 1993, did well, though not as well as expected. The band played *MTV Unplugged* to try to boost sales. The show was a hit, and a CD and video of the performance was released.

The band felt indie to their core, and the fact that they had major label success—and with it corporate expectations and public adulation—was difficult. The media attention was deafening, and for Kurt, who suffered from manic depression and drug addiction, it was too much. Though there were lots of rumors about heroin use, Kurt's close calls with overdosing were covered up by the band, their management, and the label; so music fans the world over were shocked when news got out that Kurt shot and killed himself on April 5, 1994. Kurt, in death, became the poster boy for the tortured angst of Generation X.

Courtney Love was pretty in pink in her Hollywood glamour phase, 1999.

Courtney Love

Courtney was not your average rock and roll groupie wife. She was onstage in her own group, the girl band Hole, and was far more outrageous than her famous husband. Hole's first album, *Pretty on the Inside*, released in 1991, was well received. Later that year, Courtney met Kurt at an L7/Butthole Surfers concert and in short order the two were married and expecting. The baby, a girl named Frances Bean, was born on August 18, 1992. The happy grunge family was torn apart after an article in *Vanity Fair* alleged that Courtney admitted to using heroin when pregnant. Courtney and Kurt vehemently denied this, and the baby was born healthy; but the damage was done, and child services was forced to investigate and briefly took the baby away from the couple. Hole's second album, prophetically entitled *Live Through This*, was about to be released when Kurt was found dead. A memorial service was held in Seattle, and Courtney, with tears streaming, read his suicide note, which ended with a line from a Neil Young song, "it's better to burn out than to fade away." Courtney told the fans she strongly disagreed. Hole's album, *Live Through This*, was a big success and went platinum the following year.

From left: Dave Grohl, Kurt Cobain, and Krist Novoselic on the road.

PARLIAMENT/FUNKADELIC

1970–1981

Funk veteran George Clinton decided to have it both ways in the 1970s. He stuck to the Motown-style soul for his R&B group Parliament, and he got all freaky with his other group Funkadelic. The two morphed in and out of each other throughout the decade and shared "the mothership" that took the P-Funk crew on a fantastic musical journey.

Parliament actually formed in 1955 as a vocal group in the doo-wop era. The Parliaments (as they were initially called) would not have a hit until 1967 with "I Want to Testify." Funkadelic comprised the Parliaments' backup band. Clinton recognized that he did not want to put all his eggs in one basket and he also wanted to build a stable of acts like Motown had done. He moved his core group of musicians to Detroit and began working on all kinds of projects. Among his collaborators was guitarist Eddie Hazel, who performed the monumental psychedelic licks on *Maggot Brain.* There was the rubbery, funky bass of Bootsy "Bootzilla" Collins, and perhaps most important, the classically trained keyboardist-arranger Bernie Worrell who pushed the envelope when it came to synthesizer sounds.

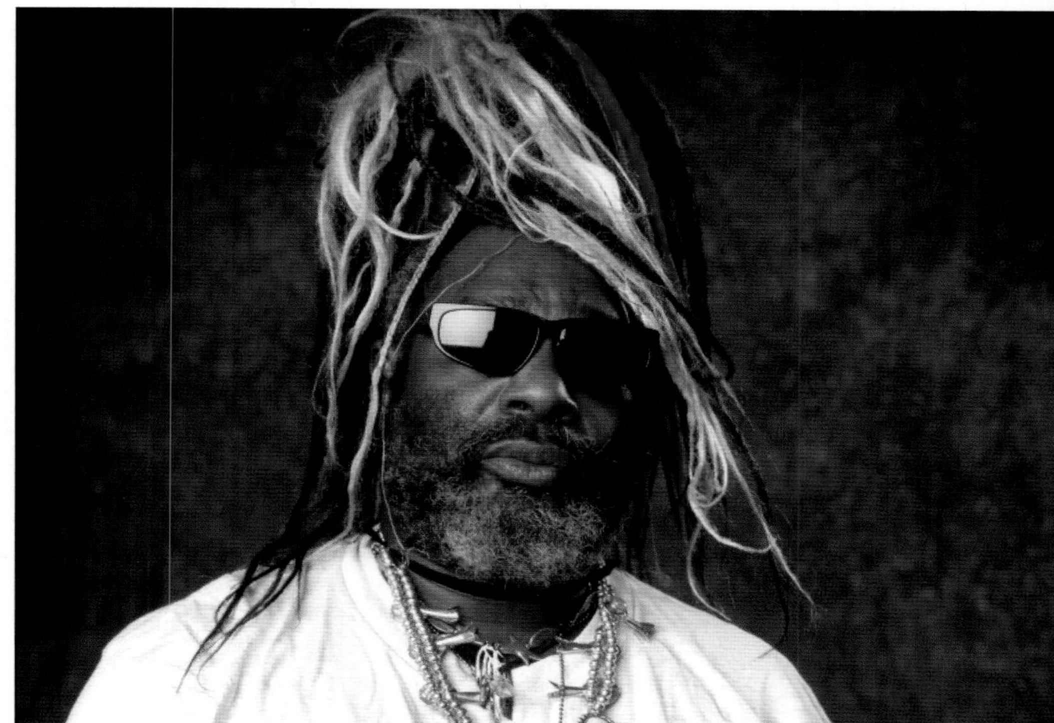

THE ICONIC GEORGE CLINTON, MANY YEARS PAST HIS BARBERSHOP DAYS IN ORANGE, NEW JERSEY.

GREATEST HITS	
YEAR	SONG
	PARLIAMENT
1974	"Up for the Downstroke"
1975	"Chocolate City"
1976	"Tear the Roof Off the Sucker (Give Up the Funk)"
1977	"Flashlight"
1980	"Agony of Defeet"
	FUNKADELIC
1970	"Free Your Mind . . . And Your Ass Will Follow"
1971	"Maggot Brain"
1973	"Cosmic Slop"
1974	"Standing on the Verge of Getting It On"
1978	"One Nation Under a Groove"

While Parliament was working on straight-up party funk like "Up for the Downstroke" and "Flashlight," Funkadelic was testing the limits with albums like *Free Your Mind . . . And Your Ass Will Follow* and *The Electric Spanking of War Babies.* But it was the 1978 album *One Nation Under a Groove* that would be their high water mark, going platinum. It was a massive crossover hit that included the throw down of "Who Says a Funk Band Can't Rock."

After three platinum albums and endless charting singles, the mothership became a little unwieldy for George Clinton with so many players in the mix. He went solo in the '80s, had more hits including the massive "Atomic Dog," and hung in to see his music embraced by a whole new generation of hip-hop acts. With his trademark rainbow-colored dreads, George Clinton remains a true icon.

Psychedelic Soul

In the late '60s many black R&B musicians, inspired by the crossover success of Jimi Hendrix and Sly and the Family Stone, started reassessing what kind of musical flavors might be added to their personal style. The Temptations opened up their sound on spacious orchestral tracks like "Papa Was a Rolling Stone." Otis Redding checked out the hippies in Monterey and wrote "Dock of the Bay." Isaac Hayes who had written a number of hits for Sam and Dave went solo and presented the epic blaxploitation classic "Shaft," and Curtis Mayfield soon followed with the wah-wah soaked "Superfly."

GRAM PARSONS

NOVEMBER 5, 1946–SEPTEMBER 19, 1973

UP-CLOSE AND DREAMY, GRAM PARSONS, THE COSMIC COWBOY WHO HELPED INVENT COUNTRY ROCK.

GREATEST HITS	
YEAR	SONG
1969	"Christine's Tune"
	"Hot Burrito #1"
1970	"Older Guys"
	"Wild Horses"
1973	"She"
	"The New Soft Shoe"
1974	"Return of the Grievous Angel"
	"Brass Buttons"
	"$1000 Dollar Wedding"
	"Ooh Las Vegas"

Gram Parsons was seen by many as an innocent angel of a man who floated into the Troubador in Los Angeles one night and made all of the waitresses swoon with his heartbreaking voice and good looks. Parsons was a Southern gentleman and an emotional soul, with a dark family history of suicide and alcoholism. He was also a type-A achiever, willing to mix it up with the rock gods of his time. Most importantly he was the architect and grand prince of country-rock.

"He was really very funny, and a very generous person. Very bright. I don't think he ever did any damage or hurt any human being except himself."—Emmylou Harris

After a semester at Harvard, Gram took the Southern soul and country he grew up with, mashed it together with rock and roll and formed the short-lived International Submarine Band. He appeared in Los Angeles in 1967 and was drafted by Chris Hillman to join the Byrds, who were a bit rudderless after firing David Crosby. His influence can be heard on the Byrd's 1968 landmark album, *Sweetheart of the Rodeo*. On tour in England, Gram met the Rolling Stones and developed a close friendship with Keith Richards, who was anxious to learn from Gram's encyclopedic knowledge of country music.

Joshua Tree

In a bizarre twist, Gram's road manager stole his body from the airport as it was being shipped to his family in New Orleans for burial. He took the body back to Joshua Tree, and lit it on fire, explaining that he had made a pact with Gram to carry out his final wish not to go in the ground. This strange story was loosely retold in the 2003 movie, *Grand Theft Parsons*.

As various Byrds began to fly the coop, Chris Hillman, Michael Clark, and Gram all ended up in the Flying Burrito Brothers, a ramshackle country-rock outfit that put on erratic live shows but made excellent albums such as *The Gilded Palace of Sin* and *Burrito Deluxe*. Though the music was great, Gram struggled with substance abuse and his unpredictable and unreliable behavior got him booted from the group he founded.

Parsons decided to give stardom a shot as a solo performer. Chris Hillman introduced him to a young chanteuse named Emmylou Harris, and with hired players who'd backed up Elvis he recorded two solo albums that are considered classics: *GP* and *Grievous Angel*. The duets with Emmylou are magical.

Gram succumbed to his demons, and overdosed in a hotel in the Joshua Tree State Park in 1973. Parsons was only 26 when he passed away, but his legacy lives on. His work is considered the cornerstone for much of the Alternative-Country that's emerged as a genre since the late '80s.

PEARL JAM

1990–

Pearl Jam was an early purveyor of grunge rock. Their sound was big and heroic, with muscular, arena-friendly riffs just dirty enough to maintain their small-venue credibility. Eddie Vedder's gruff vocal style was imitated by dozens of singers working the alt-rock scene. He developed the grunge warrior persona, snarling and wounded and ready to fight his way into the ring.

Pearl Jam grew up out of the dissolution of Mother Love Bone, one of the first Seattle bands to get a major label deal. Singer Andrew Wood had died from a heroin overdose, and guitarist Stone Gossard and bassist Jeff Ament were looking to start a new band. Drummer Jack Irons knew Vedder, who was living in San Diego, California, and sent him a tape. Eddie added his own lyrics and vocals, returned the tape, and was promptly invited to join the Seattle scene.

NUGGET: In 1995 the members of Pearl Jam played on Neil Young's album *Mirror Ball*. They were given musician credit by individual names, but there was no mention of the band name for legal reasons.

GREATEST HITS

Year	Song
1991	"Jeremy"
	"Even Flow"
	"Alive"
	"Black"
1993	"Go"
	"Daughter"
1995	"Better Man"
1996	"Who You Are"
1998	"Given to Fly"
1999	"Last Kiss"
2000	"Nothing as It Seems"
2002	"I Am Mine"
2006	"Life Wasted"

Pearl Jam's Eddie Vedder has a distinctive growl that has set the tone for many rock singers to come.

The band was originally called Mookie Blaylock, after the former NBA player, but was changed to Pearl Jam before the release of their first album, *Ten*—Blaylock's jersey number. Their first single, "Even Flow," kicked in after Nirvana's *Nevermind* made mainstream radio a safe place for alternative rock. Pearl Jam soon became the most accessible of the grunge bands, in part because their angry, post-punk aesthetic owed the most to classic rock. As further evidence, 1993's *Vs.* debuted at #1 and sold almost a million copies in its first week.

"I think celebrities suck."—Eddie Vedder

When they released *Vitalogy* in 1994, it was made available only on vinyl for the first few weeks. It still charted in the top 60, but rocketed up the charts as soon as the CD version was released. They had similar success with the 1999 cover version of the '60s song "Last Kiss." It was recorded as a fan club–only single, but popular demand got it on the radio. But, quirky releases or not, the band has a huge and loyal following.

In the early days, Pearl Jam got a lot of flack for being corporate Nirvana wannabes, but now that the dust has settled, it's clear that they have the music and the integrity for the long haul.

NUGGET: In the summer of 1994, Pearl Jam entered into a dispute with Ticketmaster, complaining that the company made it impossible for the band to keep ticket prices reasonable. The band cancelled that summer's tour rather than have their shows sold through Ticketmaster.

TOM PETTY

OCTOBER 20, 1950–

RETRO-ROCKER TOM PETTY GATHERED UP MANY STRANDS OF ROCK AND ROLL AND WOVE THEM INTO POP GOLD.

Tom Petty is an American boy, born and raised in Florida, with a talent for writing catchy songs that were a breath of roosty fresh air when he emerged in the middle of the very heavy '70s. With a Dylanesque voice and jangly Byrds-influenced guitars, it's hard not to think that Petty felt he was born a bit too late.

Tom Petty and the Heartbreakers released their self-titled first album in 1976 on Shelter Records, a label owned by ABC. It didn't go anywhere in the United States, but took off in the U.K., where Americana was a guilty pleasure. Word spread to the U.S. and the singles "Breakdown" and the Petty classic "American Girl" got added to radio playlists.

Petty's label was bought by MCA, and though he was unhappy about his new deal, he acquiesced and released *Damn the Torpedoes*—his third record with the Heartbreakers—in 1979. *Damn the Torpedoes* was a breakthrough album for Petty, with hit singles "Don't Do Me Like That" and "Refugee."

Prior to the release of the platinum *Hard Promises*, Petty squabbled with his label once again. MCA wanted to charge the then-premium price of $9.98 for the vinyl LP, but Petty withheld the record until the label agreed to charge a more reasonable $8.98. *Hard Promises* rewarded Petty with the hit single "The Waiting."

Looking for something a bit different, Petty and the Heartbreakers decided to hire Dave Stewart of the Eurythmics to produce 1985's *Southern Accents*. The record featured a variety of sounds—some soul, some new wave, some psychedelia. The video for the single "Don't Come Around Here No More" was an MTV hit, with Petty playing the Mad Hatter in a wild *Alice in Wonderland* re-creation.

Petty continues to make his own brand of American rock and roll, with and without the Heartbreakers. Nonetheless, even his solo albums—including 1989's massive hit, *Full Moon Fever*—had some or all of the Heartbreakers playing along. Now into his fourth decade of album making, Tom Petty shows no signs of backing down.

Traveling Wilburys

Tom Petty cemented his place in the rock pantheon when he got together with Bob Dylan, George Harrison, Roy Orbison, and Jeff Lynne to record a b-side for a Harrison single. The result was "Handle with Care," with George on lead vocals and the rest taking turns singing. These five guitarists had so much fun playing together; they decided to start a band. The Traveling Wilburys were born, with each band member taking the name of a made-up Wilbury brother—Petty was Charlie T. Wilbury Jr. *The Traveling Wilburys Vol. 1*, released in 1988, appealed to fans of all the artists and was a huge success.

GREATEST HITS

YEAR	SONG
1977	"Breakdown"
	"American Girl"
1979	"Don't Do Me Like That"
	"Refugee"
1981	"The Waiting"
1985	"Don't Come Around Here No More"
1989	"I Won't Back Down"
	"Free Fallin'"
1993	"Mary Jane's Last Dance"
1994	"You Don't Know How It Feels"

PINK FLOYD

1965–

They emerged in England in the summer of love passing out flowers from the stage and throwing potatoes at a huge gong. From the very beginning it was always a spectacle with Pink Floyd—maybe due to the fact that most of the members went to architecture school. They fearlessly created musical performances that were truly three-dimensional, with floating animal blimps and laser light shows. At the height of their fame, roadies constructed a giant wall around the band, brick by brick.

FROM LEFT: ROGER WATERS, NICK MASON, SYD BARRETT, AND RICK WRIGHT: THE ORIGINAL FLOYD LINEUP.

Syd Barrett

Syd Barrett made a couple of solo albums after leaving Pink Floyd that played on his image as an acid casualty. Produced by David Gilmour, who replaced Barrett in Pink Floyd, the albums, *The Madcap Laughs* and *Barrett*, had songs in the style of the first Floyd album, but stripped down to their spooky essence. The Pink Floyd album *Wish You Were Here* features the song "Shine on You Crazy Diamond," which is supposedly about Syd. He stopped making music in the early '70s and lived a quiet life, unrecognizable from the dreamy disheveled boy in the summer of love. Syd Barrett died in 2006.

GREATEST HITS

Year	Song
1967	"See Emily Play"
1968	"Set the Controls for the Heart of the Sun"
1969	"Careful with That Axe, Eugene"
1973	"Money"
1975	"Wish You Were Here"
	"Shine on You Crazy Diamond"
1979	"Another Brick in the Wall"
	"Hey You"
	"Comfortably Numb"
1987	"Learning to Fly"

Art student Syd Barrett formed the band, with a name borrowed from a pair of elder bluesmen (Pink Anderson and Floyd Council), when he met up with Roger Waters (bass), Richard Wright (keyboards), and Nick Mason (drums). In the early days, Barrett wrote most of the songs and sang lead vocals. The beautiful mysterious early single "See Emily Play" arrived in 1967 loaded with psychedelic innocence. Their first album, *Pipers at the Gates of Dawn,* is a true classic. Barrett's great melodies and strange lyrics bubbled up from his troubled inner psyche, dissecting childhood memories and the farthest reaches of time and space.

"I think it's good if a song has more than one meaning. Maybe that kind of song can reach far more people."—Syd Barrett

Unfortunately, due to mental problems exacerbated by drugs, Syd couldn't hold it together as bandleader. He was quietly removed from the front with David Gilmour coming in to play guitar. Eventually, Barrett and Pink Floyd parted ways. The albums that ensued were a bit thinner on the songwriting, but heavier on musical experimentation.

It all came together on 1973's *Dark Side of the Moon*, which went to #1, and spent more than 700 weeks on the Billboard charts. It featured the snappy single "Money" and the drifting stoner dreamscape of "Us and Them." The album took on a mythic quality. In dorm rooms and black-lit suburban basements, fans made up stories about car crashes and ghosts to go with the album.

Roger Waters became the dominant member of the group, culminating with the sprawling epic *The Wall* for which he wrote most of the material. Clashing egos between Gilmour and Waters eventually caused a rift that has never been healed.

PIXIES

1986–

The Pixies are unlikely rock and roll heroes, a group of Boston-based kids who left their mark through great songwriting and some serious innovation. Consisting of Black Francis (vocals), Kim Deal (bass), Joey Santiago (guitar), and David Lovering (drums), they were one of those bands whose sum was greater than its individual parts.

The band announced its presence with the subtlety of a sledgehammer when they recorded a demo accompanied by a poster that read DEATH TO THE PIXIES. Their unique sound got noticed. The Pixies came up with the loud-quiet-loud approach to rock, an innovation as significant as the Bo Diddley beat or the Chuck Berry riff. By bringing the music down to a simple stripped-down pulse, and then roaring back with the full band on the chorus, a formula was created that was cathartic and mosh-pit friendly.

After signing with a small English label, the Pixies released the EP *Come on Pilgrim*. Steve Albini was brought in to record their first album. The result was 1988's groundbreaking *Surfer Rosa*, which melded Albini's edgy production techniques with the band's weird hook-filled pop songs. The album *Doolittle* gained them more acclaim. The song "Here Comes Your Man," originally recorded on their first demo, received solid airplay, but the album only sold moderately.

BOSTON'S FAVORITE SONS: THE PIXIES FEATURED (FROM LEFT) KIM DEAL, JOEY SANTIAGO, BLACK FRANCIS (AKA FRANK BLACK), AND DAVE LOVERING.

GREATEST HITS

YEAR	SONG
1988	"Gigantic"
1989	"Here Comes Your Man"
	"Monkey Gone to Heaven"
1990	"Dig for Fire"
	"Velouria"
1991	"Planet of Sound"
	"Letter to Memphis"
	"Alex Eiffel"
	"Head On"
1997	"Debaser"

The band broke up in 1993, just as the grunge era they had pioneered was kicking into gear. Black Francis changed his name to Frank Black for a solo career that never quite took off, but produced many fine albums. Kim Deal re-formed her teenage band the Breeders and scored the biggest hit any of them had in the U.S., with "Cannonball." The Pixies' albums continued to sell to new generations of fans that realized *Doolittle* and *Surfer Rosa* were rock classics. When they re-formed and performed in 2003, they were shocked at the size of their crowds. While they were gone, their fan base had grown exponentially. The Pixies have yet to release anything new, but they are making a killing on the touring circuit.

Steve Albini

Steve Albini was not all that impressed with the album *Surfer Rosa* that he recorded in about 10 days. He is not even credited on early pressings. He's always been more interested in working outside the major label system, although he's made plenty of major label records. With his own bands Big Black, Rapeman, and Shellac, he made aggressive post-punk both precise and uncompromising. As a producer, or engineer as he often prefers to be called, he has created an impressive body of work, working with newcomers like Joanna Newsome and old-school rockers Jimmy Page and Robert Plant.

THE POLICE

1977–

Punk rock was an inspiration for many who had never played an instrument to make their own kind of music. It wasn't how adept you were; it was about attitude and creativity slapped together with a little snot. Punk caught on quickly at the end of the '70s, especially in the U.K. with the likes of the Sex Pistols and the Clash.

Miles Copeland was a manager who had already made a lot of money working with established '70s artists like Climax Blues Band and the prog-folk group Renaissance that were past its prime as the decade came to a close. He decided he wanted in on this punk rock game, and he started with a pub rock band called Squeeze and a trio started by his younger brother Stewart, called the Police.

Bottle-blonde, faux punks, the Police (from left: Andy Summers, Sting, and Stewart Copeland) went on to become mega arena rockers.

Sting's Publishing

Sting made a lot of money with the Police even after they broke up because he was the principal songwriter. Rap impresario Puff Daddy's tribute to Biggie Smalls, "I'll Be Missing You," used the groove of "Every Breath You Take" and borrowed the melody; Sting suddenly had the publishing on another multi-million seller. Another instance where Sting made publishing dough was on the song "Money for Nothing" by Dire Straits. Sting sings the line "I Want My MTV" at the beginning of the song, borrowing from the melody of the Police song "Don't Stand So Close to Me." Sting's publishers demanded a cut, much to Sting's embarrassment. Money for nothing indeed!

GREATEST HITS

Year	Song
1978	"Roxanne"
	"Can't Stand Losing You"
	"So Lonely"
1979	"Message in a Bottle"
	"Walking on the Moon"
1980	"Don't Stand So Close to Me"
	"De Do Do Do, De Da Da Da"
1981	"Every Little Thing She Does Is Magic"
1983	"Every Breath You Take"
	"Wrapped Around Your Finger"

The Police were not punks, but they dyed their hair platinum blonde for a collective look and hit the ground running with the single "Roxanne," barnstorming America in a van with Miles behind the wheel. "Roxanne" with its authentic reggae riff almost sounded like Bob Marley's new single. Sting had an incredible voice and knew how to write simple catchy songs like "Walking on the Moon" and "De Do Do Do, De Da Da Da." Andy Summers, a seasoned session guitarist, had a rich arsenal of licks and textures he could lay over top of things, and Stewart was a well-versed polyrhythmic drummer having spent his formative years in the prog-rock outfit Curved Air.

The hits kept coming like clockwork, but the Police were a tempestuous bunch, and one day Sting decided to walk away. Why fight with your brothers in arms when you can hire top players and not cut them in on the back end? Sting went on to have many more hits as a solo artist but without the rock bite of the Police. After he finished recording an album of lute music, Sting decided it might be time to rock again, and who better to groove with than Andy and Stewart. The Police were back and everywhere in 2007.

IGGY POP

April 21, 1947–

James Newell Osterberg Jr. was a drummer in a band called the Iguanas, which played primal rock and roll of the "Louie Louie" variety. He liked the big beat and took that love into his next band, the Stooges. This was 1967 in Ann Arbor, Michigan. The big band of the time was the MC5. They played mean Who-inspired rock and roll of a decidedly thuggish variety. James—rechristened Iggy Pop—became their mascot. The MC5 set a high bar, but Iggy and the Stooges danced on top of it. They were truly a band that wanted to get out of their heads.

If there was an original punk it was Iggy. Long before anyone else dared, Iggy dove headfirst into the crowd, sometimes cutting himself and bleeding in performance. The Stooges laid down a heavy tribal vibe that Iggy intoned over—a feral poet with some of the best lyrical ideas to spout from a young man's head. Such classics as "I Wanna Be Your Dog" and "TV Eye" have been passed down like punk heirlooms.

The Stooges made two albums for Elektra with their original lineup of the brothers Scott and Ron Ashton and David Alexander. Iggy fired Alexander and brought in James Williamson on guitar. David Bowie asked to produce the Stooges' new album, and *Raw Power* was born. "Search and Destroy" was the standout track, a song that 30-plus years later sounds like it was written yesterday.

Welcome to the fun house—Iggy Pop needs a hug in 1969. Pictured with Stooge brothers Scott and Ron Asheton.

The album received mixed reviews and the Stooges were too dysfunctional to tour. Iggy ended up drifting around Los Angeles, attempting to record an album with Williamson while badly strung out. Bowie picked him up one more time and remodeled him for the future with a pair of albums recorded in Germany and released in 1977, *The Idiot* and *Lust for Life*. Though they were not big sellers, the song "Lust for Life" became a heavily licensed standard. And when Bowie recorded Iggy's "China Girl" for his *Let's Dance* album, Iggy had his first real payday. He's made many albums since and kept his mighty roar intact. The Stooges have just re-formed after all these years for an album produced by Steve Albini.

"I like music that's more offensive. I like it to sound like nails on a blackboard, get me wild." —Iggy Pop

GREATEST HITS	
Year	Song
	IGGY AND THE STOOGES
1969	"1969"
	"I Wanna Be Your Dog"
	"No Fun"
1970	"TV Eye"
1973	"Search and Destroy"
	IGGY POP
1977	"Nightclubbing"
	"Lust for Life"
1979	"I'm Bored"
1986	"Real Wild Child"
1990	"Candy"

Iggy on the Air

There was a famous TV concert shot in Cincinnati in 1970, where the world outside of Detroit and the small rock clubs of New York caught on to the Stooges. Opening for Mountain and Grand Funk Railroad, the Stooges stole the show. Iggy—shirtless, wearing long silver gloves—smeared peanut butter on himself as he stood high above on the shoulders of the crowd, and then flung himself with reckless abandon into the sea of bodies. He was truly making it up as he went along.

ELVIS PRESLEY

January 8, 1935–August 16, 1977

He was called "the King," the man who, above all others, put rock and roll on the map as a new kind of popular music in 1956. Others came before him, but Elvis is the one who captured the world's imagination with a flick of the hip. He took the country music he heard on the radio, mixed it with the blues music he heard on Beale Street, and threw in some gospel from his Pentecostal upbringing for a breakthrough blend ultimately dubbed "rockabilly."

Sam Phillips, the man who ran the Memphis Recording Service and the Sun Records label, had been recording music by Memphis bluesmen like Howlin' Wolf and B. B. King for a number of years. Elvis Presley, a dirt-poor Memphis teenager from the wrong side of the tracks, made a couple of trips to Sam's studio to cut recordings to give to his Mom. Elvis was actually more of a crooner who admired Dean Martin than a blues shouter, but Phillips heard something on Elvis' second visit to the studio that he wanted to explore.

Setting him up with Scotty Moore on guitar and Bill Black on bass, he experimented for a while, finally hitting on something with a sped-up version of "That's All Right (Mama)," an R&B hit originally done by Arthur "Big Boy" Crudup. Eventually, the single, backed by the hillbilly rave-up "Blue Moon of Kentucky," moved from the R&B charts to the country and pop charts. The sides Elvis cut for Sun were a revelation. These songs absolutely demanded attention. Some radio stations refused to play them, but as Elvis began to tour and teenagers got to see him on shows like the *Louisiana Hayride*, public opinion would win out.

At the *Louisiana Hayride* in Nashville, Elvis met manager "Colonel" Tom Parker—a cigar-chomping impresario who became his dealmaker. Five singles recorded for Sun were sold to RCA, along with the Elvis contract for the unheard of sum of $35,000. With RCA backing him, Elvis made his way to television and made about a dozen appearances that caused a national sensation. With his backing group, which now also included drummer D. J. Fontana and the harmony group the Jordanaires, he cut singles released in 1956 like "Heartbreak Hotel," "Hound Dog," and "All Shook Up," that shot to the top of the charts. By the time he appeared on *The Ed Sullivan Show*, his hip-shaking movements were deemed so inflammatory the cameras shot him from above the waist. Sullivan assured his viewing audience that Elvis was a very nice young man.

In 1958, Elvis was drafted into the army and sent to Europe. The GI Elvis got much publicity, and while stationed in Germany he met his future wife, Priscilla, then a 14-year-old army brat. They were married in 1967. And nine months later, to the day, their daughter Lisa Marie was born.

Elvis "guitar-man" Presley plucks a twelve string.

PRISCILLA, IN HER MEMPHIS MOLL PHASE, GETS MARRIED TO THE KING ON MAY 1, 1967. THE WEDDING WAS IN LAS VEGAS, BUT THE PARTY WAS IN MEMPHIS.

Graceland

Elvis' bride-to-be, Priscilla Beaulieu, lived at Graceland—Elvis' white-columned mansion in Memphis—for a total of 10 years: Five before their marriage, under the supposed guardianship of Elvis' father and stepmother, and five years as Mrs. Elvis Presley. At the time of Elvis' death, Graceland cost a lot to keep up—approximately $500,000 a year—so Priscilla decided in 1982 to open it up to the public, as a museum. Graceland has become a veritable mecca for Elvis fans. Tourists stream in year after year, more than solving the problem of the financial drain the place put on Elvis' estate. Graceland is more than just a place, it's a state of mind, and it has been immortalized as such in song and film. It's been said that Bruce Springsteen, before he was famous, took a pilgrimage to Graceland in order to see the King, but was turned away by security guards. Paul Simon wrote a song, "Graceland," about a trip to Graceland with his son, looking for redemption after losing love—he sang, "But I've reason to believe/We both will be received/In Graceland."

"Colonel" Tom Parker seized any and all opportunities and franchised his young star. He ultimately took Elvis to Hollywood, where he would make a string of low-budget movies. Many were quite formulaic, but they almost always scored well at the box office. The movies fueled the singles, and the singles fueled the albums. It seemed like the less he tried the more he sold, which left him frustrated as an artist.

"If life was fair, Elvis would be alive and all the impersonators would be dead."—Johnny Carson

By 1968, Elvis had lost much of his credibility and hit-making ability. He hadn't had a #1 song since "Lucky Charm," six years earlier. Many wrote him off as the Beatles became the flavor of the decade. What was worse, his movies were not as successful as they once were. He needed a makeover. A TV special, called *Elvis*, but now known as the *'68 Comeback Special*, did just that. The show's high point featured Elvis and his long-time musician pals D. J. and Scotty sitting around in a circle informally singing songs and trading licks, with Elvis dressed in '50s-style black leather. He was so relaxed and charismatic that he reminded everyone of the rockabilly boy he once was.

This would prove a true rebirth for the man. He returned to Memphis for the first time to record since his Sun Records days and made the soulful *From Elvis in Memphis* album that included the hit "In the Ghetto." He focused on his rural roots for *Elvis Country* and made the excellent gospel album, *He Touched Me.*

At the end of 1971, Priscilla left Elvis and took Lisa Marie with her. The two divorced amicably the next year and remained friends. Elvis had never been a drinker, but he had relied on pharmaceuticals to get him though his grueling schedules, and the variety

ELVIS PRESLEY, THE ORIGINAL, SUN-DAPPLED ROCK GOD, COMPLETE WITH BEE-STUNG LIPS AND A COOL COIF.

ALOHA, ELVIS—THE MASTER AT WORK IN THE '70S.

of drugs he was taking began to affect him. In the final years of his life, he was caught in an endless cycle of live performances, hospital stays, and recording sessions. He died at Graceland in 1977. Fans all over the world grieved, but his legend lives on.

In popular music there are very few that can be considered in the pantheon of Elvis, as far as defining a decade: Frank Sinatra in the '40s and the Beatles in the '60s come to mind. And although cases can be made for many outstanding artists and bands as being the "best" this and the "greatest" that, make no mistake, Elvis will always be the King of rock and roll.

GREATEST HITS	
YEAR	SONG
1954	"That's All Right"
	"Good Rockin' Tonight"
	"Milkcow Blues"
1955	"Baby Let's Play House"
	"I Forgot to Remember to Forget"
1956	"Heartbreak Hotel"
	"Don't Be Cruel"
	"Hound Dog"
1957	"All Shook Up"
	"(Let Me Be Your) Teddy Bear"
	"Jail House Rock"
1958	"Hard Headed Woman"
1959	"A Big Hunk of Love"
1960	"It's Now or Never"
	"Are You Lonesome Tonight?"
1961	"Can't Help Falling in Love"
1962	"Good Luck Charm"
1969	"In the Ghetto"
	"Suspicious Minds"
1972	"Burning Love"

In the Movies

Elvis made 31 films as an actor, from 1956's *Love Me Tender* with Debra Paget, to 1969's *Change of Habit* with Mary Tyler Moore. He often made as many as three movies in any given year. Quite a few of the songs and scripts were mediocre, but Elvis' personality always shone though, and some of the films are pretty good. Many consider *King Creole* costarring Carolyn Jones to be his best. *Viva Las Vegas* is interesting for the locations, giving a real feel for the town in its heyday. *Clambake* is considered by some to be one of those films that is "so bad, it's good."

VIVA LAS VEGAS, WITH ANN-MARGRET, WAS ELVIS' 15TH FILM. SEX SYMBOL ANN-MARGRET ALSO STARRED IN THE FILM VERSION OF THE WHO'S *TOMMY*.

THE PRETENDERS

1978–

In 1973, Chrissie Hynde, a tough girl from Akron, Ohio, knew it was time to get out of town. She dug English rock, so she moved to London, where she wrote about pop music for the *New Musical Express*. With her heavy mascara and thick wave of hair, she was a throwback to the likes of Cilla Black and Dusty Springfield, with a little Keith Richards edge to keep the jerks away. She had always strummed a little and, as punk was exploding all around her in 1976, she desperately wanted to be in a band. An attempt as a guitarist in an early version of the Damned, called Masters of the Backside, did not work. But she eventually found the right formula when she helped found the Pretenders.

"I don't think it's good to be sentimental, so I try not to be."—Chrissie Hynde

Despite Chrissie's punk rock credentials, the Pretenders were probably the first true new wave band. They took the best of the mid-'60s, a dash of the New York punk sound, and added some pub rock jangle—and *voila!* Once the lineup was together—James Honeyman-Scott on guitar, Pete Farndon on bass, and Martin Chambers slamming the skins—they began to churn out a series of irresistible singles. They were immediate critics' darlings on the strength of the clever reworking of "Stop Your Sobbing," an obscure Kinks song that they gussied up with production sheen courtesy of Nick Lowe.

THE PRETENDERS IN THEIR ORIGINAL, CLASSIC LINEUP—(FROM LEFT) JAMES HONEYMAN-SCOTT, CHRISSIE HYNDE, PETE FARNDON, AND MARTIN CHAMBERS.

NUGGET: Chrissie has a pair of daughters by two different rock and roll fathers: Ray Davies of the Kinks and Jim Kerr of Simple Minds.

The Pretenders self-titled first album was loaded with excellent material including "Brass in Pocket," with its sinewy groove and Chrissie's distinctive feline sound, which went from a growl to a purr and back again. Within two years of the release of their second album, *Pretenders II*, both Honeyman-Scott and Farndon were dead of drug overdoses. Though the Pretenders were never the same, Hynde soldiered on with revamped lineups, scoring hits along the way such as "My City Was Gone" and "I'll Stand by You." Despite their name, the Pretenders are the genuine rock and roll article.

GREATEST HITS

Year	Song
1979	"Stop Your Sobbing"
	"Kid"
	"Brass in Pocket"
1980	"Talk of the Town"
1981	"Message of Love"
1982	"Back on the Chain Gang"
	"My City Was Gone"
1983	"Middle of the Road"
1986	"Don't Get Me Wrong"
1994	"I'll Stand by You"

Places and Faces

Chrissie was on the scene at a pivotal time in history. Rock and roll was her life, and she claims to have spent a lot of time going to concerts in Cleveland, seeing Iggy Pop and the Stooges and Rod Stewart among others. She was on campus on May 4, 1970, during the infamous Kent State shootings. After a brief stint in a band with Mark Mothersbaugh (later of Devo), she moved to London where, among other things, she worked as a clerk in Malcolm McLaren and Vivienne Westwood's King's Road boutique. Chrissie gave the Sex Pistols' Sid Vicious the padlock necklace he always wore. She loved rock and roll and was dying to be in a real band. She got her wish.

PRINCE

JUNE 7, 1958–

ONE OF THE GREAT, BIC-LIGHTER ANTHEMS OF THE '80S, PRINCE'S "PURPLE RAIN" APPEARED IN THE FILM AND ON THE SOUNDTRACK ALBUM OF THE SAME NAME. *PURPLE RAIN* SOLD 13 MILLION COPIES.

Prince Rogers Nelson was born with a royal name and an early vision of stardom. Following in a line of great African-American crossover artists, like Little Richard in the '50s, Sly Stone and Jimi Hendrix in the '60s, and George Clinton in the '70s, Prince started in the '80s, but he didn't stop there. His longevity is amazing: He had two albums in the Top 10 almost 30 years after his first album was released. In terms of hit singles, album sales, and sheer volume of work, Prince has outshone all of his predecessors. His music has incorporated so many elements from heavy rock and Beatlesesque pop to hard funk, rap, and new wave. While his live shows are often large ensemble affairs, Prince's solo guitar work often takes center stage. His soaring layers of feedback-soaked pyrotechnics established his place in the arena rock pantheon. Move over Chuck Berry and tell Eric Clapton the news!

Songs

Prince's songs have translated into hits for artists as varied as Chaka Khan, Stevie Nicks, and Tom Jones. At the same time as Prince's single "Kiss" was #1 on the Billboard Top 100 in 1986, "Manic Monday," a song he wrote for the Bangles under a pseudonym, was #2. Sinéad O'Connor had a huge hit in 1990 with her powerful version of Prince's "Nothing Compares 2 U."

Prince was signed at the age of 18 to Warner Brothers. His first couple of albums were R&B workouts that failed to strike a chord with a large audience, but 1980's *Dirty Mind* was something different. This was sexy, provocative music that had never been heard before, with an image to match. Prince played most of the instruments himself, with catchy pop, like "When You Were Mine," and funky freak-outs, like "Head." On the cover, he posed in an open trench coat and what looked like ladies' black underwear. Prince was opening his trench coat but also his psyche—exploring sexuality in a very explicit way. He built on this persona with *Controversy*, but his real breakthrough came in 1983 with the album *1999*. A forward-looking album, *1999* was drenched in synthesizers and featured a wide array of hits from the title track (that would

GREATEST HITS

YEAR	SONG
1980	"Dirty Mind"
1981	"Controversy"
1982	"1999"
1983	"Delirious"
	"Little Red Corvette"
1984	"Let's Go Crazy"
	"When Doves Cry"
	"Purple Rain"
1985	"Raspberry Beret"
1986	"Kiss"
1987	"Sign 'O' the Times"

make a strong reappearance at the end of the century), "Little Red Corvette," and the manically joyful "Delirious."

Prince now had some clout and he took it to the limit. His next album was a soundtrack to his own movie. *Purple Rain* the movie featured a stable of acts Prince now had under his wing including the Time, Sheila E., Vanity, and his own band the Revolution. Most were signed to his new Paisley Park imprint, named after his recording studio in Minneapolis. The album was his most adventurous to date and included the anthemic title track, the radical pop of "When Doves Cry," and the frenetic guitar licks of "Let's Go Crazy." The album sold more than 10 million copies.

Prince has released more than 25 albums in his career, some of them double and triple sets. The hits have kept coming, along with other films, like the stunning concert for *Sign 'O' the Times*, as well as flops like *Under the Cherry Moon* and the *Purple Rain* sequel, *Graffiti Bridge*.

Ever enigmatic, Prince accused his record label of enslaving him, and he released a three-disc set called *Emancipation* once he was free of his contract. He has wrestled with his religious beliefs and is always trying to balance the sacred and the profane, dancing between liturgy and libido.

Super Bowl

Prince played to the largest audience of his career when he performed—in the pouring rain—at the 2007 Super Bowl halftime show. He performed six songs, including—appropriately enough for the weather—"Purple Rain," accompanied by the driving beat of the Florida A&M University Marching Band. It's been estimated that Prince's electric, and rain-soaked, performance was seen by more than 140 million people.

Prince has worked through many pop flavors and costume changes over the course of his career.

Here the Artist formerly known as Prince cranks on his glyph guitar.

Name Change

Prince became part of the Warner Brothers Records family at a young age, but that doesn't mean he didn't want to run away from home. Prince launched a public battle with his label over ownership of his music and control over how and when it was released. He claimed that he was enslaved, and in fact appeared in public with the word SLAVE emblazoned across his cheek. The label, he felt, co-opted the man, so he changed his name in 1993 to an unpronounceable glyph—an icon that looks like a cross between the symbols for male and female. Since there was no way to pronounce his new "name," he became known as "The Artist Formerly Known as Prince" or, for short, "The Artist." He finally tired the Warner folks out and they freed him from his contract. In 2000, when his publishing deal expired as well, he was able to take back his name.

QUEEN

1971–

THEY WERE THE CHAMPIONS—FROM LEFT: ROGER TAYLOR, FREDDIE MERCURY, BRIAN MAY, AND JOHN DEACON.

Queen came of age when rock gods ruled the Earth, and they were desperate to play on that hallowed turf. They came out as a full-blown spectacle, having practiced and refined their act for 18 months, ready to take on the likes of Led Zeppelin riff for riff. They could play faster and more accurately that anyone on the U.K. pop scene, and their harmonies were more daring than Yes or any other progressive rockers. In all their pomp and glory, Queen ruled Britannia and the world, firing many a multiplatinum disc off across the pond.

"What will I be doing in 20 years' time? I'll be dead, darling! Are you crazy?"—Freddie Mercury

With a monster guitar player in Brian May and a fearless rhythm section, they were all in service to the king of Queen, Freddie Mercury, one of the most over-the-top front people to ever grace a stage. It is hard to think of anyone more impressive when you consider his athletic abilities, his four-octave range, and his Renaissance man mane of hair.

Queen's first couple of albums went largely unnoticed, but with *Sheer Heart Attack*, the glammy gutsy wail that emanated from Freddie on "Killer Queen," along with Brian Mays' pummeling riffs, won the hearts of hard rock enthusiasts the world over. It was that ability to meld all the popular genres of the day—glam, progressive rock, and heavy metal—into something listenable and grander than the sum of its parts, that made them superstars.

It was a surprise how many twists and turns Queen would take. Every one of their big hits was unique. There was the operatic chorale of "Bohemian Rhapsody," the stadium chants of "We Are the Champions" and "We Will Rock You," the progressive funk of "Another One Bites the Dust," and even the surprising rockabilly song near the end of their reign, "Crazy Little Thing Called Love."

When Mercury passed away in 1991, he took the heart and soul of Queen with him. Though his incredible voice can never be replaced, Queen has recently begun touring and recording with former Bad Company lead singer Paul Rodgers.

Freddie Mercury

Freddie Mercury was born Farrokh Bulsara in Zanzibar, then a British Colony, in 1946. His parents were Indian Parsis, descendants of Persian Zoroastrians who'd emigrated to India more than a century ago to escape religious persecution. The Bulsara family moved to London in 1964, and the newly nicknamed Freddie (he later picked Mercury as a stage name) enrolled in art college and started to pursue music. Freddie was bisexual and had a long-time relationship-turned-friendship with a woman named Mary Austin, who inherited his estate including his music copyrights. He died of AIDS in 1991, 24 hours after confirming rumors of his being stricken with the disease. The remaining members of Queen threw a benefit concert for Mercury, with many special guests, and raised millions of dollars for AIDS charities.

GREATEST HITS

YEAR	SONG
1973	"Keep Yourself Alive"
1974	"Killer Queen"
1975	"Bohemian Rhapsody"
1976	"Somebody to Love"
1977	"We Are the Champions"
	"We Will Rock You"
1979	"Crazy Little Thing Called Love"
1980	"Another One Bites the Dust"
1981	"Under Pressure" (with David Bowie)
1984	"Radio Ga Ga"

RADIOHEAD

1991–

Radiohead was started in the mid-'80s, under the name On a Friday, by a bunch of budding musicians who didn't know each other that well but were all interested in being in a band. Formed at a boys-only grammar school outside of Oxford, they were together for nearly seven years before they got signed.

They seemed like a one-hit wonder when they found themselves with a popular MTV hit, "Creep," from their debut album *Pablo Honey*. Lead vocalist Thom Yorke's eerie, self-loathing performance in the video helped sell what was probably the most straight-ahead song that they ever recorded. Their career might have ended after "Creep," but with their second album, *The Bends*, Radiohead suddenly became important. They became the thinking man's guitar band of the '90s, filling a spot R.E.M. held the decade before.

NUGGET: The band's original name, On a Friday, was appropriated from a song title on the Talking Heads' album *True Stories*. Talking Heads, R.E.M., and the Fall were early influences on the band.

Radiohead raised the bar again with 1997's *OK Computer*. Engineered by Nigel Goodrich, the disc took inspiration from disparate sources such as the Beach Boys' *Pet Sounds*, the Beatles' *White Album*, and Miles Davis' *Bitches Brew*. A year-long tour ensued, as well as a documentary, ironically entitled *Meeting People Is Easy*.

After the critical and commercial success of *OK Computer*, the band looked for new inspiration. They cut *Kid A* amid much hand-wringing and remixing. The album was an overthought, overwrought work of brilliance that borrowed heavily from the dance music underground. It also proved difficult to perform live, because they hadn't rehearsed the material before recording, and much of it had gelled out of endless overdubs and samples.

After they released *Hail to the Thief* in 2003, they were free of their record deal and this new-found independence raised the question, "What next?" In 2006 Yorke released *The Eraser*—a solo album where he accompanied himself on a number of samples and guitar—but maintained that he was not leaving the band. Radiohead continues to mull their next move. The only pressure is the pressure they put on themselves. Something Radiohead is very good at.

"Creep"

"Creep" borrows some chords and melody from "The Air That I Breathe" a song made popular by the Hollies but recorded by many artists. The song, originally written by Albert Hammond and Mike Hazelwood, was intended for Phil Everly of the Everly Brothers. Hammond is the father of Albert Hammond Jr. of the Strokes and also wrote "It Never Rains in Southern California." Hammond and Hazelwood received songwriting credit on "Creep," along with all the members of Radiohead.

Bathed in blue, the morose, yet manic Thom Yorke pours it out for the crowd.

GREATEST HITS

Year	Song
1993	"Creep"
1995	"Fake Plastic Trees"
	"Just"
	"High and Dry"
1997	"Let Down"
	"Paranoid Android"
	"Karma Police"
1998	"No Surprises"
2001	"I Might Be Wrong"
2003	"There There"
	"Go to Sleep"

THE RAMONES

1974–1996

1-2-3-4. Joey, Marky, Johnny, and Dee Dee Ramone are ready for rock and roll high school.

Many bands succeed by trying to be all things to as many people as possible. The Ramones succeeded by being only one thing: a bare-bones band with a sound stripped down to the very heart and soul of rock and roll. No band has more to do with the legacy of punk rock than this one. Originally perceived by many as a thin cartoon joke wrapped in leather, the Ramones endured for three decades with songs that have influenced scores of other artists. By keeping it simple, they showed people that you could make moving, energetic music that drove the kids wild.

The Ramones were a bunch of knucklehead friends who grew up in Queens, New York, and had a mutual fascination with the Stooges and the New York Dolls. Dee Dee could barely play an instrument but had the soul of a street poet, penning most of the band's songs that started with "I Don't Wanna . . ." Johnny was a teetotaling conservative who was all business. Joey was the

Today

Kids today all know the Ramones; they are in the air. "I Wanna Be Sedated" is played on the radio all the time, and "Blitzkrieg Bop" is used in beer commercials. In fact, the Ramones are more popular now than they were in their heyday, with kids who weren't even born in the '70s listening to their music and wearing the omnipresent T-shirt. Some of the band members' leather jackets are on display in the Rock and Roll Hall of Fame.

GREATEST HITS

Year	Song
1976	"Blitzkrieg Bop"
	"Beat on the Brat"
	"I Wanna Be Your Boyfriend"
1977	"Sheena Is a Punk Rocker"
	"Pinhead"
	"Rockaway Beach"
	"Cretin Hop"
	"Teenage Lobotomy"
1978	"I Wanna Be Sedated"
	"Needles and Pins"
1979	"Rock 'N' Roll High School"
1980	"Do You Remember Rock 'n' Roll Radio?"
2002	"The KKK Took My Baby Away"

sweethearted front man with a limited but pure voice—a low-grade croon between Brian Ferry and Ronnie Spector. Tommy was the brains who realized that they needed a drummer who could keep it stupid-simple but also in time. He was very involved in the production of the band's first four albums, and if they had stopped there, the Ramones' place in rock history would have been safe. And they'd yet to work with Phil Spector!

"They're actually fairly long songs played very, very quickly."—Johnny Ramone

The Ramones used classic rock beats, added a wall of noise for guitar and a throbbing bass, and Joey's cool dork croon overtop. Few bands have made four albums so perfect as *The Ramones* (1976), *The Ramones Leave Home* (1977), *Rocket to Russia* (1977), and *Road to Ruin* (1978).

They kept making albums and touring endlessly—it's been said that they performed 2,263 concerts over 22 years—until *Adios Amigos* in 1994 (although the reunion tour went on for quite some time). As soon as they were off the road, the Ramones began to fade away: Joey succumbed to lymphatic cancer in 2001, a year before the band was inducted into the Rock and Roll Hall of Fame. Dee Dee lost his long battle with drug addiction just two months after the induction, and Johnny died from prostate cancer in 2004. Only the drummers, Tommy and Marky, remain.

THE ORIGINAL LINEUP: JOHNNY, TOMMY, JOEY, AND DEE DEE.

ROCKIN' AROUND NYC, THE BAND'S HOME BASE. JOEY RAMONE WAS SUCH A FIXTURE, THAT THEY EVEN NAMED A STREET (NEAR THE SITE OF CBGBS) AFTER HIM—THE CORNER OF EAST SECOND STREET AND THE BOWERY IS KNOWN AS JOEY RAMONE PLACE.

No, They're Not Brothers

Allegedly inspired by a rumor that Paul McCartney registered in hotels under the name "Paul Ramone," Dee Dee, whose real name was Douglas Colvin, was the first to start using the last name Ramone. The rest of the band followed suit: Jeffrey Hyman became Joey Ramone, John Cummings became Johnny Ramone. Originally Joey was the drummer, but found it too hard to sing and play drums. When they discovered that then manager Tommy Erdelyi had the beat, he became Tommy Ramone. Tommy was replaced by Marc Bell, aka Marky Ramone, who put in the most years in the chair. All wore the Ramones uniform—sneakers, ripped jeans, T-shirt, and leather biker jacket—until the end.

RED HOT CHILI PEPPERS

1983–

They grew up in the center of the entertainment business, attending Fairfax High in Los Angeles. It was where celebrities and street punks brushed up against one another, where a punk scene was inadvertently injected with some funk, thanks to Flea's mad love of popping bass lines and Anthony's half-sung rap. The Red Hot Chili Peppers loved to get naked on stage (save for a well-placed tube sock) and loved intense physical shows that combined skate-punk energy with steamroller funk. Often imitated by lesser men, their punk-funk sound has endured and kept them rolling past the wannabes. To date, they've sold more than 50 million albums worldwide.

FROM LEFT: ANTHONY KIEDIS, JOHN FRUSCIANTE, CHAD SMITH, AND FLEA.

The Chili Peppers were an almost immediate local sensation, quickly snapped up by Capitol Records. After a couple of albums that didn't get off the ground—one produced by Andy Gill of the Gang of Four and another produced by George Clinton—the band lost their guitar player, Hillel Slovak, to a heroin overdose. Shortly after, drummer Jack Irons abruptly quit, and it was down to Anthony and Flea to put it all back together. John Frusciante, a fan of the band, immediately jumped in, and Chad Smith took the seat as drummer. This new lineup would prove to be their most durable.

Pushing the more metallic elements of their sound, the band finally generated a hit from *Mother's Milk*, getting on the radio with a cover of Stevie Wonder's "Higher Ground" and "Knock Me Down," an ode to their fallen comrade.

Warner Brothers Records picked up the band's contract from Capitol for a hefty sum, and it was time for the Chili Peppers to step it up. With Rick Rubin as producer, they truly came into their own, developing a large body of work while holed up in an old mansion (purported to be haunted) in the Hollywood Hills. *Blood Sugar Sex Magik* was an almost immediate success thanks to "Give It Away," a song that was hard-hitting, muscular funk accompanied by a crazed manic video with the band all painted silver and writhing around in the hot desert sun like devil beings from a Hollywood B movie.

After nearly losing another member—Frusciante—to a drug addiction, Dave Navarro from Jane's Addiction came in for the somewhat disappointing *One Hot Minute*, which still sold 5 million copies. Frusciante emerged from rehab and rejoined the band for the best-selling *Californication*. From there, they've continued to enjoy massive success on a level achieved by few others in the last 20 years.

Frusciante

The album *Blood Sugar Sex Magik* also included "Under the Bridge," a ballad about life as a homeless drug addict taken from Anthony Kiedis' own experiences. Sadly it would become the story of John Frusciante's life. All the success and touring was too much for John. He drifted away from the band in a haze of heroin, selling all of his guitars and almost dying on the streets. The Peppers were adrift until John went to rehab and rejoined them. Frusciante is one of the great guitarists of his generation, and the Peppers came roaring back hotter than ever with *Californication*. The video for "Scar Tissue" shows them driving through the desert beaten up and bleeding—a far cry from the silver devils of "Give It Away."

GREATEST HITS

YEAR	SONG
1989	"Higher Ground"
1991	"Give It Away"
	"Under the Bridge"
1992	"Behind the Sun"
1995	"My Friends"
1999	"Scar Tissue"
2000	"Californication"
2002	"By the Way"
2006	"Dani California"
	"Tell Me Baby"

R.E.M.

1980–

Although R.E.M. was one of the great American rock bands of the '80s, they didn't start to really sell lots of albums until the '90s. It has been suggested that they kept their growth slow on purpose, releasing songs with mumbled, nonsensical vocals, accompanied by obscure arty videos, often without the band appearing. But it worked—after many other jangle rockers of the '80s had long since lost their luster, R.E.M. broke in 1991 with their album *Out of Time* and the massive hit single "Losing My Religion." They followed it in 1992 with the even more popular—and quadruple platinum—*Automatic for the People*. The band had been together for a decade by then and had made a lot of friends and had a lot of fun along the way.

"I think there were early critics who wanted us to change the world because the Sex Pistols failed."—Michael Stipe

Adopting a disturbingly French look, R.E.M. shows how they caught the eyes of many a coed.

R.E.M. was formed in Athens, Georgia, the college town south of Atlanta that became a hotbed for musical talent in the '80s with bands like the B-52's and Pylon leading the way. R.E.M. settled into this rock and roll community and became its greatest champions. Drummer Bill Berry and bassist Mike Mills had played in Allman Brothers cover bands and had a good arsenal of licks behind them when they met record-store clerk Peter Buck. Buck possessed an encyclopedic knowledge of rock and especially drew guitar inspiration from '60s groups like the Byrds and Love. Lead singer Michael Stipe was just one of those otherworldly kids: angelic looking with a large mop of curls, pouty lips, and bad skin. But his voice could growl like Elvis or soar like a choirboy's. The band members knew how to get out of one another's way, and in no time they were wandering up and down the eastern seaboard making friends with other bands, such as the dB's in New York and the Neats in Boston. They were always inviting other bands up for encores, absorbing all the new music that was seeping out of the indie-rock underground. Impressed with his work on the second dB's album *Repercussions*, R.E.M. hooked up with producer Scott Litt, and he remained by the band's side for a decade. Peter Holsapple from the dB's joined R.E.M. as an auxiliary player for *Out of Time* and had a major effect on their sound, helping to score their first #1 album. They were at the height of their careers, and from there, the band could sell out arenas.

R.E.M.'s Start

Their first single, "Radio Free Europe," was an underground smash followed by "Chronic Town," the EP recorded at Mitch's Drive-In Studio in Winston-Salem, North Carolina, by Mitch Easter, who later formed Let's Active and toured regularly with R.E.M. By the time *Murmur* came out in 1983, R.E.M. was the critic's favorite band in America. Many young bands began to copy their style, which tended to feature danceable grooves with hypnotic jangly picked guitar on top and Michael's distinctive, emotional singing. You didn't necessarily know what he was going on about, but it hit you at the center of your being. Peter Buck used his fame to produce endless bands in the '80s. It became a bit of a joke as sticker after sticker appeared on albums by young hopeful indie bands that read "Pete Buck's favorite band!"

GREATEST HITS

Year	Song
1981	"Radio Free Europe"
1984	"(Don't Go Back to) Rockville"
1985	"Can't Get There from Here"
1986	"Fall on Me"
1987	"The One I Love"
	"It's the End of the World as We Know It (And I Feel Fine)"
1988	"Stand"
	"Orange Crush"
1991	"Losing My Religion"
	"Shiny Happy People"
1992	"Drive"
1993	"Man on the Moon"
1994	"What's the Frequency, Kenneth?"
2007	"#9 Dream"

THE REPLACEMENTS

1979–1991

It's chilly in Minneapolis! Paul Westerberg and the Replacements try to beat grunge to all the best flannel.

America's greatest songwriters will pop up in some unlikely places. For instance, Paul Westerberg emerged from the suburbs of Minneapolis to lead the nation's greatest underdogs to the heights of . . . well, cult status.

The self-professed rebels without a clue came together after punk broke, a bunch of all-around dysfunctional outcasts who somehow banded together to start a garage band and ended up making some of the finest rock and roll albums ever. Besides Westerberg with his mighty pen and off-kilter, heartfelt howl, there was Bob Stinson, a metal head with a limited repertoire of high-speed licks; his brother Tommy, on bass, who was 12 when the band started in 1979; and Chris Mars, a quiet visual artist with a flair for hooky, up-tempo beats.

> **NUGGET:** They Might Be Giants paid homage to the Replacements and life on the road with their 1986 song "We're the Replacements."

Sorry Ma, Forgot to Take Out the Trash, the first album by the 'Mats (as they were called after a detractor dubbed them the "Placemats") flies by at a furious clip with punky, suburban youth classics. It came out just as the hardcore style was solidifying, and the next album, *Stink*, was a conscious attempt to reach its audience. When it succeeded, the 'Mats then confounded their fans with *Hootenanny*, a wildly eclectic album that tried to cover all genres, from synth pop ("Within Your Reach") to power pop ("Color Me Impressed"). Word spread about the band, and *Let It Be*, with an appearance by R.E.M.'s Peter Buck, was the album of the year for most rock critics. Songs like "Unsatisfied," "I Will Dare," and "Answering Machine" put them in the category of the great. If *Let It Be* had been released on a major label, the 'Mats might have broken through as a power band, but mainstream success might have killed them. Lack of cash was the only thing controlling their drink and drug consumption.

Signed to Sire Records, Tommy Erdelyi of the Ramones produced their first major album, *Tim*. One classic album after another followed, but radio never gave them their due; despite all the critical raves, they weren't able to break into the big time. Bob Stinson was kicked out first and later succumbed to the rock and roll lifestyle. Tommy ended up in Guns 'n' Roses for a while, Paul recently scored a major Disney film, and Chris shows his paintings in museums. But the 'Mats legacy is there for future generations to discover.

Big Star

"Alex Chilton," one of the Replacements best-known songs, is named after the Memphis musician who was an early champion of the band and also produced demos that led to their major label deal. When he was 16, Chilton had a hit as lead singer of the Boxtops with the 1966 song "The Letter." He went on to front the highly influential cult band Big Star, which influenced R.E.M., Wilco, and many others. The song "Alex Chilton" helped him establish a solo career, and he now does shows occasionally with re-formed versions of both the Boxtops and Big Star. "I never travel far without a little Big Star," sang Westerberg.

GREATEST HITS

Year	Song
1984	"I Will Dare"
	"Unsatisfied"
1985	"Bastards of Young"
	"Kiss Me on the Bus"
	"Left of the Dial"
	"Here Comes a Regular"
1987	"Can't Hardly Wait"
	"Alex Chilton"
1988	"Skyway"
1989	"I'll Be You"
	"Achin' to Be"
1990	"Merry Go Round"

JONATHAN RICHMAN AND THE MODERN LOVERS

1970–

Before its 1976 release, the Modern Lovers debut album languished on the shelf for a number of years. Yet even with the delay out of the gate, it was an album ahead of its time. The Modern Lovers, much like the Ramones, figured a way to bring rock and roll back to its essence, paving the way for all the punks and new wavers of the late '70s. Much of their greatness is manifested in the song "Roadrunner," lead singer Jonathan Richman's ode to driving in the Boston suburbs. The simple two-chord riff is worked through a number of permutations before finally resolving while Jonathan waxes poetic about the glory of the modern world, of the power lines and pine trees racing by in the dark, and how he preferred driving (to walking) by the Stop & Shop because he had his radio on. Every time the song plays, the listener is transported alongside Jonathan to that moment of epiphany.

NUGGET: Jonathan's most high-profile moment came with the 1998 Farrelly Brothers film *There's Something About Mary*, where he plays a wandering troubadour commenting on the story through song.

The Modern Lovers formed in Boston in 1970, around singer Jonathan Richman, bassist Ernie Brooks, and his Harvard pal Jerry Harrison on guitar/keyboards, along with drummer David Robinson. The Velvet Underground was surprisingly popular in Boston, receiving lots of radio play and regularly selling out the Boston Tea Party. Jonathan was their #1 fan.

Using the simple chord progressions and hypnotic rhythms of the V.U. as a base, the band created a sweet but sinister sound. Jonathan sang about wanting a girlfriend while looking at the paintings in the Museum of Fine Arts in Boston. He sang about wanting to get back into a girl's life after she got out of the hospital. He sang about Pablo Picasso, and in "I'm Straight" he sang about a drug-free guy who tries to convince a gal that she should break up with her stoned boyfriend "hippie Johnny." It was a straight-edge anthem that flew in the face of the era's counterculture.

A chance meeting at a wake for Gram Parsons led Matthew Kaufman to sign them to his Beserkley Records. Jonathan went on making albums that grew progressively quieter, with an emphasis on '50's doo-wop. A re-recording of "Roadrunner" was a hit in England, and it was covered by the Sex Pistols on *The Great Rock 'n' Roll Swindle*. His unique lyrical style, captivating showmanship, and iconoclastic approach make him a true original.

An earnest young Jonathan gazes into the cameras, and his listeners' souls.

The Modern Lovers

John Cale produced their first album (he also covered "Pablo Picasso," as did David Bowie), but there were no takers and the original band broke up without ever releasing an album. Jerry Harrison joined Talking Heads and David Robinson, the Cars. They took the lessons that they learned in the Modern Lovers and brought stripped-down rock and roll back to platinum glory.

GREATEST HITS

Year	Song
1976	"Roadrunner"
	"She Cracked"
	"Girl Friend"
	"Pablo Picasso"
	"Hospital"
1977	"Egyptian Reggae"
	"Ice Cream Man"
	"I'm a Little Airplane"
1992	"I Was Dancing in the Lesbian Bar"
1992	"Velvet Underground"

THE ROLLING STONES

1962–

They started out in their early teens backing up Alexis Korner as they learned to play rhythm and blues; an unlikely, motley crew of little London boys who loved the music made by African-American artists in the United States—such as Chuck Berry and Little Walter—and wanted to somehow pull from that powerful foreign source for inspiration. This was the early '60s, when the teen idols had taken over the airwaves, and if you wanted to find something a little deeper, you had to go to folk and blues because you would not find it in the Top 40.

When the Beatles hit, the Rolling Stones, named after a Muddy Waters song, saw a way into the game with a little conceptual help from manager Andrew Loog Oldham. They copied aspects of the Beatles while playing against their squeaky-clean image, turning themselves into unkempt street thugs, arrested for urinating in public and experimenting with marijuana. It is ironic that the Beatles were originally leather-clad toughs themselves.

"Anything worth doing is worth overdoing." —Mick Jagger

The band solidified with Mick Jagger on lead vocals, Keith Richards on guitar, Brian Jones on guitar and assorted auxiliary instruments, Bill Wyman on bass, and Charlie Watts on drums. Ian Stewart played piano for the group but was banned from photos because he didn't have "the look." With Jagger's and Richards' girlfriends, Marianne Faithfull and Anita Pallenberg, they were rock and roll royalty.

THE BOYS, BACK IN THE DAY: BILL WYMAN, MICK JAGGER, KEITH RICHARDS, CHARLIE WATTS, AND BRIAN JONES SHOW HOW THEY GOT TO BE THE EPITOME OF COOL.

GREATEST HITS

YEAR	SONG
1964	"Not Fade Away"
1965	"(I Can't Get No) Satisfaction"
1965	"Get Off of My Cloud"
1966	"As Tears Go By"
	"Nineteenth Nervous Breakdown"
	"Paint It Black"
	"Mother's Little Helper"
1967	"Ruby Tuesday"
1968	"Jumpin' Jack Flash"
	"Street Fighting Man"
1969	"Honky Tonk Women"
1969	"You Can't Always Get What You Want"
1970	"Brown Sugar"
1972	"Tumbling Dice"
1973	"Angie"
1974	"It's Only Rock and Roll"
1978	"Miss You"
	"Beast of Burden"
1980	"Emotional Rescue"
1981	"Start Me Up"
	"Waiting on a Friend"

Their early albums were mostly covers: Their first single was a Chuck Berry song. But originals such as "The Last Time" emerged, culminating in their international #1 hit "(I Can't Get No) Satisfaction," highlighted by Keith's fuzzed-up guitar—the inspiration for garage bands all over the United States. The writing team of Jagger/Richards became a powerhouse team in the ranks of Lennon/McCartney.

Four albums from their middle period seemed to mimic the Beatles' moves. The 3-D cover of *Their Satanic Majesties Request* rivaled the cover of *Sgt.*

KEITH RIPS ONE OUT ON THAT LONG SUFFERING '50S TELECASTER.

Pepper (although the album was a bit of a mess, it included songs like "We Love You," "Mother's Little Helper," and "Paint It Black"). *Flowers* was a U.S. release, a grab bag of psychedelic singles that mimicked the grab bag that was *Magical Mystery Tour*. *Beggars Banquet*, with its album cover designed to look like a dinner invitation on cream-colored stock, was very close to the Beatles plain, embossed *White Album*. *Let It Bleed* and the Beatles' *Let it Be* followed. Enough said.

By 1969 the group was at the height of its powers, and after an increasingly unreliable Brian Jones was replaced by guitarist Mick Taylor they were truly firing on all cylinders with the #1 hits "Honky Tonk Women" and "Brown Sugar." At the infamous Altamont concert in 1969, their image as dangerous rebels was solidified when they hired Hells Angels as security and a man was murdered while they played. The Woodstock dream faded as "Sympathy for the Devil" played on.

After the brilliant, if somewhat unfocused, *Exile on Main Street*, the Stones settled into a groove of making solid albums—some better than others. Ron Wood replaced Mick Taylor after *It's Only Rock 'n' Roll* and shone on *Some Girls*, with its massive disco-tinged hit "Miss You."

Sex symbol Mick may be technically a senior citizen, and Keith recently fell out of a palm tree (but came away unscathed), but the Stones nonetheless endure as the last band from the '60s still standing, making music people care about, and mounting the highest-grossing concerts out there year after bleedin' year.

Brian Jones

It's been said Brian Jones was the original leader of the group, the best musician with the most ideas. But Keith stole Brian's girlfriend Anita Pallenberg, and as the team of Jagger and Richards wrote more and more hits, Brian was marginalized until he finally quit. Less than a month after his departure, Jones was found floating in his swimming pool, dead at the age of 27. The coroner labeled it "death by misadventure."

MARIANNE FAITHFULL SHOWING THE SASS AND APPEAL THAT CAUGHT JAGGER.

Cool Girls

Marianne Faithfull and Anita Pallenberg were more than just rock and roll groupies with ties to the Stones: they were great friends and powerful creative forces. Anita was a fashion icon and actress who went from Brian Jones to Keith Richards. She co-starred in the films *Barbarella* with Jane Fonda and *Performance* with Mick Jagger, where the pair wound up naked in a bathtub together. Anita, who was obsessed with black magic, had a powerful hold over the band, and it's been said that tracks from *Beggars Banquet* were remixed due to Anita's criticisms. Anita and Keith had a tumultuous, drug-filled relationship and three children together (though their third child died shortly after birth), finally splitting up in 1980. Discovered by producer Andrew Loog Oldham, singer Marianne Faithfull had her first hit with "As Tears Go By," a song written by Oldham, Jagger, and Richards. She inspired Mick to write "Sympathy for the Devil"—said to be based on a book she gave him—and co-wrote "Sister Morphine." She also abused drugs, which culminated in her losing everything, including the custody of a son, and winding up on the streets for a time. Marianne released her masterpiece, the album *Broken English*—complete with drug-ravaged vocals—in 1979, though she was still battling her addiction well into the '80s. Marianne and Anita appear as god and the devil, respectively, in an episode of the TV series *Absolutely Fabulous*.

THE RONETTES

1959–1966

RONNIE SPECTOR (RIGHT) AND THE RONETTES BROUGHT BIG HAIR AND ANGELIC VOICES TO THE MASSES.

It's a tribute to Ronnie Spector and her talent that so many years after her heyday with the Ronettes, she still has many fans and is releasing albums. Her soaring, vibrato-tinged voice put a signature stamp on Phil Spector's mighty "wall of sound" recordings but she has continued on, jamming regularly with Keith Richards and working with the likes of Bruce Springsteen, and the late Joey Ramone and George Harrison.

The Ronettes were Veronica Bennett (aka Ronnie Spector), her sister Estelle, and their cousin Nedra Talley. After a few singles that didn't go anywhere, this girl group from New York City hooked up with Brill Building producer-writer Phil Spector for a string of hits including "Baby I Love You," "Walking in the Rain," and the truly massive "Be My Baby." They partied with the Beatles, toured with the Stones, and were a mainstay on the rock and roll TV shows of the day such as *Shindig!* and *Hullabaloo*.

GREATEST HITS	
YEAR	SONG
1963	"Be My Baby"
1964	"(The Best Part of) Breakin' Up"
	"Do I Love You?"
	"Baby I Love You"
	"Walking in the Rain"

Phil Spector got his start when his tune "To Know Him Is to Love Him" (a song inspired by the inscription on his father's gravestone) was a big hit for his own group, the Teddy Bears. In no time, he put together the Phillies record label, created a stable of stars, and developed a unique recording style. Working at the Gold Star Studios in Los Angeles with top session players known as the Wrecking Crew, as well as with arranger Jack Nitzsche and overseer Sonny Bono (before he hooked up with Cher), Spector built his wall of sound using multiple drummers, keyboards, horns, and backing vocals. He blended the instruments together on the limited number of recording tracks available at the time until it was very difficult to distinguish which instrument was playing what. It was an effect that produced the maximum amount of sound on an AM radio or jukebox. Spector had an incredible string of hits in the early '60s with the Crystals, Bob B. Soxx and the Blue Jeans, and the Righteous Brothers, but the wall of sound's signature act was the Ronettes.

Phil married Ronnie, his muse, but once she was his wife he forbid her to sing, keeping her caged up in the Hollywood mansion where they lived. Ronnie eventually had enough of the marriage and slipped out in the middle of the night. She then launched a solo career.

NUGGET: Ronnie Spector released a new album in 2006, *The Last of the Rock Stars*.

A number of lawsuits have been filed in recent years, with the Ronettes suing for back royalties. As the case goes back and forth in the courts, Spector faces deeper trouble. Always an eccentric guy with a penchant for weird wigs, toupees, and handguns, he was accused of shooting actress Lana Clarkson, and in the spring of 2007 went on trial for murder. As for the Ronettes, in March 2007, their long-time fan Keith Richards inducted them into the Rock and Roll Hall of Fame.

When the Wall Came Down

Some say the wall of sound era ended with the release of *River Deep–Mountain High* by Ike and Tina Turner, a grandiose song that turned the wall of sound into the wall of mud. Spector had maxed-out what you could get out of a small set of speakers, and he shifted gears, working with people who revered him, such as the Beatles on *Let It Be*, George Harrison on *All Things Must Pass*, John Lennon on his debut album, and the Ramones on *Rock and Roll High School*. The sound on Lennon's album is interesting: With limited instrumentation, it takes the wall of sound and strips it down, leaving space for a cavern of reverberation.

ROXY MUSIC

1971–

While groups like Iggy and the Stooges and the Velvet Underground led the way into punk rock, it was Roxy Music that took a stylish art-rock approach, prefiguring everyone from Talking Heads to such New Romantic bands as Duran Duran and Spandau Ballet. With lead man Bryan Ferry, the elegant crooner, and Brian Eno, the most flamboyant soundman ever (for their first two outings), Roxy Music made a number of beautifully crafted albums from 1972 through 1982. They evolved from a quirky tinker-toy glam outfit to making artworks that were note-perfect temples of sound.

The unique lineup was initially put together through a newspaper ad, with Brian Ferry on vocals and keyboards, Brian Eno on synthesizer and manipulated tapes, Phil Manzanera on guitar, Andy Mackay squawking on sax, and Paul Thompson on drums. The original sound combined pulsing grooves with Eno and Andy layering slabs of noise over Ferry's piano parts and Manzanera's treated guitar. Eno's position was as much sound supervisor as band member—although with his peacock-plumed outfits, he was eye-catching enough to steal the spotlight from the suave Ferry, who had a look that hovered between a contemporary fashion model and an uppercrust crooner playboy of the '50s. But Ferry's high-profile romance with model Jerry Hall (before she ran off with Mick Jagger) and the highly styled album covers that imitated upper-class sensuality struck a nerve. Roxy Music spent as much time on their music as they did on their glossy image, which made for a truly solid package.

Brian Ferry, in white suit and cigarette, making the rest of his band look homely.

Ferry's vocal style would be widely imitated by endless British bands that wanted an alternative to the Cockney snarl of the punks. Eno left as tensions developed with Ferry and both parties were the better for it, with Roxy Music making the more focused recordings of *Stranded*, *Country Life*, and *Siren* (which featured the international hit "Love Is the Drug"). Eno went off to work on a series of excellent solo albums, several collaborations, and production projects. The band broke up for a bit, and Ferry released numerous solo albums, often with radical reworkings of other artists' songs, making them completely his own, including "A Hard Rain's A-Gonna Fall" and "Let's Stick Together."

Roxy reconvened for *Manifesto* and developed their sound even further, releasing such hits as "Dance Away" and culminating with their final album to date, *Avalon*. There's a rumor of a full-blown Roxy reunion in 2008, which will include Brian Eno for the first time since his departure.

Brian Eno

Brian made four remarkable song-based solo albums after he left Roxy: *Here Come the Warm Jets*, *Taking Tiger Mountain (by Strategy)*, *Another Green World*, and *Before and After Science*. These albums inspired many other bands and led Eno to find production work with the likes of Talking Heads, Devo, the B-52's, David Bowie, and ultimately U2. He is considered one of the most important record producers of all time. He also developed, with Robert Fripp and others, a new approach to record making, taking drones and computer-generated music to create his ambient series, including the 1978 album *Music for Airports*.

GREATEST HITS

Year	Song
1972	"Virginia Plain"
1973	"Pyjamarama"
	"Street Life"
1974	"All I Want Is You"
1975	"Love is the Drug"
1979	"Dance Away"
	"Angel Eyes"
1980	"Over You"
1981	"Jealous Guy"
1982	"More Than This"
	"Avalon"

SANTANA

1966–

CARLOS SANTANA'S SOUND TECH HAS SAID THAT CARLOS' ONLY INSTRUCTIONS TO HIM WERE TO MAKE HIS GUITAR SOUND LIKE THE OPENING OF A LOTUS PETAL. SANTANA IS SHOWN HERE INDULGING IN THAT SOUND.

The band Santana formed in San Francisco at the tail end of the psychedelic era. Named after lead guitarist Carlos Santana, the group was more of a collective, taking a democratic approach to songwriting and performing. Over the years, the group members shifted, with Carlos the only permanent member. He in turn alternated the group's rock and pop releases with more experimental solo and collaborative efforts that were skewed toward jazz and the exploration of his spiritual side.

With vocalist Gregg Rolie and drummer Michael Shrieve in the lineup in 1969, Santana recorded their first album just in time for the Woodstock festival, where their electrifying performance of "Soul Sacrifice" was a highlight. A cover of Peter Green's Fleetwood Mac song "Black Magic Woman" was an immediate hit. One of the first albums released after Woodstock, *Santana* featured a trippy drawing of a lion's head with all sorts of imbedded creatures in the image, allowing stoners to stare at the cover for hours. The album went double platinum and was followed up by *Abraxas* with the cover of Tito Puente's "Oye Como Va" and more platinum success. Santana collaborated with many artists, including adding guitarist Neal Schon (who would found Journey) as a member on their third album.

As the '70s wore on, the music leaned more toward jazz fusion. But Carlos periodically pulled back the reins, covering the Zombie's "She's Not There" in 1975 and recording some of the music he grew up on in Mexico with Booker T. and the MGs and Willie Nelson in 1983 for *Havana Moon*. That album included covers of Bo Diddley's "Who Do You Love?" and the Latin-tinged Chuck Berry title song.

In 1999 he proved what a solid brand the Santana moniker was when he signed to Arista and worked with president Clive Davis, who'd been involved with his career at Columbia in 1969. Forty years later he had the biggest hit of his career with *Supernatural*, selling 15 million copies. The album was a series of collaborations with many young artists, some of whom were not even born when Santana played that fateful show at Woodstock.

The Santana Sound

Santana's signature guitar sound revolved around clean, sustained, high-pitched notes that seemed to hang in the air of their own accord, using very controlled feedback from his Mesa/Boogie amp. Added to this was the Latin rhythm section of drums, congas, and timbales. Although the band started out as a blues-rock outfit, the Latin flavors were slowly added in. It has been suggested that jamming with various Latin-influenced musicians, and the effects that the percussion had on the hips of the young ladies in the audience, were responsible for Santana coming up with the Latin-rock hybrid.

GREATEST HITS

YEAR	SONG
1969	"Evil Ways"
1970	"Black Magic Woman"
	"Oye Como Va"
1971	"No One to Depend On"
1977	"She's Not There"
1978	"Stormy"
1979	"You Know That I Love You"
1981	"Winning"
1982	"Hold On"
1985	"Say It Again"
1999	"Smooth" (featuring Rob Thomas)
2000	"Maria Maria" (featuring The Product G&B)
2002	"The Game of Love" (featuring Michelle Branch)
2006	"Illegal" (featuring Shakira)

THE SEX PISTOLS

1975–1978

They flamed brighter and faster than perhaps any band in rock and roll, punching a safety pin hole through the polite fabric of popular music. There were other punks before and since, but the Sex Pistols played it to the hilt. They were the real deal, flying in the face of convention wherever they stumbled. With Johnny Rotten, aka John Lydon, as their antagonistic front man and an audience of disaffected youth that spat on them as a sign of approval, the Sex Pistols soon became an immediate sensation.

"Ever get the feeling you've been cheated?"—Johnny Rotten

Their first single released on EMI, "Anarchy in the UK," changed the face of rock and roll, dividing the old guard of '70s FM rock from an underground culture that didn't yet know what it was trying to be. Like "Great Balls of Fire" and "Tutti Frutti" before it, this was something completely new. The group was immediately dropped and re-signed for more money to A&M and then dropped again and re-signed to Warner Brothers Bassist Glenn Matlock left the group before their album was recorded and his replacement, Lydon's friend Sid Vicious, could barely play bass, but he looked the part. Sid was a shy young man who suddenly saw himself as "a toughie," as Lydon once put it, and he proved it when he got his ass kicked from coast to coast. Sid ended up believing that he was the embodiment of "punk." But the Pistols' one-and-only album, *Never Mind the Bollocks*, doesn't feature Sid's bass playing because he was in the hospital at the time it was recorded. Guitarist Steve Jones played all of the parts.

A terrifying U.S. tour supporting their album through the redneck South was a trial by fire for the Pistols, who had purposely booked themselves into cowboy saloons in Texas and avoided places like New York City, where they might have been properly received. It all came to an end at the Winterland in San Francisco. The band members were at odds: with themselves, their audiences—with everything. Lydon left the stage in disgust, and the Sex Pistols were history.

Lydon soon started Public Image Ltd., and Sid, with his girlfriend, Nancy Spungen, tried to put something together in New York City but lost it all in a heroin haze. They were dead within three months of each other.

Sex Pistol's Public Image

The Pistols started with guitarist Steve Jones and drummer Paul Cook. They scored some of their first gear when Bowie was doing his Ziggy Stardust gig in London in 1972, and they actually broke into the theater and stole his amplifiers. They spent some of their time hanging around Malcolm McLaren's Teddy Boy clothing shop, which went through a variety of names and permutations. McLaren had briefly managed the New York Dolls and passed on a Les Paul guitar to Jones—like passing the torch to the next generation. At McLaren's shop they met Glen Matlock and auditioned one John Lydon for lead singer. Borrowing from the look created by Richard Hell in New York, with torn clothes and safety pins, the band was off and running almost immediately with a handful of their own songs and covers of the Who, Small Faces, and the Monkees.

GREATEST HITS

Year	Song
1976	"Anarchy in the UK"
1977	"God Save the Queen"
	"Pretty Vacant"
	"Holidays in the Sun"
1978	"No One Is Innocent"
1979	"Something Else"
	"Silly Thing"
	"C'mon Everybody"
	"The Great Rock 'n' Roll Swindle"
1980	"(I'm Not Your) Steppin' Stone"

Sid Vicious and Johnny Rotten have no use for you, and will cheerfully tell you just that.

THE SHANGRI-LAS

1963–1968

(Clockwise, from bottom left) Marge Ganser, Mary Weiss, and Mary Anne Ganser in the bedroom thinking about boys.

NUGGET: English new waver Joe Jackson adopted the first line of "Leader of the Pack" as the title of his 1978 hit, "Is She Really Going Out With Him?"

GREATEST HITS

Year	Song
1964	"Remember (Walking in the Sand)"
	"Leader of the Pack"
	"Give Him a Great Big Kiss"
	"Wishing Well"
1965	"Out in the Streets"
	"Give Us Your Blessings"
	"I Can Never Go Home Anymore"
1966	"Sophisticated Boom Boom"
	"He Cried"
	"Past, Present and Future"

The truly great artists somehow transcend their genres. The Shangri-Las were lumped in with the girl groups of the '60s, but if they were part of that, they were indeed the leaders of the pack. They sang songs that were incredibly inventive as far as structure, with a shot of over-the-top melodrama that was always tempered by heartfelt vocals. Playing on the image of tough city girls, with hoodlum boyfriends just off-screen, they played out teen dramas that were worldly and wise beyond their years. Mary Weiss lost her dad when she was 6 months old, and perhaps her fatherless childhood really did toughen her up.

The group formed in Queens, New York, from two sets of teenaged sisters, Mary and Betty Weiss and twins Marge and Mary Ann Ganser. Betty sang lead on their first couple of singles but was soon reduced to a more auxiliary role when they were discovered by George "Shadow" Morton and signed to the Red Bird label. Shadow was a young hustler who was trying to convince Red Bird owners, benevolent gambler George Goldner and songwriters Jerry Leiber and Mike Stoller, that he too was a songwriter. He wasn't, but somewhere out of his psyche he cooked up "Remember (Walking in the Sand)." The unorthodox chorus of handclaps and finger snaps and the voice of Mary Weiss all angst and heartbreak (along with some prerecorded seagulls) made the song a smash. It was almost as if Morton created sonic movies that were incredibly visual and emotionally stirring.

For two years the Shangri-Las held their own with the Beatles on the charts. They toured on many road shows, played the *Soupy Sales Show*, and were every teenaged boy's dream. Sadly, internal problems at Red Bird saw the collapse of the label due to gambling debts. Lawsuits kept the girls from recording for almost 10 years.

The Ganser sisters passed away without ever making another album. Shadow Morton produced Janis Ian's "Society's Child" and recordings for Vanilla Fudge and the New York Dolls. When Johnny Thunders covered "Give Him a Great Big Kiss," the Shangri-Las became a touchstone for punk rockers the world over. Aerosmith upped the ante with their version of "Remember (Walking in the Sand)," and Bette Midler appropriated "Leader of the Pack." In 2007, Mary Weiss came back with an album on Norton records and performed at South by Southwest in Austin to an ecstatic crowd. She still has great hair.

Leader of the Pack

For the follow-up to "Remember," Shadow Morton collaborated with the hit songwriting team of Jeff Barry and Ellie Greenwich to come up with "Leader of the Pack," a groundbreaking girl group song with conversation parts. The other girls call out to Mary, playing the part of Betty, and ask her a series of questions about the ring she's wearing, culminating with asking how she met the leader of the pack. Mary bursts out like she can't hold back any longer, "I met him at the candy store . . ."

SIMON AND GARFUNKEL

1957–2004

Simon and Garfunkel originally broke up in 1959, and they've been breaking up ever since. But the best part of breaking up is getting a new reunion album and a repackaging of your greatest hits, and fans are happy to buy them all over again.

The actual S&G catalog is small, just a little over four full-length albums of material, but what a catalog! Their songs are some of the most memorable and best-selling of the '60s. They cleaved themselves emotionally to the events of those times, and the nation's nostalgia will forever be set off in the bloodstream when those songs play. The songs are also great outside of their historical context, so subsequent generations have rediscovered them as well.

NUGGET: The large reverb-laden sound on "Bridge Over Trouble Water" was supposedly made by a baseball bat hitting the side of the vocal booth.

Paul Simon and Art Garfunkel were childhood friends in Forest Hills, Queens. In their junior year of high school they released a single, "Hey Schoolgirl," under the moniker Tom and Jerry that owed a debt to the Everly Brothers' close-harmony style of singing. The song took off and sold 100,000 copies, but subsequent efforts were a bit too noveltylike. Simon and Garfunkel broke up for the first time and went off to college, only to get back together to sing in Greenwich Village nightclubs.

Paul Simon (left) enjoys a smoke while studiously ignoring Garfunkel's considered opinion.

Their early folk efforts were collected on *Wednesday Morning, 3 A.M.*, but it was not a success, so they broke up again. Simon headed off to England and started cutting a solo album called *The Paul Simon Songbook*. But while they were away, folk rock hit in the form of the Byrds' reworking of Dylan's "Mr. Tambourine Man." Dylan's original was a solo acoustic folk song to which the Byrds added 12-string Rickenbacker guitar four-part harmony and a full Beatlesque backbeat. Simon and Garfunkel's and Dylan's producer, Tom Wilson, had gotten word from some radio stations that they liked a song on *3 A.M.*, called "The Sound of Silence." Without asking for permission, he had Dylan's backing band add a Byrds-style backing track to the acoustic "The Sound of Silence." It rocketed to #1. Simon came back from England and re-formed his duo with Garfunkel. He grabbed from songs he'd recorded solo, went back into the studio, and created pop band arrangements for songs such as "I Am a Rock." From here they made a trio of classic '60s albums: *Parsley, Sage, Rosemary and Thyme*; *Bookends*; and

The Graduate

A song written for Mike Nichols' 1967 film *The Graduate*—the coming-of-age anthem "Mrs. Robinson"—appeared on the soundtrack album as well as on *Bookends*. The film was a touchstone for a generation and the song was forever engraved in the shot of Mrs. R. slipping her stocking off as a young Benjamin gaped into his future.

Simon and Garfunkel, a fresh faced, young duo.

their finale *Bridge over Troubled Water.*

By time they released *Bridge over Troubled Water*, the duo was barely speaking, but they came together especially on "Cecilia," which coupled American rhythms to their Everly Brothers' roots. But the title track was the standout, with Garfunkel's high, quavering tenor somehow speaking for all the lost souls of the decade.

Garfunkel later explored acting as well as recorded with famed writer Jimmy Webb. Simon went on to a very successful solo career, with many hits culminating in *Graceland*. The duo together recorded one more new song, "My Little Town," for release on both of their solo albums in 1975, and they get back together every half a decade or so to wheel out their classic songs one more time.

Simon (right) and Garfunkel perform during one of their many reunions.

Simon Solo

Paul Simon was inducted into the Rock and Roll Hall of Fame twice—the first time as half of Simon and Garfunkel and again for his solo performances. Going solo didn't slow down Paul Simon's hit-making abilities, and he churned out iconic songs like "Mother and Child Reunion," "Me and Julio Down by the Schoolyard," "Kodachrome," and "50 Ways to Leave Your Lover." And if the man hadn't done enough already, 1986's massively successful *Graceland* put him right back on top of the heap. Simon is on record as believing that the title track is the best song he's ever written. The album was controversially recorded in part in South Africa and featured many South African musicians, including the singing group Ladysmith Black Mambazo, who acquired an audience of their own from the exposure. That year the album and title track were both awarded Grammys for best in their categories.

GREATEST HITS

Year	Song
1964	"The Sound of Silence"
1966	"I Am a Rock"
	"Scarborough Fair"
	"Homeward Bound"
	"For Emily, Whenever I May Find Her"
	"The Dangling Conversation"
1967	"At the Zoo"
1968	"A Hazy Shade of Winter"
	"Mrs. Robinson"
	"Fakin' It"
	"America"
1970	"Bridge over Troubled Water"
	"El Condor Pasa"
	"Cecilia"
	"The Boxer"
1975	"My Little Town"

SLY AND THE FAMILY STONE

1967–1983

He was his own creation; a larger than life crazy pimped-out "playah" of the first order, who drew together so many disparate musical forms and piled them into an ever-changing brew that America loved—black, white, and blue.

Born and raised in Texas and brought up strongly Christian, Sylvester Stewart, his brother Freddie, and sisters Rose and Vaetta started a gospel group when the family moved to Vallejo, California. They released one single in 1959 as the Stewart Four, "Walking in Jesus' Name." Sly went on to release a number of failed singles as Danny Stewart before morphing into the more flamboyant Sly Stone as a deejay on the San Francisco soul station KSOL.

After leaving the studio as a producer for Autumn Records, where he made recordings with the Beau Brummels and the Great Society (Grace Slick's first band) and had a hit producing Bobby Freeman's "C'mon and Swim," he was ready to strike out on his own. He combined his own band with a band of his brother's to create Sly and the Family Stone. A regional hit led Clive Davis to sign the group to Epic, and in his inimitable style he begged, cajoled, and worked on Sly to write a hit. "Dance to the Music" was the song that put them on the charts. By the time they got to their glorious performance at Woodstock, they had laid a number of songs on the radio and everybody loved them: soul audiences, hippies, and Top 40 radio listeners. They began selling out Madison Square Garden on a regular basis (in 1974, Sly married Kathleen Silva, mother of Sly Jr., onstage at the Garden) with record attendance numbers. In 1970 things grew dark just as they were at the height of their fame; heavy drug abuse kicked in and politics went from "let's all live together" to black power, Panthers, and the icy "Thank You (Falettinme Be Mice Elf Agin)." "There's a Riot Goin' On" is considered his masterpiece, but it was recorded with only minimal help from the band and instead used the talents of such edgy characters lurking in the background as Ike Turner and Billy Preston. Sly and the Family Stone grew paranoid and split into different camps.

SLY STONE (SECOND FROM LEFT) AND THE FAMILY, ONE OF THE FIRST SUCCESSFUL INTERRACIAL GROUPS OF THE '60S, ENJOY A CALMER MOMENT.

GREATEST HITS

YEAR	SONG
1968	"Dance to the Music"
	"Life"
	"M'Lady"
	"Everyday People"
1969	"Stand!"
	"Hot Fun in the Summertime"
1970	"Thank You (Falettinme Be Mice Elf Agin)"
	"I Want to Take You Higher"
1971	"Family Affair"
1972	"Runnin' Away"
1973	"If You Want Me to Stay"
1974	"Time for Livin'"

Sly kept things rolling for a little while with *Fresh*, a more friendly album than *Riot*, with the great songs "If You Want Me to Stay" and "Que Sera Sera." Sly looks like he's taking a flying karate kick on the cover, but he's actually sprawled on a piece of Plexiglas.

Sly disappeared after a series of disappointing albums and was eventually arrested and convicted of cocaine possession. Nonetheless, a crazy appearance at the Grammys in 2006 left fans yearning for some of the old audacity.

The Sly Sound

As a disc jockey on KSOL, Sly mixed up the music and added Beatles and Stones in with Stax and Motown. In a sense, on that radio station he created the mix that would turn into the music of Sly and the Family Stone. It was a great multiracial "family of man" band, with everyone interjecting lines in a call-and-response style, and it featured hip women who played instruments. It was a groundbreaking family affair, or as the live-and-let-live ethos of "Everyday People" said, "different strokes for different folks."

PATTI SMITH

DECEMBER 30, 1946–

PATTI SMITH IN MAN-TAILORED SHIRT AND TIE MESSES WITH GENDER EXPECTATIONS.

Somewhere between sleep and awakening exists the place from where Patti Smith pulls her songs; a rock-and-roll dreamland with stallions coming in on waves that lapse into seahorses, where gang fights around a locker end in hysterical laughter, and where the sea of possibilities are there for the taking.

GREATEST HITS	
YEAR	SONG
1974	"Hey Joe"
	"Piss Factory"
1975	"Gloria"
1975	"Free Money"
1976	"Pissing in a River"
	"Ain't It Strange"
1978	"Because the Night"
	"Rock 'n' Roll Nigger"
1979	"Frederick"
1979	"Dancing Barefoot"
1988	"People Have the Power"
1997	"1959"

Horses

Patti befriended Tom Verlaine of Television and found herself part of the fledgling New York City CBGB rock community. Where she had been a starry-eyed kid around the Warhol crowd, she was now an elder statesman, and with drummer Jay Dee Daugherty and bassist Ivan Kral the Patti Smith Group was the first to get signed out of the club. The album *Horses*, with Mapplethorpe's distinctive black-and-white cover portrait of Patti, was a tour de force. Produced by John Cale of the Velvet Underground, the album fused V.U.– and Television-style grooves with Patti's unique poetic delivery. This was before rap, but she accessed songs like Van Morrison's "Gloria," "Land of a Thousand Dances," and even the groove from "I Only Have Eyes for You" for the track "Birdland." The album takes the listener to other worlds fused with her Rimbaud-style rants; she's a rock and roll priestess conjuring up the spirits of a primitive god—a rock god.

Patti Smith developed an early fascination for rock and roll as a child in South Jersey, growing up as a member of the working poor with parents who cared about art. She knew she had to get out of Jersey and make her mark on the world (her early years at a dead-end job are chronicled in her first single "Piss Factory"). She ended up in New York, rooming with the photographer Robert Mapplethorpe, hanging out on the fringes of the Warhol Max's Kansas City scene, dreaming and writing about rock stars like Dylan, Hendrix, and Keith Richards.

"[Horses] tore my limbs off and put them back on in a whole different order."—Michael Stipe

She found a kindred spirit in Lenny Kaye, a part-time rock critic like herself, who played guitar after getting off work at Village Oldies, the Greenwich Village record store. They started playing a bit, Patti with her poetry accompanied by Lenny in a cabaret-style group. They added pianist Richard Sohl and, after a while, began to make a bit of a name for themselves. With producer John Cale, Patti and the band recorded their landmark first album, *Horses*, and although it wasn't a major commercial success, it's influenced a generation of bands and listeners. Patti made a number of albums, none ever quite as breathtaking or groundbreaking as *Horses* but excellent all the same, including *Radio Ethiopia* and *Easter*.

The Patti Smith Group was disbanded when she fell in love and married Fred "Sonic" Smith from the MC5. In between raising children they cowrote the album *Dream of Life*, which included their anthem "People Have the Power." She first lost her good friend Robert Mapplethorpe to AIDS in 1989, and then in 1990 her bandmate Richard Sohl passed away. In 1994, her husband and brother both died of heart attacks. Encouraged by friends Michael Stipe and Allen Ginsberg, she put a group back together that included old friends Lenny Kaye and Tom Verlaine and recorded *Gone Again* as a way to deal with all of her losses. In 2007, she was inducted into the Rock and Roll Hall of Fame and sang "People Have the Power" backed up by Keith Richards and many others.

THE SMITHS

1982–1987

Morrissey and his band, the Smiths, brought a new attitude to rock and roll. They were the first of the mope rockers, the ambassadors of "twee." Where Bowie had been outrageous and defiant in his stance that the kids were all right no matter what their sexual preference, Morrissey took the stance that it was all right to feel bad about yourself, and perhaps it was better to dream from the safety of one's bedroom than interact with the rest of the human race. "I should go out tonight," he mused, "but I haven't got a thing to wear." Heaven knows, he loved being miserable.

The Smiths might not have pulled it off if it weren't for Morrissey's keen, exact use of language and a world-weary voice that was ready to yawn at a moment's notice. Morrissey's voice crooned like something heard on an old wind-up phonograph from the '20s, but it was also a distinctively modern instrument that could stretch words and melodies in unique directions. Add to that the post–R.E.M. guitar work of Johnny Marr, and you had a killer combination that flew in the face of all the pretentious synth rock of the day. They hit their stride particularly well on the monster groove of "How Soon Is Now," a song that took an old Eno riff and updated it into U2 arena rock proportions. Marr and the rhythm section of Mike Joyce on drums and Andy Rourke on bass worked up tracks that Morrissey could take home to develop words and melodies.

Morrissey gave great controversial interviews in the music press and his matinee idol image gave them an edge on MTV. They also had distinctive album art that utilized duotone photos of '60s iconic types like Warhol superstars Joe Dallesandro and James Dean. They were stylized, adroit, and they rocked even while they moped. And who couldn't love songs with titles like "The Boy with the Thorn in His Side," "Shoplifters of the World Unite," and "Girlfriend in a Coma."

The difficult personalities in the Smiths led them to break up after a five-year run. Fans are always hoping that they will reunite. Morrissey has admitted that he hates hearing other people add their lyrics to Marr's music. The cult of Morrissey has continued to grow and evolve over time, and he's released successful solo albums. Meanwhile, Marr has quietly collaborated with many artists including Talking Heads and Beck. He's also had chart success with New Order's Bernard Sumner in a collaborative effort called Electronic and most recently a #1 album as a member of Modest Mouse in 2007.

The Name

Morrissey and Marr came up with the name the Smiths, because it was such a bland name; it set them apart from the more outlandishly named bands of the day such as Spandau Ballet and Kajagoogoo. The Smiths led English bands back to the guitar-based Brit-rock sound, making the world safe for the likes of Belle and Sebastian, Blur, and Oasis. Before he started the Smiths, Morrissey was attempting to be a writer, often penning letters to the *New Musical Express* and *Melody Maker*. He was also the English fan club president for the New York Dolls and helped convince them to re-form in 2004.

GREATEST HITS

Year	Song
1983	"Hand in Glove"
1984	"What Difference Does It Make?"
	"Heaven Knows I'm Miserable Now"
	"William, It Was Really Nothing"
1985	"How Soon Is Now?"
	"That Joke Isn't Funny Anymore"
	"The Boy with the Thorn in His Side"
1986	"Bigmouth Strikes Again"
1987	"Sheila Take a Bow"
	"Girlfriend in a Coma"
	"I Started Something I Couldn't Finish"
	"Last Night I Dreamt That Somebody Loved Me"

The Smiths, (from left) Johnny Marr, Morrissey, Andy Rourke, and Mike Joyce, grimly contemplate their fate.

BRUCE SPRINGSTEEN

September 23, 1949–

Bruce Springsteen didn't want to be a successful musician. He wanted to be part of the mythology of rock and roll, and he spent more than a decade living in that place. It was more than just an image, but it was less than real life. For as long as Bruce has been around, his output has been very small, with every album a carefully honed gem.

"In all my years in this business he is the only person I've met who cares absolutely nothing about money." —John A. Hammond

Discovered by John Hammond in 1972, Bruce started out as a solo performer with a mouthful of lyrics and a great group—the E Street Band—waiting in the wings. *Greetings from Asbury Park* was an overly wordy affair: pumped up and bursting at the seams with ideas, some slightly half-baked. Nonetheless, there were songs on this album that stood him in good stead, such as "Hard to Be a Saint in the City" (think Scorsese's *Mean Streets*), "Growin' Up" (a lost boy waiting to turn into Peter Pan), and "Spirit in the Night," featuring a great cast of teenage ne'er-do-wells mucking it up in Greasy Lake.

Even if you think he is, please don't call Springsteen "The Boss"; he doesn't like it.

The E Street Band was front and center on his next release, *The Wild, the Innocent and the E Street Shuffle*, an album that would mythologize Springsteen's Jersey shore life. In some ways it was his most ambitious album. The E Street Band could play anything, and on this album they prove it, doing everything from Ray Charles and Van Morrison R&B grooves to Steely Dan ersatz jazz to sprawling epic rock and roll constructions like "Rosalita" and Tom Waits hipster poetics in "Wild Billy's Circus." Unfortunately, they forgot to come up with a single.

Music critic and producer Jon Landau, the man who'd famously proclaimed Bruce as "rock and roll's future," came on the scene to help out with the next album, pushing aside Springsteen's manager,

From left: Clarence Clemons, Bruce, Max Weinberg, and Steve Van Zandt like to give their audience a good show.

GREATEST HITS	
YEAR	SONG
1973	"Blinded by the Light"
	"Spirit in the Night"
	"Fourth of July, Asbury Park (Sandy)"
	"Rosalita"
1975	"Born to Run"
1976	"Thunder Road"
	"Jungleland"
1978	"Prove It All Night"
	"Badlands"
	"The Promised Land"
1980	"Hungry Heart"
	"The River"
1984	"Dancing in the Dark"
	"Born in the U.S.A."
1985	"Glory Days"
1987	"Tunnel of Love"
	"Brilliant Disguise"
1993	"Streets of Philadelphia"
2002	"The Rising"
	"Mary's Place"

Mike Appel. The epic *Born to Run* of 1975 launched Springsteen to stardom, landing him on the cover of *Time* and *Newsweek*. The E Street Band toured the world and all was good.

Unfortunately former manager Mike Appel did not go gently into the night, and although everything was ultimately resolved, there was a long period where Springsteen couldn't step foot in the studio. When he finally emerged from it all, he came up with *Darkness on the Edge of Town*—and gone was the runaway gypsy rocker from *Born to Run* with the big man at his side. In his place was a haunted-looking young man, standing alone in a drab, barely furnished house, looking somewhat

BRUCE SPRINGSTEEN WAS AMERICA'S HERO DURING THOSE LOFTY DAYS AFTER THE RELEASE OF *BORN TO RUN*.

beaten down. The production of the album knocked some holes in the previous album's wall of sound, leaving more room for reverberation. The language was pared down—from a "highway jammed with broken heroes on a last chance power drive," we now had a guy stuck in traffic in his car. With his voice raspier and more desperate, *Darkness on the Edge of Town* was larger-than-life, but somehow still more real.

NUGGET: The sprawling *Live/1975–85* showed the world just what Bruce was made of and included songs he had given away over the years, such as "Fire," a hit for the Pointer Sisters, and "Because the Night," a hit for Patti Smith.

Springsteen continued to boil down what he was doing to some kind of essence. *The River*, a sprawling set that found his vocals buried in the mix on a lot of songs, relied on primitive production values. Fixated on Gary U.S. Bonds recordings like "Quarter to Three," he was trying to get things to sound like the rock and roll records he dug in his youth. The album included the haunting title track and the hit "Hungry Heart." It was a song originally written for the Ramones that was closer in spirit to "Born to Run," with more of a pop sheen than the rest of the album. Lyrically, the songs revolved around each other, with words like *hearts*, *cars*, and *girls* all showing up repeatedly.

The Early Days

Bruce got his start in a post-Beatles America, playing in Freehold, New Jersey, in bands like the Castiles, doing all the requisite Stones and garage band covers of the day, and occasionally making a foray into Greenwich Village to try his luck at the big time. His next band, Child, morphed into Steel Mill, a blues-based, Cream-style, heavy rock trio. After adding more musicians they became Dr. Zoom and his Sonic Boom, and finally the E Street Band, one of the greatest rock and roll outfits ever to hit a stage.

The Making of *Born to Run*

Bruce found a champion in the guise of Jon Landau, who slowly inserted himself into the E Street camp as producer. Original manager Mike Appel had worked on the title song for the next album, and he'd also kept the fragile economics together for this band. But while he was busy in the trenches, Landau was showing Springsteen new horizons. *Born To Run* was where it all came together for the band. They were at the top of their playing abilities, and Bruce and Landau came up with a new set of parameters. The album was more of a throwback to an earlier time, to the epic wall of sound approach of Phil Spector, the big power chords of the Who, a little Duane Eddie guitar, Clarence Clemons blowing like a storm, Roy Orbison, and *West Side Story*. Springsteen was Peter Pan luring Wendy to take his hand and escape from the ordinary life. They would get out while they still had their youth—just a couple of tramps that were born to run.

Where could he go from here? His next album stripped things down to just a man and his guitar. *Nebraska* was just Bruce in his bedroom with a tape recorder, writing some of the best and starkest songs of his career. It was a great artistic achievement and, in part, it was the story of a legend with nowhere else to go.

And so reduced to a man and a guitar, he reinvented himself and came bursting out with an album, *Born in the U.S.A.*, that married the big production values of *Born to Run* (note the similar titles) to what he had learned on his journey to *Nebraska* about stripping things back to their essentials. The E Street Band plays the songs aggressively: Max Weinberg's snare drum is the dominant instrument, Danny Federici's organ stabs out big notes, Clarence keeps the sax fat and on the back end of songs. Bruce had been pumping iron at the time and appeared in a new, buff, weight lifter's physique, and the music had the muscle to match. It exploded beyond anything he had ever done, selling more than 15 million copies in the United States and cementing his superstar status.

After his divorce from model-actress Julianne Phillips and subsequent marriage to E Street Band backup singer and guitarist, Patti Scialfa, Springsteen the man diverged from Springsteen the myth. There was the sense that, from the late '80s onward, he was more interested in real life than rock-and-roll warrior status. He broke up the E Street Band for a while and started a family. He delivered a couple of lackluster albums with new players. He made an acoustic Woody Guthrie–style affair that took a journalistic approach to music. He caused some stir when he reconvened the E Street Band for *The Rising*, an album that tapped right into the nation's psyche after 9/11. Most recently, he discovered the music of Pete Seeger, someone he'd missed at the beginning of his career as a young rock and roller, and made *The Seeger Sessions* album perhaps the most spontaneous, joyful album he ever cut. We'll see where he goes from here. He's always got another chance to make it even more real.

THE FACE THAT LAUNCHED A THOUSAND RIFFS? BACKUP SINGER, GUITARIST, AND WIFE, PATTY SCIALFA BRINGS MANY TALENTS TO THE TABLE.

Hungry Heart

His failed marriage to Julianne Phillips made Bruce rethink things a bit. He was at the top of his game with nowhere else to go, and so he found a Jersey girl (and member of the E Street Band), someone perhaps more real than the magazine image that had enamored him the first time around. With Patti Scialfa, he got married, settled down, and had three children. *Tunnel of Love*, the album that followed *Born in the U.S.A.*, was a quiet romantic coda to his journey, with keyboard washes the prominent instrument, dominating over the guitars and snare. It was an intimate exploration of the heart.

STEELY DAN

1971–

There was no one in the '70s who made pop music as suave and sophisticated as Steely Dan. Like top-shelf liquor, their music was made from the finest players, working obsessively in the finest studios, with Donald Fagen and Walter Becker, one of the finest songwriting teams ever. Fagen did the lion's share of the work, doing most of the composing and lyric writing; Becker was a friend and foil, who motivated him to put in the long hours to create the sleek, perfected works that made up the Steely Dan oeuvre.

Becker and Fagen began their partnership playing in a variety of college bar bands, while attending Bard in upstate New York. One of the bands featured comedian Chevy Chase on vocals. After a stint as backing musicians for Jay and the Americans, the duo ended up with a songwriting contract with ABC Dunhill. It was there that they met up with producer Gary Katz, who'd be the other constant in the Steely Dan story. Their first album, *Can't Buy a Thrill*, contained two of their biggest hits "Do It Again" and "Reelin' in the Years." It was a more aggressive musical version of the soft rock popular on early '70s AM radio.

GREATEST HITS	
YEAR	SONG
1972	"Do It Again"
	"Reelin' in the Years"
1973	"My Old School"
1974	"Rikki Don't Lose That Number"
1976	"Kid Charlemagne
	"Haitian Divorce"
1977	"Deacon Blues"
	"Josie"
	"Peg"
1978	"FM (No Static at All)"
	"Hey Nineteen"
2000	"Cousin Dupree"

KNOWN FOR THEIR STUDIO PERFECTIONISM, STEELY DAN WAS ABLE TO BRING THAT SOUND TO LIVE AUDIENCES ONLY WITH CONSIDERABLE EFFORT.

Steely Dan always worked to create phenomenal-sounding albums—on an almost Olympian level. But the group's meticulous attention to sonic details made touring an unpleasant experience. It would be decades before the live sound technology would catch up to and approximate what they achieved in the studio. After 1974 they stopped touring, and band members Jeff "Skunk" Baxter and sometimes vocalist Michael McDonald went off to join the Doobie Brothers. Steely Dan's albums became increasingly sophisticated, bringing in more jazz and R&B influences and leaving the rock trappings behind. Their singles charted: never at the top of the charts, but they were a staple of the FM radio band. With albums like *Katy Lied*, *The Royal Scam*, and *Aja* their base continued to slowly grow, even though they didn't tour. *Aja* was their first album to go platinum.

Steely Dan sat out most of the '80s, concentrating on production work for Becker and a single solo album for Fagen. As the compact disc came to dominate the recording industry, the Steely Dan catalog flew off the shelves. For people looking for the pristine sound quality of digital audio, Steely Dan's vinyl albums were the first listeners chose to replace. In 1993, Steely Dan began performing for the first time in almost 20 years, as well as making new albums.

FM

Steely Dan contributed the song "FM" to the movie soundtrack of the same name. The film was about a '70s rock station in the era between '60s idealistic underground radio and the eventual aging of the format into "classic rock." Not to be left out, AM radio stations spliced the first note of the chorus of the Steely Dan song "Aja" (the sustained "A") and cut out the F of the chorus of "FM," so they could play the song and promote their own format.

STEVE MILLER BAND

1968–

There's no hard-luck story at the beginning of the Steve Miller saga. His father was a doctor in Dallas, Texas, who loved jazz. Les Paul, inventor of the self-named guitar and the multitrack tape recorder, was his godfather. Paul even taught Steve his first chords. That said, Steve Miller worked hard for everything he got, even if he did travel in some rarified circles.

His formed his first band with childhood friend Boz Scaggs (who later rejoined him in the Steve Miller Band). After a stint in college he moved to Chicago and started a group with Barry Goldberg of the Electric Flag. When the Miller–Goldberg Blues Band didn't take off after an initial single, he picked up and headed to San Francisco, where it seemed all of the bands were being signed. He got signed, too, and was soon playing the Monterey Pop Festival. Next, he traveled to England because George Martin, the Beatles' brilliant producer, wanted to work with him. But Martin was busy making such albums as *Sgt. Pepper* and *Magical Mystery Tour* so Steve "settled" for the Rolling Stones' producer Glyn Johns.

> **NUGGET:** "Fly Like an Eagle" and "The Joker" have been sampled in a number of hip-hop songs, including "Angel" by Shaggy.

It seemed as if Miller lived a charmed life, but then the hard work set in. Despite solid albums like *Brave New World* and the occasional FM turntable hits such as "Living in the USA" and "Space Cowboy," the Steve Miller Band couldn't break into the really big time. Boz Scaggs left to go solo. Then after seven albums, Steve was in a horrific car accident that broke his neck. While he was recovering, he came up with a thin batch of songs. One of them, however, proved to be a great one: "The Joker" was his first hit single. After three more years of hard touring, he had a platinum album and enough money to stay off the road for a while.

At this point, he took a break, bought a farm, and wood-shedded in his Marin County home studio, recording enough material for two albums. The first, *Fly Like an Eagle*, contained the ambitious title track along with such other hits as "Rock 'n' Me" and "Take the Money and Run." When he released the second half of the stockpile as *Book of Dreams*, the album went quadruple platinum, with three more massive hits in "Jet Airliner," "Swingtown," and "Jungle Love." He then collected the best of his recent work and called it *Greatest Hits 1974–78,* which sold more than 14 million copies.

McCartney Guest Appearance

"My Dark Hour" on *Brave New World* features Paul Ramone on bass, drums, some backup vocals, and a bit of guitar. Ramone, however, is actually Paul McCartney, credited under an assumed name. One listen to the track, recorded in 1969, and you can hear echoes of "Helter Skelter" on the coda, as well as the kind of playing McCartney attempted on his first solo album the following year.

More often seen behind an electric axe, Miller is shown here playing a rare acoustic gig.

The Steve Miller Band continues to tour and wow the crowds. "Fly Like an Eagle" is always the centerpiece, with Steve and the band soaring and bending it in many different directions, improvising something new every time it's played.

GREATEST HITS

Year	Song
1968	"Living in the USA"
1969	"Space Cowboy"
1973	"The Joker"
1976	"Rock 'n' Me"
	"Take the Money and Run"
	"Fly Like an Eagle"
	"Wild Mountain Honey"
1977	"Jet Airliner"
	"Jungle Love"
1982	"Abracadabra"

T. REX

1967–1977

A true rock and roll visionary, Marc Bolan was the person most responsible for developing the glam rock movement. While many think it was David Bowie, the thin white duke was actually taking his cues from the electric warrior himself. Early in Bowie's career he actually did mime as part of Bolan's entourage.

"I feel there is a curse on rock stars." —Marc Bolan

It was the time of Donovan and the Incredible String Band, and Bolan, as one half of the swirling hippie duo Tyrannosaurus Rex, was a bohemian prince on the scene. With album titles like *My People Were Fair and Had Sky in Their Hair . . . but Now They're Content to Wear Stars on Their Brows*, it was obvious that Bolan was the pied piper. It was also obvious that he needed to find a bigger flock to lead, so with the help of producer Tony Visconti, he retooled himself as a teen pop superstar going electric. He shortened his songs, kept the bongos, and added a rhythm section as well as the wild wail of the Turtles' Flo and Eddie on backing vocals. He sang about cars in "Metal Guru" and girls in "Jeepster" and all the young dudes in "Children of the Revolution." Suddenly he was banging out hit after U.K. hit. He grew so popular that Ringo Starr took notice and made a documentary about him, called *Born to Boogie*. Now kids from the post-hippie '60s had a hero of their own—and a movement to go along with it.

Marc Bolan is often under-heralded for his role in showing an entire generation the sartorial possibilities available to the motivated rock star.

GREATEST HITS	
YEAR	SONG
1970	"Ride a White Swan"
1971	"Get It On"
	"Jeepster"
1972	"Metal Guru"
	"Children of the Revolution"
1973	"20th Century Boy"
	"The Groover"
1974	"Teenage Dream"
	"Light of Love"
	"Zip Gun Boogie"
1975	"New York City"
1976	"I Love to Boogie"
1977	"The Soul of My Suit"

In no time there were other stars like Bowie, Mott the Hoople, and David Essex all working the glam angle. But Bolan was king, especially with a trio of releases, *Electric Warrior*, *Bolan Boogie*, and *The Slider*. While he continued to tweak his formula, he never strayed too far from what made him famous. Not unlike Captain Beefheart, he had a set of grooves that were truly his own. But the times moved on. Bolan never truly caught fire in the United States, but did have a TV show in the U.K., and introduced to the world such bands as the Jam and the Damned.

In 1977, with girlfriend Gloria Jones at the wheel, Bolan's Austin Mini crashed into a tree. Bolan was killed instantly. Over time, however, his music took on a life of its own: The quality was there and songs like "20th Century Boy" and "Jeepster" continue to show up in films and advertisements, their boogie grooves too catchy to be discarded by future generations.

Tyrannosaurus Rex

As a youngster in the '50s, Bolan grew up on rockabilly such as Gene Vincent, Eddie Cochran, and Elvis. As a musician in the '60s he went though his folk phase (covering Dylan and Fred Neil), his mod phase as a sharp-dressed fashion model, his psychedelic phase (digging Syd Barrett and performing in John's Children), and finally his hippie phase, wowing the London underground drop-out, hippie set with his acoustic guitar and percussion duo Tyrannosaurus Rex, with Steve Took. Their high-spirited shows were intense and tribal, with Bolan masquerading some of those rockabilly licks in the driving rhythms of his acoustic guitar.

TALKING HEADS

1974–1991

THE NAMES OF THESE PEOPLE ARE DAVID BYRNE, JERRY HARRISON, CHRIS FRANTZ, AND TINA WEYMOUTH. THE NAME OF THIS BAND IS TALKING HEADS.

The trio of Rhode Island School of Design students who made up Talking Heads was an unlikely cast of characters. A woman playing something other than an acoustic guitar? A preppy-looking kid on drums? A spastic twitching front man with short hair, singing about being a psycho killer? Not the crew you'd want to hang with at the local biker bar.

Yes, Talking Heads were an anomaly when they showed up at CBGB in the mid-'70s. David Byrne wrote strange, wonderful songs about buildings, loving the government, and being a boy in motion, mystified and dazzled by the world around him. Tina Weymouth, sporting short blond hair, moved seductively with her oversized bass, and her boyfriend, Chris Frantz, in his shirts with the

Tom Tom Club

When the Tom Tom Club appeared on the scene, they were light-hearted fun that everyone, and their boyfriend, wanted to dance to. Originally a side project for Talking Heads members Tina and Chris, the project gained momentum and before they knew it their self-titled album was a hit with a Top-40 single, "Genius of Love." The single has been widely sampled by dozens of artists, including Mariah Carey in her single "Fantasy" and Grandmaster Flash in "It's Nasty." "Genius of Love" extols the virtues of a boyfriend who is "the maven of funk mutation."

GREATEST HITS

YEAR	SONG
1977	"Psycho Killer"
1978	"Don't Worry About the Government"
	"Take Me to the River"
1979	"Life During Wartime"
1980	"Once in a Lifetime"
1983	"Burning Down the House"
1984	"Slippery People"
1985	"Stop Making Sense (Girlfriend Is Better)"
	"And She Was"
	"Road to Nowhere"
	"Stay Up Late"
1986	"Wild Wild Life"
1991	"Sax & Violins"

David Byrne illustrates his art-school panache.

David Byrne

Even though he dropped out of the prestigious Rhode Island School of Design after only a year, it's hard to take the artist out of David Byrne. He looks at the world through artist's eyes and is adept at sharing what he sees. Over the years he's released varied solo records, starting with a highly acclaimed collaboration with Brian Eno, *My Life in the Bush of Ghosts*. He's collaborated with dance choreographer Twyla Tharpe and playwright Robert Wilson. He has a "disco opera" in the works about Imeldo Marcos and he recently created a body of visual art using Power Point software.

"I couldn't talk to people face to face, so I got on stage and started screaming and squealing and twitching." —David Byrne

little alligator, banged out an arsenal of funky drum licks. The Heads melded disco to bubblegum to Velvet Underground minimalism, filtering it all through a Warholian art-school perspective. When they added Jerry Harrison from the Modern Lovers, the picture was complete.

Their first album, *Talking Heads: 77*, contained many of their herky-jerky classics, including "Don't Worry about the Government," "Pulled Up," and "Psycho Killer." The songs were outstanding, but the production was lacking. Enter Brian Eno, late of Roxy Music, who became their close collaborator and made their next album a sonic masterpiece. *More Songs about Buildings and Food* contained the slinky cover of Al Green's "Take Me to the River," which was their first big hit. Having exhausted most of the stockpile of songs they had gathered since 1974, *Fear of Music*, again produced by Eno, contained shorter, tighter songs with less quirk in them. It spawned the radio hit "Life during Wartime," with that classic line: "This ain't no Mudd Club, or CBGB, I ain't got time for that now."

Remain in Light, the band's last collaboration with Eno, explored the complex world of African rhythms while asking the existential question: "How did I get here?" Gone were the odd song structures, replaced by a fascination for Afro pop. Eno and Byrne were figuring out how to layer a groove, rather than create different sections with different chord patterns. Talking Heads surprised everyone when they showed up live with an expanded lineup that included backup singers and Bernie Worrell and Steve Scales. *Remain in Light* and *Speaking in Tongues* worked the funk and Afro pop with their own art-rock vision, bringing the band massive popularity with songs like "Once in a Lifetime" and "Burning Down the House," the band's first Top 10 hit. It all culminated with *Stop Making Sense*, a concert by Jonathan Demme, with David Byrne in an oversized suit that played up his awkwardness.

On *Little Creatures*, the group returned to their rock roots and their original four-piece lineup. *True Stories* followed as a soundtrack to a David Byrne film/travelogue. Their final album, *Naked*, was a collaborative album with all four band members receiving songwriting credit.

Tina Weymouth gave girlfriends everywhere hope by picking up a bass and rocking it harder than any of the boys.

TELEVISION

1973–

Their output was small, but their influence was great. Television was the band to see at CBGB, the club on New York City's Bowery. The band literally helped build CBGB—they worked on constructing the original stage. Television created transcendental rock and roll that made you feel teleported to another world, while really you were just inside a long dirty bar, laced with neon signs.

Tom Miller and Richard Meyers were a couple of ne'er-do-well boarding-school dropouts, who supposedly got in trouble for setting fire to a field. Like Huck Finn and Tom Sawyer, they needed adventure and where better to find it than New York City in the early '70s, a place ripe for new dreamers.

Each considered himself a poet, and Meyers, now renamed "Hell," started a small press. Miller, who adopted poet Paul Verlaine's surname, listened to a lot of jazz and practiced guitar. Rock and roll somehow seemed like a better way to be heard in the urban din, and the Neon Boys were born with Billy Ficca on drums. Verlaine taught Hell how to play bass, and Ficca brought a jazz style of playing to the band. Verlaine himself fooled around with *Blonde on Blonde* Dylan licks and mixolydian scales and drew inspiration from Coltrane's sax solos. When they met the young guitarist Richard Lloyd, the lineup for Television was complete. Hell wrote the period classic, "Blank Generation," about a young man who saw himself as an empty canvas devoid of history. "I was saying let me out of here before I was even born," he wailed. Verlaine was working on equally ambitious fare, such as a love song about falling into the arms of the Venus de Milo, the goddess of love and beauty famous for her armless statue.

Richard Hell

Richard Hell left Television to form the Heartbreakers with ex-New York Dolls Johnny Thunders and Jerry Nolan. He left that band after a short while but collaborated on the song "Chinese Rocks" with Thunders and Dee Dee Ramone. He then formed his own band, the Voidoids with Marc Bell, aka Marky Ramone, and the killer guitarists Robert Quine and Ivan Julian. He delivered the classic album *Blank Generation* in 1977. Hell invented much of punk's visual style. He was the first to cut his hair to different lengths, and he also came up with the idea of safety-pinning his clothes together. Many mistook *Blank Generation* to be about the nihilistic hatred for life, which was also a central idea for much of punk.

Hell left before any proper recordings came out. He was replaced by bass player Fred Smith, who left Blondie when they were still a struggling opener unlike Television, who were then kings of the scene. Their first single was the sprawling "Little Johnny Jewel" that stretched over the two sides of a seven-inch 45 and was released on their patron Terry Ork's record label, Ork Records. The song shared a sensibility with Verlaine's former girlfriend Patti Smith's music. To this day, Verlaine often performs with Smith.

It was the monumental first album, *Marquee Moon*, which truly left their mark. The guitar solo on the title track is one of the greatest pieces of guitar architecture ever built.

GREATEST HITS	
YEAR	SONG
1976	"Little Johnny Jewel"
1977	"Venus"
	"See No Evil"
	"Marquee Moon"
	"Prove It"
1978	"Foxhole"
	"Glory"

Tom Verlaine (center) builds some structured guitar-solo edifices on his Lucite axe, with Fred Smith (left) and Richard Lloyd (right).

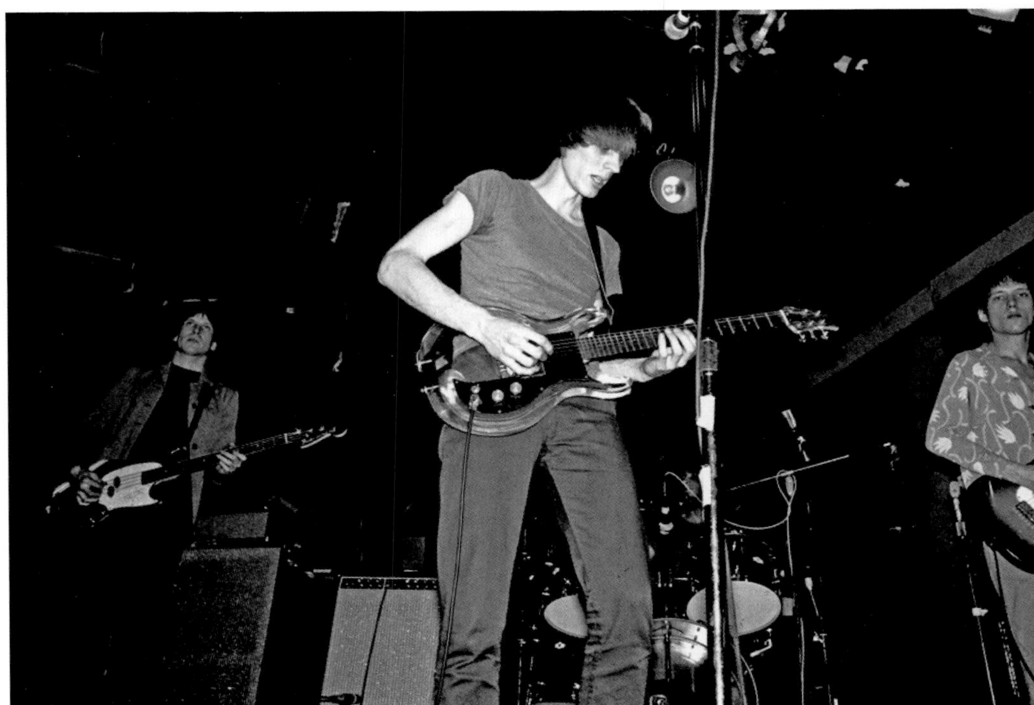

TRAFFIC

1967–1974

FROM LEFT: JIM CAPALDI, STEVE WINWOOD, RIC GRECH, AND CHRIS WOOD.

GREATEST HITS	
YEAR	SONG
1967	"Dear Mr. Fantasy"
	"Paper Sun"
1968	"Medicated Goo"
	"Feelin' Alright"
	"Forty Thousand Headmen"
1970	"Freedom Rider"
	"Glad"
	"Empty Pages"
1971	"Light Up or Leave Me Alone"
	"The Low Spark of High Heeled Boys"
	"Rock and Roll Stew"

In 1966, teenaged Steve Winwood was a keyboard wunderkind and blue-eyed soul singer who had 'em all dazzled as a member of the Spencer Davis Group. "Little Stevie" astonished the crowds with full-throttle Ray Charles–like pipes pouring from his tiny frame. He also played some mean blues guitar, impressing the likes of Eric Clapton. Despite big hits with the group like "Gimme Some Lovin'" and "I'm a Man," Winwood heard destiny calling him to the countryside, where he lived for six months in a communal setting, with three other smelly guys jamming and partying into the night. His compadres were guitarist Dave Mason, drummer Jim Capaldi, who also wrote very trippy lyrics, and flute and sax man Chris Wood.

Traffic, as this new group called themselves, moved through the styles of the day, starting with the full-blown psychedelia of "Paper Sun," into more blues-based material and mixing in some traditional folk styling along the way. The title track of their first album, *Mr. Fantasy*, set the tone for their signature style: Traffic excelled at dreamlike grooves perfect for the swaying stoners of the day. Young musicians in cover bands used the song to stretch out on, fitting perfectly with such other elongated classics as Neil Young's "Down by the River," Hendrix's "Hey Joe," and Donovan's "Season of the Witch." Play those four songs and you had an entire set.

John Barleycorn

Traffic's "John Barleycorn" was a cover of an old English folk song. John Barleycorn was a little devil representing barley, from which beer and whiskey are made. In the song, John Barleycorn gets processed like a barley crop—that is, cut down with scythes, rolled and tied, pricked with pitchforks, and eventually ground between two stones. "John Barleycorn must die." The song tied in with the return to traditional English folk music as legitimate roots music for these young English musicians to plunder, as opposed to inspiration from the African-American bluesmen.

Dave Mason bailed before they could tour the United States but rejoined for a second album and gave them one of their bigger hits, "Feelin' Alright." Winwood then left to join the overhyped super group Blind Faith with Eric Clapton. When Clapton bailed on Blind Faith, Winwood launched a solo project after a short stint in Ginger Baker's Airforce, but looking for lyrical help from Capaldi, he suddenly had a Traffic reunion on his hands. Wood returned and Rick Grech came over from Blind Faith, and in 1970 they made their finest album, *John Barleycorn Must Die.*

The album was the first to go gold with such exuberant workouts as "Freedom Rider" and "Empty Pages." The band was stretching out and getting jazzier, and their follow-up album, *The Low Spark of High Heeled Boys*, contained the song "Rock and Roll Stew." It was a stew that had more to do with blues and jazz than rock and roll, but who cared—especially when Traffic was coming up with songs like "Light Up or Leave Me Alone," perfect for standing around in the rain and mud, watching bands play half a mile away.

IKE AND TINA TURNER

1959–1976

As a young man, Ike Turner was fearless; driving up and down Highway 61 making connections with different music scenes. His band, the Kings of Rhythm, was cutting sides in the early '50s. Ike was discovering talent and producing recordings for B. B. King, Howlin' Wolf, and Bobby "Blue" Bland. He was working for Chess and any other label that would hire him, playing the angles and constantly on the move. Eventually he settled down in St. Louis, where his group became a major draw on the local scene.

Anna Mae Bullock, from Nutbush, Tennessee, had been bugging Ike for a chance to sing. He ignored her, but she just snatched the mike one night and let it wail. Ike renamed the gutsy singer "Tina" and brought her into his show. When another singer didn't show up for a session one night, the pair cut a record by "Ike and Tina Turner"—even though they weren't actually married at the time. "A Fool in Love" became their first hit in 1960, and Ike made sure they were officially married by 1962.

Tina's distinctive raspy voice could cut through anything, and Ike developed a whole soul review around Tina, with three shimmying backup singers known as the Ikettes. Together they had a number of hits, among them a reworking of "Proud Mary" that started out at half tempo with Tina warning the crowd, "we nevah do nothin' nice and easy." Phil Spector worked with them in 1966 to make "River Deep—Mountain High," a song considered by some the greatest production in his career and by others his biggest failure. It didn't chart in the United States, and he stopped producing for three years. Mick Jagger invited them to open for the Stones, and he credited Tina and James Brown for teaching him how to move. Tina also played the Acid Queen in the film version of the Who's *Tommy*.

IKE AND TINA'S TURBULENT RELATIONSHIP LURKED BEHIND THEIR COMMERCIAL SUCCESSES.

Ike, always a jealous man, consumed ever-increasing quantities of drugs, hanging out with Sly Stone and developing a fortified recording compound in which Tina Turner felt that she was a prisoner. He was physically abusive, and in 1976 she fled in the middle of the night—never to return. She had 36 cents in her pocket and was forced to live on food stamps for a time.

GREATEST HITS

Year	Song
1960	"Whole Lotta Love"
1961	"It's Gonna Work Out Fine"
1966	"River Deep—Mountain High"
1971	"Proud Mary"
	TINA TURNER (Solo)
1984	"What's Love Got to Do with It"
1984	"Better Be Good to Me"
	"Private Dancer"
1985	"We Don't Need Another Hero"
1993	"I Don't Wanna Fight"

Tina Goes Solo

After leaving Ike, Tina slowly made a comeback. She worked her way up from appearing at corporate functions where they only wanted to hear the old hits to becoming a solo dynamo on such hit songs as "What's Love Got to Do with It" and "Private Dancer." In her divorce settlement she had asked for nothing but the rights to her stage name. Brilliant move: As simply "Tina Turner," she sold many more albums than she ever did with Ike.

U2

1976–

At the New Music Seminar in New York City in 1982, a panel of radio specialists discussed the idea of breaking in new music by editing songs down to half their lengths, so they could play more of them. Radio time is expensive, after all. A voice in the crowd piped up, "I'm Paul McGuinness, the manager of U2, and all I can say is don't you dare edit their songs!" The radio expert retorted, "Well, if they'd made a strong album they might be getting some airplay" (referring to U2's *October*). "Don't count them out yet," replied McGuinness. "They're still young."

There isn't a band on the planet to rival U2. They have seemingly done everything right. Hard-working, artistically sound, morally centered, while still enjoying a pint, they've crafted a body of work that hasn't been matched by anyone in the last 20 years. Balancing credibility and Top 40 hits is not an easy trick. U2 has done it with their original lineup still intact: Bono, he of the hurricane lungs; Edge, the great rhythm guitarist; Adam Clayton, with the steady throb of their punk-rock roots; and band leader Larry Mullen, who's kept the big-snare sound alive way past its '80s heyday.

FROM LEFT: LARRY MULLEN, ADAM CLAYTON, THE EDGE, AND BONO IN THEIR YOUNGER DAYS; BOTH THEIR LOOKS AND THEIR MUSIC HAVE ONLY GOTTEN BETTER.

Listening to *U2 18 Singles*, the 2006 hits collection, it's surprising how little they have changed sonically from their earliest albums. They write big songs with great grooves in the verses. They always have big choruses with Bono putting it out there in simple declarative catchphrases, emoting in the name of love that he still hasn't found what he's looking for, but oh she moves in mysterious ways down the streets with no name. "Excuse me miss but did I tell you it's a beautiful day?"

U2 made three albums with producer Steve Lillywhite. Their third collaboration, 1983's *War*, yielded the hits "Sunday Bloody Sunday" about the troubles in Northern Ireland and "New Year's Day." The album went to #12 in the U.S. The group switched over to a combination of Daniel Lanois, known for his work with Bob Dylan, and Brian Eno (coming off his successful collaborations with Talking Heads). Both were producers who knew a lot about making artistic, atmospheric music. They woodshedded with the band for great lengths of time, producing two of their finest releases, *The Unforgettable Fire*, out in 1984, and the Grammy-winning 1987 Album of the Year, *The Joshua Tree*. A documentary and double album with mixed live and studio recordings included help from Bob Dylan and B. B. King. It yielded a hit with the Bo Diddley-style workout "Desire."

The band's output slowed down in the '90s as the band grew their families and experimented with more electronics than they had on their guitar-oriented '80s work. The results were promising:

Punks at Heart

The Irish group came together at Dublin's Mount Temple High School. Inspired by the punk-rock ethos, they were nonmusicians who learned along the way. The Edge developed his wide variety of heavily treated rhythm licks because he couldn't figure out how to play lead guitar. They have often cited influences like the Velvet Underground, the Clash, and the Ramones.

"The world is more malleable than you think and it's waiting for you to hammer it into shape."—Bono

Achtung Baby was more sophisticated in its rhythms than anything they had so far put out. The album was their first to go to #1 on the strength of such singles as "Mysterious Ways" and "One," written about the Edge's divorce. The album showed a side to the band never before revealed—vulnerability.

The Zoo TV tour that followed was an elaborate, technologically advanced affair with Bono flying in the face of his earnest Christian persona to craft a new edgy look, wearing sunglasses and gangster hats and appearing at press conferences as "The Fly." In the current decade, there has been a return to the '80s guitar rock that made them famous.

GREATEST HITS	
YEAR	SONG
1983	"New Year's Day"
	"Two Hearts Beat as One"
	"Sunday Bloody Sunday"
1984	"Pride (In the Name of Love)"
1987	"With or Without You"
	"I Still Haven't Found What I'm Looking For"
	"Where the Streets Have No Name"
1988	"Desire"
	"All I Want Is You"
1992	"One"
2000	"Beautiful Day"
2001	"Stuck in a Moment You Can't Get Out Of"
2004	"Vertigo"
	"City of Blinding Lights"

BETTER STYLING IN THE '90S LED TO HUGE SUCCESS FOR THE EDGE AND BONO.

Steal from the Rich to Give to the Poor

Early on, U2 was pegged as a Christian band, and although a number of the members were practicing Christians, they weren't rigid in their beliefs. Bono's view is that you don't need a building—you just need to live your life according to the basic tenets of Christianity. If you see hunger and sickness in the world, you need to help. And Bono has put his money where his mouth is, spending much of his free time campaigning heavily for relief for Africa, rallying many Westerners to the cause, including Republican senators and movie stars like Brad Pitt.

It does make it easier to help if you, like U2, live in a country such as Ireland where artist income has not been heavily taxed. It's been said by some that U2's massive earnings have caused the Irish government to rethink their artist-friendly taxation laws. Since the late '60s, Irish artists—musicians, painters, novelists, sculptors—have been exempt from paying any taxes at all on certain kinds of income. For a musician, the tax-exempt portion is royalties, which can cover record sales, publishing rights including film licensing, soundtracks, and advertising. Basically, it's the major portion of any musician's income—and quite an impressive figure when the musicians are U2 with a net worth estimated at more than $900 million.

Beginning in January 2008, Irish tax laws will reflect an attempt to even the playing field a bit. Any artist's royalty income higher than 250,000 euros (or just over $300,000) will be taxed on a sliding scale. Of course, a band like U2, which earns its money internationally, is not happy about the change and have chosen—like fellow rockers the Rolling Stones—to take their money to the land of the windmills and tulips, the Netherlands, where artist royalties are not subject to tax.

You can't blame them—no one wants to pay any more taxes than absolutely necessary—but some critics view it as ironic considering Bono's message of fiscal responsibility to the governments of the world. Certainly, from the government's point of view, there's less to spend when major earners are not contributing to the tax pot.

VAN HALEN

1974–

Eddie Van Halen and David Lee Roth at the height of their big-hair, bare-chested '80s glory.

They were never the heaviest, but Van Halen ruled the hard rock/heavy metal roost in the '80s. The group came together in Southern California when Dutch brothers Eddie and Alex Van Halen met up with the charismatic vocalist David Lee Roth (who happened to own his own PA system). The band learned more than 300 songs, mostly covers, including side one of the Kinks' greatest hits and lots of Led Zeppelin. When bassist Michael Anthony auditioned, the lineup was complete.

Eddie is a guitar virtuoso who'd turn his back to the audience in the early days so that they wouldn't see the unique two-hand hammering techniques he'd invented. Smart move—it's been widely imitated ever since.

The band developed a huge following without having a record contract and decided to let the big labels come to them. Two players that checked them out early were Gene Simmons of Kiss and Ted Templeman, a staff producer with Warner Brothers. Simmons produced a demo but couldn't get much interest. Dazzled by David Lee Roth's showmanship, but more important, by Eddie Van Halen's guitar playing, Ted Templeman immediately offered them a record deal. Their first album, *Van Halen*, in 1978 was a huge success, selling more than 10 million copies. *Van Halen II* and *Women and Children* did not do quite as well. After Eddie Van Halen helped Michael Jackson out with a searing solo on his big crossover hit "Beat It," Van Halen retooled their sound and delivered in 1984 with the synth-driven monster "Jump" and the testosterone-fueled car song "Panama." The album put them back in the 10-million-range once again.

The Name

The Van Halen brothers and David Lee Roth originally worked together in a band with the heavy moniker Mammoth. When another metal Mammoth reared its ugly head, Roth suggested that they change the name to Van Halen because it sounded strong and could mean whatever they wanted it to mean. "It's named after human beings, and they're expected to grow. But if you call yourself the Electric Plotz, three years from now you're supposed to sound like an Electric Plotz."

Eddie's Son

In 2006, Van Halen announced a new bass player—Wolfgang Van Halen. Wolfgang is Eddie's son with actress—and estranged wife—Valerie Bertinelli, who appeared opposite Mackenzie Phillips (daughter of John and Michelle from The Mamas and The Papas) in the long-running television show *One Day at a Time*. Eddie and Valerie were married in 1981 and separated in 2001.

At the height of their fame, Roth was dismissed from the group and replaced by Sammy Hagar. He's been fighting to get back in ever since. There have been a couple of minor reunions with the outspoken Roth, but nothing has stuck. Most recently they were scheduled to reunite for a tour to coincide with their entrance into the Rock and Roll Hall of Fame. Unfortunately, Eddie recognized a need to enter rehab, and the reunion was cancelled. Fans are still hopeful that Van Halen will rock again.

GREATEST HITS	
Year	Song
1978	"Runnin' with the Devil"
1979	"Dance the Night Away"
1980	"And the Cradle Will Rock . . ."
1984	"Jump"
	"Panama"
	"Hot for Teacher"
1986	"Why Can't This Be Love"
1998	"Love Walks In"

THE VELVET UNDERGROUND

1965–1994

FROM LEFT: NICO, MAUREEN TUCKER, STERLING MORRISON, LOU REED, JOHN CALE.

The Velvet Underground never burned brightly, but they never burned out. The Velvets were one of the most important American rock and roll bands, as much for their influence as for their sales—their first album only went gold 20 years after its initial release. Built around simple hypnotic grooves that borrowed from '50s and '60s R&B and rock and roll, they added a modern urban twist with the lyrics of Lou Reed (the best rock poet after Dylan) and the edgy classical flavorings of John Cale. Maureen Tucker's unique trance-inducing drumming style and Sterling Morrison's beautifully crafted blues stylings played so well off Reed's manic outbursts of feedback catharsis.

"Only a few thousand people bought that record, but all of them formed a band of their own." —Brian Eno

The group formed when Syracuse University student Lou Reed met up with John Cale at the Pickwick Records song factory, cranking out surf and biker songs and faux dance craze numbers like "The Ostrich" and "Cycle Annie." Cale was intrigued by Lou's edgier material, which took Dylan's poetic vision and gave it a decadent twist on songs like "Venus in Furs" and "Heroin." They holed up with Angus MacLise (soon replaced by Maureen "Mo" Tucker) and Sterling Morrison and worked up a set of songs. Andy Warhol saw one of their first shows and immediately invited them into his world, teaming them up with the beautiful German chanteuse Nico. Their first album was a bit of a sensation with the peel-off banana sticker Andy designed for the cover and the wild light shows that they employed as part of Warhol's Exploding Plastic Inevitable, a

NUGGET: It's been said that the Velvet's fourth album, *Loaded*, was so called in answer to the record label's request that they deliver an album "loaded with hits."

GREATEST HITS

Year	Song
1967	"I'll Be Your Mirror"
	"Sunday Morning"
	"Femme Fatale"
1967	"Heroin"
1968	"White Light/White Heat"
	"I Heard Her Call My Name"
1969	"Candy Says"
	"Beginning to See the Light"
	"I'm Set Free"
	"After Hours"
1970	"Rock and Roll"
	"Sweet Jane"

Lou Reed plays his heavily customized Telecaster.

Lou Reed Solo

Lou Reed had a big break when David Bowie produced his second album, *Transformer*. It included the massive international hit "Walk on the Wild Side" that looked back on the cast of characters from his days in the Warhol scene. This led to interest in the VU catalog, as well as a number of live releases that showed how great the band had been. Lou Reed re-recorded some of the Velvets' classic songs, including "Heroin," "Rock and Roll," and "Sweet Jane" for his *Rock and Roll Animal* album with a band made up of former Alice Cooper players. It was one of the biggest albums of his solo career, and the big rock arrangements were built on the solid roots of the Velvets. Lou put aside past differences with John Cale to pay tribute to past mentor Andy Warhol after his accidental death during surgery in 1987. The resulting album, *Songs for Drella*—so named for Andy's nickname, a contraction of Dracula and Cinderella—celebrated Andy's life in song.

multimedia road show complete with "whip dancers" Mary Woronov and Gerard Malanga writhing and snapping their way through the audience.

What's amazing about the Velvet Underground is how diverse their four proper studio albums were. After the decadent pop of the first album, they came back and made an album of long Marshall-revved feedback-bleeding noise rock. *White Light White Heat* was utterly uncompromising in its sound and sold accordingly but would inspire many, including Bowie (who often covered the title song), and Sonic Youth, who made the album a touchstone for what they did in the future.

John Cale left the group after the second album to go solo and produce. Doug Yule, a more conventional musician, replaced Cale. When their amps were stolen right before they made their self-titled third album, they plugged into the board directly for a very clean sound. It is perhaps their most beautiful recording, with great songs and carefully laid-out parts. The fourth album, *Loaded*, has some of their strongest songs, including "Sweet Jane" and "Rock and Roll," and their most fleshed-out production. It's the band's most accessible album. Lou Reed left the band before *Loaded* was finished, and Doug Yule put the tracks in shape. A picture of Yule alone in the studio, facing away from the camera, graces the album's back cover. Sterling was off finishing school and Maureen was having a baby.

After the initial love for their Warhol album, the Velvets slogged around the country on tours that did little to grow their base. The Velvets might have been forgotten, but Lou Reed marched on as a solo artist. Although Nico had died in 1988 as a result of a brain hemorrhage, the band re-formed in 1992 and recorded an album for Warner Brothers. Since most of their fans had never seen them play—they had never done much television in their original day—it was a real treat. Sterling Morrison died of cancer shortly after.

The Velvet Underground changed rock forever with their unusual orchestrations and arrangements. Here, John Cale and Nico in a post-Velvets performance.

TOM WAITS

DECEMBER 7, 1949–

He's a real character, the guy you see at the end of the bar at last call, or at the diner at 2 A.M. chatting up the waitress over a breakfast special. Cigarettes and coffee and a flask in the back pocket, he's the people's poet: one part Kerouac, one part Bukowski, with some Ray Charles and a piano that drinks too much. And just when you think you have him pinned down, he's gone into the last of the night, just before the blue lights of dawn.

"My wife says I write two types of songs: Grand Weepers and Grim Reapers." —Tom Waits

With the seedy demeanor of a man beyond his years, Tom Waits got his start in L.A., playing piano at the famed Troubadour. At 21, he got his first record deal, signed to Asylum by Herb Cohen, Frank Zappa's manager and made some noise with "I Hope That I Don't Fall in Love with You." Audiences took notice when the Eagles covered his car song, "Ol' 55," and he created his first masterpiece with the release of *Heart of Saturday Night* in 1974.

NUGGET: Other artists may have had hits with his songs—Springsteen's cover of "Jersey Girl" or Rod Stewart's version of "Downtown Train"—but Waits has instead developed a huge cult, especially among songwriters.

With *Nighthawks at the Diner,* his voice changed a bit, as if he'd been coughing up blood from too many nights of whiskey and cigarettes. Was he putting it on, or was he slowly killing himself? His albums rose in popularity when he adopted that ersatz jazz approach—all strings and wandering piano. And directors cast him in films, where he played bartenders and barflies, including Francis Ford Coppola's *One from the Heart*, where he met future wife Kathleen Brennan—they married in 1980—on the set.

He then tossed out some of his signature elements, the cornier parts of his act, and made simpler, more bluesy albums, with strange instrumentation—bent saws and cardboard boxes and buzzing guitars. *Swordfishtrombones* in 1983, *Rain Dogs* in 1985, and *Frank's Wild Years* in 1987 all boiled his songs down to their essences. Over the years, he's tried everything from waltzes to tribal stomps—creating a diverse American songbook. There were stints when his wife (who's been a collaborator on much of his later music) booted him out of the house. Where he had to peer through the schoolyard fence to get a glimpse of his kids. There was the drying out and more writing and woodshedding and more movies. America is grateful to have Tom Waits as one of our greatest dreamer bards.

TOM WAITS MAKES HIS POINT.

Not a Sell Out

Tom Waits has made it clear he does not want his music to be used in conjunction with advertising campaigns; so when something sneaks through, it makes him mad. He sued Frito-Lay for using a sound-alike to imitate his distinctive vocal sound to accompany music based on an early song, "Step Right Up," that he did not control the publishing rights to. He was awarded more than $2 million dollars in compensation and became the first artist to successfully sue a corporation for using a vocal impersonator. Levi's licensed Screamin' Jay Hawkins' cover version of his song "Heartattack and Vine." When Waits sued, they immediately withdrew the commercial and apologized in a full-page ad in the industry magazine *Billboard*.

GREATEST HITS

YEAR	SONG
1973	"Ol' 55"
	"I Hope That I Don't Fall in Love with You"
1974	"Looking for the Heart of Saturday Night"
1975	"Big Joe and Phantom 309"
1976	"Tom Traubert's Blues"
	"The Piano Has Been Drinking (Not Me)"
1977	"I Never Talk to Strangers"
1980	"Jersey Girl"
1985	"Downtown Train"
1987	"Innocent When You Dream"
1999	"Big in Japan"

WEEZER

1992–

RIVERS CUOMO AND FIRST BASS PLAYER, MATT SHARP, ROCK THE HOUSE WITH THEIR BRAND OF QUIRKY POWER POP.

Weezer exploded onto the scene with a friendlier version of grunge than the one offered by the likes of Geffen label mates Nirvana and Sonic Youth. This was pop grunge that rocked but also had pretty harmonies and moments when lead singer and guitarist Rivers Cuomo seemed to be tapping into the classic rock of Queen. With such massive MTV hits as "Undone—The Sweater Song," "Say It Ain't So," and "Buddy Holly" (with a Spike Jonze video, complete with the band playing in the pop shop from the TV show *Happy Days*), they were multiplatinum right out of the box.

Their follow-up, *Pinkerton*, was quickly dismissed by their massive fan base and rock critics as "too rough and unfocused." Taking a page from the Nirvana playbook, they'd tried to make their second album harder edged and more in your face. The plan backfired—or so they thought.

Pinkerton

After the lukewarm reaction to *Pinkerton*, the group immediately broke up with Rivers Cuomo going off to Harvard. But in the ensuing years, the hardcore Weezer fans kept extolling the virtues of *Pinkerton* and turned their friends on to it. On closer examination, *Pinkerton* was a cycle of songs loosely based on the Puccini opera *Madama Butterfly*, and although it is raw and slightly careening, the songcraft is impeccable and the passion behind the singing and playing is truly cathartic. It influenced a generation of young musicians coming of age in the grunge era. Along with Sunny Day Real Estate, it is the cornerstone of what became known as Emo.

Weezer broke up, deeming itself a failure. An invitation to play the Warp tour in 2000 showed the guys that they'd been wrong. Fans had sorely missed 'em, and all the new young punks loved 'em. They began work on a new album, *Weezer*. Its cover was a copy of the first album except for the color; hence album one became known to fans as *The Blue Album* and album three *The Green Album*. *The Green Album* dispensed with most of the grunge trappings in favor of short, catchy pop songs, like an updated version of early Beatles. Only "Hash Pipe," which led Weezer back to platinum status, evoked the harder rock of their earlier fare.

Their next album, *Maladroit*, was beautifully crafted but didn't produce any monster hits, and it sold accordingly. With producer Rick Rubin at the helm, they again went for the most commercial sound they could muster. It was rumored that they were writing with Fred Durst of Limp Bizkit and were making a rap metal album. Instead they came up with *Make Believe*, which contained the megahit "Beverly Hills," complete with a video shot at the Playboy Club. What little credibility they had was gone, but then in 2007 an MP3 was leaked of a new song called "Pig," with Cuomo singing along with an acoustic guitar and minimal instrumentation. It proved that there was more in store for their fans.

GREATEST HITS

YEAR	SONG
1994	"Undone—The Sweater Song"
	"Buddy Holly"
1995	"Say It Ain't So"
1996	"El Scorcho"
2001	"Hash Pipe"
	"Island in the Sun"
	"Photograph"
2002	"Dope Noise"
	"Keep Fishin'"
2005	"Beverly Hills"
	"We Are All on Drugs"
	"Perfect Situation"

THE WHITE STRIPES

1997–

The White Stripes are a successful rock duo from Detroit, Michigan. Jack and Meg White pretend to be a brother-and-sister act, a postmodern Donny and Marie, dressed only in red, white, and black, but Jack White's real name is Jack Anthony Gillis. A long-time rumor that Meg and Jack were married and now divorced has been proven true.

The White Stripes are a stripped-down, stylized affair, with songwriter Jack on guitar, keyboards, and vocals, and Meg on drums and vocals. Their first two albums, the self-titled debut and *De Stijl*, are rough and ready and decidedly lo-fi. In fact, they recorded *De Stijl* on a small analog recorder in Jack's living room.

They started to gain national attention with their third album, *White Blood Cells*, in 2001. For the single "Fell in Love with a Girl" they made a Lego-themed music video directed by Michel Gondry that brought them a lot of attention, first in the U.K. and then in the U.S. They followed that with *Elephant* in 2003. With the hit single "Seven Nation Army," the band rose to the top of the charts and won a Grammy for best rock song. *Under Blackpool Lights*, a live DVD with songs recorded at the Empress Ballroom in Blackpool, featured the band's extreme take on Dolly Parton's "Jolene."

Popular with the rock press, *Q* magazine named the band one of the "50 Bands to See Before You Die," and Jack was named number 17—between Johnny Ramone and Red Hot Chili Pepper John Frusciante—in *Rolling Stone's* Greatest Guitarists of All Time list. The next album, 2005's *Get Behind Me Satan*, was critically acclaimed, featuring singles "Blue Orchid" (with an appearance by Jack's new wife, Karen Elson, in the video), "My Doorbell," and "The Denial Twist." In May of 2005, Jack and fellow Detroit musician Brendan Benson formed the Raconteurs and released their debut album *Broken Boy Soldiers*. Jack toured with this outfit for the rest of the year, but it was not the end of the White Stripes. White Stripes fans got *Icky Thump*, the new album they'd all been waiting for, in 2007. It was recorded in three weeks in Jack's new hometown of Nashville. It is the longest they have ever taken to make an album. Jack described it to *Rolling Stone* as "very heavy."

NUGGET: "We're Going to Be Friends," the anthem for kinder, gentler relationships, appeared in the opening credits of the 2004 hit film *Napoleon Dynamite*.

EXES? SIBLINGS? WHATEVER THEIR RELATIONSHIP, MEG WHITE (LEFT) AND JACK WHITE ROCK THE RED AND WHITE STRIPES.

GREATEST HITS

YEAR	SONG
2001	"Hotel Yorba"
2002	"Fell in Love with a Girl"
	"We're Going to Be Friends"
2003	"Seven Nation Army"
	"I Just Don't Know What to Do with Myself"
2004	"Jolene"
2005	"Blue Orchid"
	"My Doorbell"
	"The Denial Twist"

The Number Three

If you know anything about White Stripes, you know that the pair is famously eccentric. When Jack and Meg married, he did the unusual and took her last name. Taxidermy is one of Jack's hobbies, and they are both obsessed with the number three. Three as in the band's three favorite colors—red, white, and black—which Jack calls "the most powerful color combination of all time, from a Coca-Cola can to a Nazi banner." Three also comes into their music. Most songs have only three sounds—drums, guitar, and vocals—and the band philosophy holds their three truths—storytelling, melody, and rhythm—in the highest regard.

THE WHO

1964–

FROM LEFT: PETE TOWNSHEND, ROGER DALTREY, JOHN ENTWISTLE, AND KEITH MOON ANSWERED THE MUSICAL QUESTION "WHO?" IN THE AFFIRMATIVE.

As culturally important as they are, it's surprising to realize that the Who released very few albums: a mere eight studio albums with their original lineup of Roger Daltrey, he of the Greek god curls and lariat microphone technique; Pete Townshend, known for his slash-and-burn guitar; Keith Moon, the manic drummer who created and held down the chaos; and John Entwistle, the ox-solid bassist, steady yet complex, who also played a mean French horn. Together, these guys cornered the market on explosive energy.

Townshend wrote the songs that put them on the map: "My Generation" with Daltrey sneering "hope I die before I get old . . ." and "The Kids Are Alright," a heartfelt rocker about how it's okay if his friends dance with his girl because they're all part of the same group until he has to leave 'em all behind.

Each album had its own character. *A Quick One* was intensely ambitious with a mini rock opera included in the nine-minute "A Quick One While He's Away." This is the song the Who performed as part of the BBC's *Rolling Stones Rock and Roll Circus* television show, a program that was shelved for more than 20 years because the Stones thought that the Who had blown them away. Subsequent viewings proved that the Rolling Stones were actually at the height of their powers.

The Who Sell Out, released in 1967, is many fans' favorite. A clever wink at pop culture, they interspersed songs with radio commercials created for such products as baked beans, deodorant, and

Lifehouse

Townshend, the group's ambitious main songwriter, won the next go-round after *Tommy* with an idea for a concept album, called *Lifehouse*, about a magical chord that would change the world. But much like the Beach Boys' *Smile* album, it proved to be beyond their grasp. A simplified *Who's Next*, released with some of the material from the project, proved to be their biggest album. Around this time, the itch to go his own way hit Townshend. He released the excellent *Who Came First* that included "Pure and Easy" from *Lifehouse* and a duo album, *Rough Mix*, with Ronnie Lane of the Small Faces. In 1980, he released *Empty Glass*, with the Top 10 single "Let My Love Open the Door."

GREATEST HITS

YEAR	SONG
1965	"I Can't Explain"
	"My Generation"
	"The Kids Are Alright"
1966	"Happy Jack"
1967	"I Can See for Miles"
1968	"Magic Bus"
1969	"Pinball Wizard"
	"I'm Free"
1970	"See Me, Feel Me"
	"The Seeker"
1971	"Won't Get Fooled Again"
	"Baba O'Riley"
	"Behind Blue Eyes"
1972	"Join Together"
1973	"Love Reign O'er Me"
	"5:15"
1975	"Squeeze Box"
1978	"Who Are You"
1979	"Long Live Rock"

NUGGET: Townshend, who suffers from partial hearing loss and tinnitus from over-exposure to loud music, helped to found H.E.A.R.—Hearing Education and Awareness for Rockers.

"We lived the life with Keith Moon. It was all Spinal Tap *magnified a thousand times."*—Roger Daltrey

pimple cream. This album contained stellar songs like "Pictures of Lily" and the transcendental rocker "I Can See for Miles" that seemed to bust out of the haze of psychedelia into a higher consciousness.

From 1966 through 1969, the Who toured endlessly, but there were cash flow and management problems. Practically broke, they cobbled together a masterpiece, a rock opera double album about a deaf, dumb, and blind boy—a pinball savant who becomes the head of a huge but ultimately ill-fated religious cult. *Tommy* was a smash hit. It was followed by *Live at Leeds*, the elaborately packaged live album designed to look like a bootleg album, loaded with all kinds of goodies: tour posters, a receipt for fireworks, and the band's contract to play Woodstock. It proved that without any studio trickery the Who were a great live band that could bash away with the best of them.

Who's Next, with the explosive, synth-driven "Baba O'Riley" and the megawatt political rager "Won't Get Fooled Again" came out of the failed *Lifehouse* project. The Who also started to recycle its biggest hits; there was the symphonic version of *Tommy*, the movie version of *Tommy*, the Broadway show version of *Tommy*, the movie of *Quadrophenia*—all with their own album versions and greatest hits, and expanded editions of their eight studio albums as well.

Who Are You was the last album by the original lineup. In 1978, the self-destructive, notoriously hard-partying Keith Moon died from a drug overdose. Surprisingly, John Entwistle passed on in a similar manner—an overdose of cocaine—in 2002. In 2006, the Who released a credible new album, *Endless Wire*, with just Daltrey and Townshend sparring away. There's also talk of Townshend finally finishing *Lifehouse*.

Entwistle (left) rocks while Daltrey works his trademark microphone magic.

One has to wonder if that Rickenbacker knows how short its lifespan just became, what with Townshend tuning and getting ready to "windmill."

The Mods

The Who arrived in those rhythm and blusey days of 1964 as a group of mods called the High Numbers. Mods were a subset tribe of British youth who liked to dress sharp in tailored suits—working-class kids trying to outdo the bankers and rich kids. In contrast to the opposing group, the rockers, who dressed in black leather jackets and drove heavy motorcycles, the mods drove Vespas, popped amphetamines, and wore those thick oilcloth raincoats. The Who created a whole rock opera about the tribe in 1973 with their album *Quadrophenia*. The name *Quadrophenia* was a nonscientific riff on the main character's multiple-personality disorder, or schizophrenia. Each one of Jimmy's four personalities represents a band member, illustrated by four different theme songs—the tough guy is Daltrey, the romantic is Entwistle, the bloody lunatic is Moon, and the beggar and hypocrite is Townshend.

WILCO

1994–

Music category alt-country started to coalesce in the early '90s. Aging punk rockers still trying to keep it real, even if they didn't want to scream so much, joined disgruntled Nashvillians who liked Dwight Yokum, Gram Parsons cultists, and Rolling Stone fans and mixed it up with the aging outlaw clan of Willie and Waylon. Into this stew, came a young band called Uncle Tupelo with the songwriting guitarists Jeff Tweedy and Jay Farrar. It was music for regular folks who liked to raise a little hell now and again—if only on the weekends. Uncle Tupelo traveled heavily with the likes of Freedy Johnston and got signed to Warner Bros. before splitting into two camps: Farrar's Son Volt and Tweedy's Wilco.

Wilco, with its solid debt to the Replacements, was the more rock oriented of the two. Brash and swaggering, they threw deli platters at the fans for their encores. They rocked with a Stonesy swagger and Tweedy's great raspy voice took the Paul Westerberg model of singing to new places.

After the relative failure of *A.M.*, the ragged glory of *Being There*, and the pop-friendly *Summerteeth*, the band was ready to make their masterpiece. With Jim O'Rourke coming on as producer, they created the sprawling *Yankee Hotel Foxtrot*. The end result elated them—and here is where the story took an interesting turn. Filmmaker Sam Jones documented the whole process of cutting the album. First, they fired long-time guitarist Jay Bennett. Then their A&R man didn't hear a hit and wanted them to go back into the studio and record some more. They refused, and their record company turned the album down (but gave them their masters back). Warner Brothers' move outraged fans and critics. The album was leaked on the Internet, and the story grew. It was obvious that the music business had changed: Art was now secondary. What mattered were the bottom line and the quarterly stockholder reports. And all this drama was caught on tape for the acclaimed documentary *I Am Trying to Break Your Heart.*

In the end, the band sold their album to Nonesuch, a subsidiary of the Warner Music Group distributed through Warner Brothers Records; in essence Warner bought the album twice. It went on to sell more 300,000 copies. And Wilco continues to record and keep it real, even if they'll never be the Backstreet Boys.

"I think somehow you need to get to a certain point in your life where the notion of failure is absurd." —Jeff Tweedy

GREATEST HITS

Year	Song
1995	"Box Full of Letters"
1996	"Outtasite (Outta Mind)"
1999	"Can't Stand It"
	"A Shot in the Arm"
2002	"War on War"

Jay Bennett and Jeff Tweedy of Wilco had the last laugh with *Yankee Hotel Foxtrot*.

Mermaid Avenue

When American folk musician Woody Guthrie passed away in 1967, he left behind lyrics to more than 1,000 songs that had never been put to music. According to Bob Dylan, it was Guthrie's intention that these words pass on to him, but the family was reluctant to give them up. Years later, in 1995, Woody's daughter, Nora, was inspired to give these songs some life—in a way relevant in the present, not archivally—and decided an English singer/songwriter Billy Bragg was the man for the job. Bragg in turn invited Wilco to join in, and they wrote modern music for the vintage songs. The result was 1988's *Mermaid Avenue*, named after the Coney Island street where Guthrie lived. The critically and commercially successful album was a beautiful tribute to the man who inspired so many, including a young Bob Dylan. *Mermaid Avenue II* was released in 2000.

STEVIE WONDER

May 13, 1950–

One of the top Motown stars of the '60s, Stevie Wonder went on to bring the album art form to a whole new level in the '70s. He was a platinum hit machine in the '80s and much sampled by hip-hop artists in the '90s. He was a child prodigy, signed to Motown records when he was only 12 years old, a junior Ray Charles—born poor, blind, and wise beyond his years. He could play any instrument set before him.

Between 1963 and 1970, a dozen of his singles hit the Top 10, including "Uptight (Everything's Alright)," "My Cherie Amour," and "Signed, Sealed, Delivered I'm Yours." He wrote for other artists, produced sessions, and toured on the road, but the ambitious young Stevie wanted more. When he turned 21, he renegotiated his Motown contract, demanding greater creative control, choosing to abandon Motown's tried-and-true formula of mixing hits and B-side filler to quickly turn out albums. Wonder wanted to bring the Motown sound into the modern post–*Sgt. Pepper's* world, taking whatever time needed to make a credible artistic statement. The first fruits would be "Superwoman (Where Were You When I Needed You)" from *Music of My Mind*, where he developed a new, more sophisticated sound.

He opened for the Stones on their 1972 U.S. tour, just as he was delivering some of his finest work. *Innervisons* tapped into the unrest of the day, as well as to the sounds of the new synthesizers. Using synth programmers from Tonto's Expanding Headband, he created such synth/soul masterpieces as "Superstition," "Higher Ground," and "Living for the City" while still coming up with romantic ballads like "You Are the Sunshine of My Life" that always assured him a slot on the charts.

A freak car accident set him thinking about deeper spiritual concerns, and he worked harder, crafting more ambitious works. His peak as a commercial artist was the far-reaching *Fulfillingness' First Finale* in 1974 and *Songs in the Key of Life in* 1976. Although he didn't hit those artistic peaks again, he continued charting platinum with some of his biggest hits, like the absurdly catchy "I Just Called to Say I Love You." "Ebony and Ivory," the song he wrote with Paul McCartney, was #1 on the charts for seven weeks in 1982. In 2007, the longevity of his work and mass appeal was made evident when a whole episode of *American Idol* was dedicated to his music.

Little Stevie Wonder grew up and lost the "Little" forever when people got a listen to his soulful voice.

NUGGET: His song "Happy Birthday" was an anthem for his pet cause—to get Martin Luther King Jr.'s birthday celebrated in the United States as a national holiday.

GREATEST HITS

Year	Song
1965	"Uptight (Everything's Alright)"
1967	"I Was Made to Love Her"
1968	"For Once in My Life"
1969	"My Cherie Amour"
	"Yester-Me, Yester-You, Yesterday"
1970	"Signed, Sealed, Delivered I'm Yours"
1971	"If You Really Love Me"
1972	"Superstition"
1973	"You Are the Sunshine of My Life"
	"Higher Ground"
	"Living for the City"
1974	"Boogie on Reggae Woman"
1976	"Sir Duke"
1979	"Send One Your Love"
1980	"Master Blaster (Jammin)"
1982	"That Girl"
1984	"I Just Called to Say I Love You"
1985	"Part-Time Lover"

NEIL YOUNG

NOVEMBER 12, 1945–

One of the most unblocked writers of his generation, Neil Young has kept the well-crafted classics coming, consistently and continuously making relevant music since the '60s. Neil's songs don't always top the charts, but he keeps the idea of art connected to the popular song form.

After a stint in '60s group Buffalo Springfield, Young went solo with the album *Neil Young*, which featured the self-confessional "The Loner." But in his next album, *Everybody Knows This Is Nowhere*, the Neil Young sound truly came together. Here he was joined by Crazy Horse, a rough-and-ready bar band. They weren't great musicians in a traditional sense, but they made gritty rock and roll that grooved and snarled. The album contained the signature workouts "Cinnamon Girl" and "Down by the River," his answer to Hendrix's "Hey Joe."

Meanwhile, former band mate Stephen Stills was having success in his new outfit, playing with the Hollies' Graham Nash and the Byrds' David Crosby. When Ahmet Ertegun, the head of Atlantic records, suggested getting Neil Young involved, Crosby, Stills, Nash & Young and the classic album *Déjà Vu* were born. Young contributed some searing guitar and the maudlin, plodding "Helpless," a surprising fan favorite. *Déjà Vu*'s success spurred interest in his solo career and his next album (perhaps his strongest artistically), *After the Goldrush*, was a huge hit as the Woodstock counterculture spread out into suburban America. The back-cover photo of Neil's blue-jeaned butt sent a generation to the ragbag to sew patches on their jeans.

NEIL YOUNG RIPS OUT ANOTHER LEGENDARY NOISY SOLO ON A GIBSON LES PAUL.

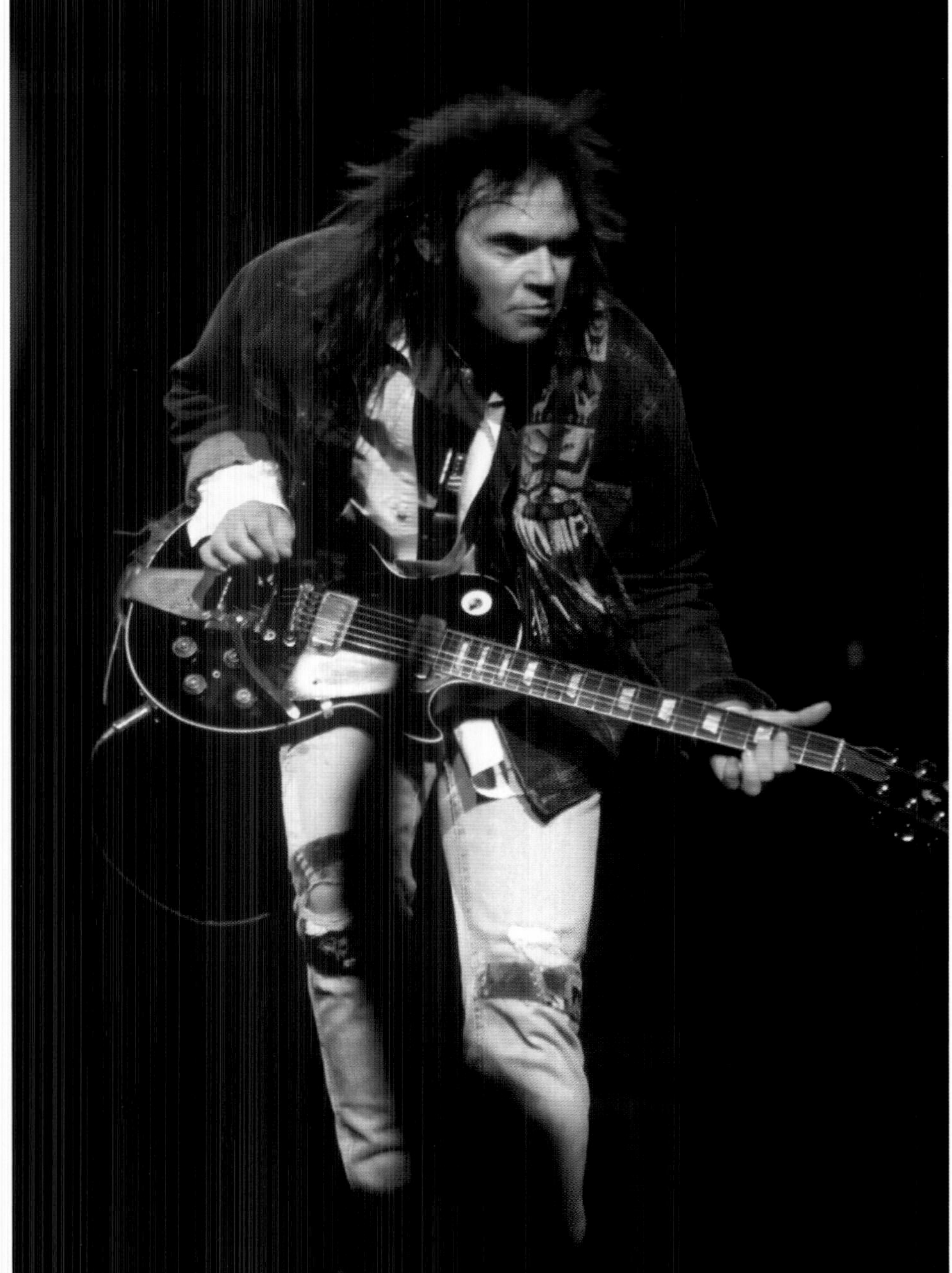

GREATEST HITS

YEAR	SONG
1969	"Cinnamon Girl"
1970	"Only Love Can Break Your Heart"
	"Southern Man"
	"When You Dance I Can Really Love "
1972	"Heart of Gold"
	"Old Man"
	"The Needle and the Damage Done"
1976	"Long May You Run"
1979	"Hey Hey, My My (Into the Black)"
1982	"Little Thing Called Love"
1989	"Rockin' in the Free World"

Young was on fire, banging out classic song after classic. The concert album *Live at Massey Hall 1971*, with Neil on acoustic guitar and piano, shows how solid a set of songs he was then delivering. Next, he recorded some material in Nashville with the Stray Gators and some with backing from the London Symphony Orchestra and packaged it as *Harvest*, which included the giant seller "Heart of Gold."

Harvest's massive success freaked Neil out a bit. He spent more time on his ranch, releasing a confusing documentary soundtrack *Journey through the Past* and generally messing with fans' expectations. As

"That's what rock 'n' roll is becoming. It's your parents' music." —Neil Young

he says in the liner notes to *Decade*, "'Heart of Gold' put me in the middle of the road. Traveling there soon became a bore so I headed for the ditch." His next proper release was not all that proper, a drunken, careening live album of all new material. *Time Fades Away* is actually a forgotten classic that hasn't been re-issued in many years, with some of the songs left from his great outburst delivered in a slightly shambolic manner. The stark *On the Beach* followed, which included a song written from the perspective of Charles Manson. The even more harrowing *Tonight's the Night* was next, telling the tales of Crazy Horse guitarist Danny Whitten and roadie Bruce Berry, who both died of drug overdoses.

Neil once said that he wanted to be in a band that combined the attitude of Dylan with the sound of the Stones, and he was at that place with Crazy Horse. He scored another radio hit with "Like a Hurricane" from the collected hodgepodge of different sessions called *American Stars 'n' Bars*. He delivered the outstanding *Zuma*, a driving guitar record with Crazy Horse, and he made an excellent acoustic affair, *Comes a Time*. At Geffen Records he made the most eclectic albums of his career, abandoning old formulas. He worked though a series of genre exercises—sythn pop on *Trans*, '50s rockabilly and doo-wop on *Everybody's Rockin'*, straight country on *Old Way*, blues on *This Note's for You*, and on and on until he had Geffen tearing his hair out. He returned to Warner and delivered his best album in years, *Freedom*, with the hit "Rockin' in the Free World."

Neil is still going strong. After a brush with death, he returned for the album and film *Prairie Wind* and followed it up with the politically charged *Living with War* a year later. He even persuaded Crosby, Stills & Nash to join him on the road to help promote it. Neil Young, long may you run.

Crazy Horse, pictured here in their original lineup without Neil Young. Modified versions of the group have backed up Neil on various albums over the years.

Clockwise from top: Buffalo Springfield members Neil Young (in the fringe jacket), Richie Furay, Bruce Palmer, Dewey Martin, and Stephen Stills.

Buffalo Springfield

Young came out of Canada as a folksinger of the Bob Dylan school in 1965. On a trip to L.A., in a hearse he met up with Stephen Stills, a friend from the folk circuit. The legendary story has it that Stills was just about to leave town when he saw Young's hearse, and the band Buffalo Springfield came together on a traffic island. Buffalo Springfield had only one hit with Stephen Stills, the song "For What It's Worth," but Young wrote a number of classics, including "Mr. Soul" and "Flying on the Ground Is Wrong." Since Young's high, keening voice was an acquired taste, fellow band member Richie Furay, who later formed Poco, sang many of his songs. Neil, always an introspective loner, had trouble in the group setting and quit rather than play the Monterey Pop Festival. The band only put out two albums, but along with the Byrds they were the basis for the evolving West Coast sound.

FRANK ZAPPA

December 21, 1940–December 4, 1993

Frank Zappa (front center) shares a light moment with the Mothers of Invention.

Frank Zappa was unique. With a love for avant-garde classical music, '50s doo-wop and R&B, free jazz, and Spike Jones, Zappa landed in the pop market at the height of psychedelia and made weirdness very hip. Incredibly industrious, innovative, and prolific, he left a massive catalog of recordings behind when he died from prostate cancer in 1993. There were few genres he feared working in.

"There are more love songs than anything else. If songs could make you do something we'd all love one another." —Frank Zappa

In 1966, Tom Wilson, who had produced Dylan and Simon & Garfunkel, signed his band, the Mothers of Invention, to Verve after seeing a couple of songs at Hollywood's Whiskey a Go Go. At Verve, the Mothers banged out *Freak Out!*, *Absolutely Free*, and *We're Only in It for the Money*—three stone-cold classics that put them at the center of the super freaky side of the late-'60s hipster underground. Zappa became the epicenter of a wild array of L.A. crazies, conducting his biz with his wife, Gail, from their Laurel Canyon mansion.

Tour From Hell

A European tour in 1971, in support of his film *200 Motels*, was a textbook disaster when a fire broke out and burned up all of Zappa's equipment as well as the theater. In the song "Smoke on the Water," Deep Purple recounted the incident, claiming that someone with a flare gun set the fire. After canceling a bunch of shows, the band soldiered on to London, where a crazy fan who thought Zappa was making eyes at his woman threw him off the stage, breaking his ankle and crushing his larynx among other injuries. Zappa walked with a limp after that and the throat injury lowered his voice.

GREATEST HITS

Year	Song
1967	"Son of Suzy Creamcheese"
1968	"Who Needs the Peace Corps?"
1973	"Dinah-Moe-Humm"
	"Montana"
1974	"Don't Eat the Yellow Snow"
1976	"Disco Boy"
1981	"Bamboozled by Love"
1982	"Valley Girl"
1984	"In France"
1988	"Zomby Woof"

NUGGET: Zappa testified at Senate hearings against Tipper Gore and her fight for the government censorship of music.

Warner Brothers decided to fund a label for him, and Zappa recorded for Bizarre and signed acts like Captain Beefheart (a teenage music buddy and major inspiration) and Wild Man Fischer (a raving street singer). Bizarre bled money.

As much as he was a rebel, he was also a record man constantly trying to figure out a way on to the charts. The Mothers broke up in 1969, and Zappa released the solo *Hot Rats*, a mostly instrumental affair with Beefheart doing vocals on "Willie the Pimp." He then streamlined his act with a new version of the Mothers that included such top session players as guitarist Adrian Belew and singers like Flo and Eddie from the Turtles. The new band had a slicker, Steely Dan sheen, but the lyrics were still surreal. "Montana" and "Don't Eat the Yellow Snow" proved to be FM radio successes.

When a live tour lost a quarter of a million dollars, he decided to concentrate on studio work, spending 12-hour days there. Ironically, his daughter, Moon Unit, in a bid to get some quality time with her dad, collaborated on the song "Valley Girl." It was his only Top-40 single.

ZZ TOP

1970–

Rock and roll bands don't get much more iconic than ZZ Top. With their big hats, cheap sunglasses, and long pioneer beards, the three sharp-dressed men came up with a musical formula that they modified like new additions to a classic car. ZZ Top played slow-burnin' boogie blues, Texas style. Always tasteful, always cool in a cartoon kind of way, ZZ Top has cruised slow and steady up the charts, time and time again.

The band toured extensively in the South, trying to break as a regional act on their first couple of releases. It was their third album, *Tres Hombres*, that put them on the map with the classic John Lee Hooker riffage of "Le Grange." It was their first album to go gold; many more albums and tours followed. It was a slow-building process, and after nine albums they were still a mid-level band.

In 1983, the band took a break, and Gibbons refurbished a classic hot rod that became the visual centerpiece for their next album, *Eliminator*. A series of three videos featured the classic cherry red Deuce Coupe, along with glamorous girls and the band appearing as phantom helpers dangling the ZZ Top keys to offer to a gas station attendant, a waitress, and a parking valet. The videos are perfect metaphors for their music. "Gimme All Your Lovin'," "Legs," and "Sharp Dressed Man" invited regular folk to the coolest party in town. Beneath the boogie riffs, the band customized their music as well. Carefully layered synthesizers bolstered their signature grooves and created a new kind of ear candy. People ate it up.

By 2003, the four-CD box set *Chrome, Smoke & BBQ* showed how far the band had come. They were inducted into the Rock and Roll Hall of Fame in 2004, and hold the record for being the longest-running band to operate with its original members. Three decades and going strong—the little ol' band from Texas has done good.

A Mysterious Bearded Stranger

Guitarist Billy Gibbons made some noise with a psychedelic '60s band called the Moving Sidewalks. Another competing band from the era, American Blues, contained the ZZ Top rhythm section. When members of the Moving Sidewalks were drafted, the ZZ Top lineup came together with Gibbons (who has a distinctive sound due to using a quarter or peso for a guitar pick) joined by bassist Dusty Hill and drummer Frank Beard. They picked the name because they liked the sound of B. B. King, and thought if you are "king" you are also the "top." Originally, they looked like any other longhaired rock group, but it's been said that a meeting one night with a mysterious bearded stranger convinced Gibbons and Hill to grow their facial hair. Oddly the man with the last name Beard is the one without one.

NUGGET: Gibbons and Hill are so attached to their long beards that they reportedly turned down $1 million each to shave them in a Gillette razor commercial.

GREATEST HITS	
YEAR	SONG
1973	"La Grange"
1979	"Cheap Sunglasses"
1983	"Gimme All Your Lovin'"
	"Legs"
	"Sharp Dressed Man"
1985	"Sleeping Bag"
1990	"Doubleback"
1994	"Pincushion"
1996	"What's Up with That"
2000	"36-22-36"

FROM LEFT: DUSTY HILL, FRANK BEARD, AND BILLY GIBBONS MAKE UP ZZ TOP.

SELECT DISCOGRAPHY

AC/DC

1975 High Voltage
T.N.T.
1976 Dirty Deeds Done Dirt Cheap
1977 Let There Be Rock
1978 Powerage
1979 Highway to Hell
1980 Back in Black
1981 For Those About to Rock
1983 Flick of the Switch
1984 '74 Jailbreak
1985 Fly on the Wall
1986 Who Made Who
1988 Blow Up Your Video
1990 The Razors Edge
1995 Ballbreaker
1997 Volts
2000 Stiff Upper Lip

Aerosmith

1973 Aerosmith
1974 Get Your Wings
1975 Toys in the Attic
1976 Rocks
1977 Draw the Line
1979 Night in the Ruts
1982 Rock in the Hard Place
1985 Done With Mirrors
1987 Permanent Vacation
1989 Pump
1993 Get a Grip
1997 Nine Lives
2001 Just Push Play
2004 Honkin' on Bobo

The Allman Brothers Band

1969 The Allman Brothers Band
1970 Idlewild South
1971 At Fillmore East
1972 Eat a Peach
1973 Brothers and Sisters
1975 Win, Lose or Draw
1976 Wipe the Windows, Check the Oil, Dollar Gas
1979 Enlightened Rogues
1980 Reach for the Sky
1981 Brothers of the Road
1990 Seven Turns
1991 Shades of Two Worlds
1994 Where It All Begins
2003 Hittin' the Note

The Band

1968 Music from Big Pink
1969 The Band
1970 Stage Fright
1971 Cahoots
1972 Rock of Ages
1973 Moondog Matinee
1975 Northern Lights—Southern Cross
1977 Islands
1978 The Last Waltz
1993 Jericho
1996 High on the Hog
1998 Jubilation

with Bob Dylan

1974 Planet Waves
1974 Before the Flood
1975 The Basement Tapes

The Beach Boys

1962 Surfin' Safari
1963 Surfin' USA
Surfer Girl
Little Deuce Coupe
1964 Shut Down Volume 2
All Summer Long
The Beach Boys' Christmas Album
1965 The Beach Boys Today!
Summer Days and Summer Nights!!
Beach Boys' Party!
1966 Pet Sounds
1967 Smiley Smile
Wild Honey
1968 Friends
Stack-O-Tracks
1969 20/20
1970 Sunflower
1971 Surf's Up
1972 Carl and the Passions—"So Tough"
1973 Holland
1976 15 Big Ones
1977 The Beach Boys Love You
1978 M.I.U. Album
1979 L.A. Light Album
1980 Keepin' the Summer Alive
1985 The Beach Boys
1992 Summer in Paradise
1996 Stars and Stripes Vol. 1

Brian Wilson solo

1987 Brian Wilson
1995 I Just Wasn't Made for These Times
1998 Imagination
2004 Gettin' in Over My Head
SMiLE

The Beatles

1963 Please Please Me
With the Beatles
1964 Introducing . . . The Beatles
Meet the Beatles!
The Beatles Second Album
A Hard Day's Night
Beatles for Sale
Something New
1965 Beatles '65
The Beatles VI
Help!
Rubber Soul
1966 Yesterday . . . and Today
Revolver
1967 Sgt. Pepper's Lonely Hearts Club Band
Magical Mystery Tour
1968 The Beatles The White Album
1969 Yellow Submarine
Abbey Road
1970 Let It Be

Beck

1994 Mellow Gold
Stereopathic Soulmanure
One Foot in the Grave
1996 Odelay
1998 Mutations
1999 Midnite Vultures

2002 Sea Change
2005 Guero
2006 The Information

Chuck Berry

1958 After School Session
One Dozen Berry
1959 Chuck Berry is on Top
1960 Rockin' at the Hops
1961 New Juke-Box Hits
1964 Two Great Guitars with Bo Diddley
St. Louis to Liverpool
1965 Chuck Berry in London
1966 Fresh Berry's
1967 In Memphis
1968 From St. Louie to Frisco
1969 Concert of B Goode
1970 Back Home
1971 San Francisco Dues
1972 The London Chuck Berry Sessions
1973 Bio
Sweet Little Rock and Roller
1974 Wild Berrys
Flashback
Chuck and His Friends
1975 Chuck Berry
1979 Rock It
1982 Chuck Berry

Black Sabbath

1970 Black Sabbath
1971 Paranoid
Master of Reality
1972 Black Sabbath, Vol. 4
1973 Sabbath Bloody Sabbath
1975 Sabotage
1976 Technical Ecstasy
1978 Never Say Die!
1980 Heaven and Hell
1981 Mob Rules
1983 Born Again
1986 Seventh Star
1987 The Eternal Idol
1989 Headless Cross
1990 Tyr
1992 Dehumanizer
1994 Cross Purposes
1995 Forbidden

Blondie

1976 Blondie
1977 Plastic Letters
1978 Parallel Lines
1979 Eat to the Beat
1980 Autoamerican
1982 The Hunter
1999 No Exit
2003 The Curse of Blondie

David Bowie

1967 David Bowie
1969 Space Oddity
1970 The Man Who Sold the World
1971 Hunky Dory
1972 The Rise and Fall of Ziggy Stardust and the Spiders from Mars
1973 Aladdin Sane
Pin Ups
1974 Diamond Dogs
1975 Young Americans
1976 Station to Station
1977 Low
Heroes
1979 Lodger
1980 Scary Monsters and Super Creeps
1983 Let's Dance
1984 Tonight
1987 Never Let Me Down
1993 Black Tie White Noise
1995 Outside
1997 Earthling
1999 Hours . . .
2002 Heathen
2003 Reality

James Brown

1959 Please Please Please
Try Me
1960 Think
1961 The Amazing James Brown
James Brown Presents His Band/Night Train
1962 Shout and Shimmy
James Brown and His Famous Flames Tour the USA
1963 Live at the Apollo
Prisoner of Love
Excitement—Mr. Dynamite
1964 Pure Dynamite: Live at the Royal
Showtime
The Unbeatable James Brown
Grits and Soul
Out of Sight
1965 Papa's Got a Brand New Bag
1966 I Got You (I Feel Good)
James Brown Plays James Brown Today and Yesterday
Mighty Instrumentals
James Brown Plays New Breed
The Boo-Ga-Loo
Soul Brother No. 1: It's a Man's Man's Man's World
James Brown Sings Christmas Songs
Handful of Soul
1967 The James Brown Show Sings Raw Soul
James Brown Plays the Real Thing
Cold Sweat
1968 James Brown Presents His Show of Tomorrow
I Can't Stand Myself
I Got the Feelin'
Jams Brown Sings Out of Sight
Thinking About Little Willie John and a Few Nice Things
A Soulful Christmas
1969 Say It Loud, I'm Black and I'm Proud
Gettin' Down to It
The Popcorn
It's a Mother
1970 Ain't It Funky
Soul on Top
It's a New Day—Let a Man

Come In
Sex Machine
Hey America
1971 Super Bad
Sho' Is Funky Down Here
Hot Pants
Revolution of the Mind/ Live at the Apollo, Volume 3
1972 There It Is
Get on the Good Foot
1973 Black Caesar
Slaughter's Big Rip-Off
1974 The Payback
Hell
1975 Reality
Sex Machine Today
Everybody's Doin' the Hustle and Dead on the Double Bump
1976 Hot
Get Up Offa That Thing
Bodyheat
1977 Mutha's Nature
1978 Jam 1980's
1979 Take a Look at Those Cakes
The Original Disco Man
1980 People
Hot on the One
Soul Syndrome
1981 Nonstop!
1983 Bring It On
1986 Gravity
1988 James Brown and Friends
I'm Real
1991 Love Over-Due
1993 Universal James
Funky President
1998 I'm Back!
2002 The Next Step

The Byrds

1965 Mr. Tambourine Man
Turn! Turn! Turn!
1966 Fifth Dimension
1967 Younger Than Yesterday
1968 The Notorious Byrd Brothers
Sweetheart of the Rodeo
1969 Dr. Byrds & Mr. Hyde
Ballad of Easy Rider
1970 Untitled
1971 Byrdmaniax
Farther Along
1973 Byrds

Captain Beefheart

1967 Safe as Milk
1968 Strictly Personal
1969 Trout Mask Replica
1970 Lick My Decals Off, Baby
1971 Mirror Man
1972 The Spotlight Kid
Clear Spot
1974 Unconditionally Guaranteed
Bluejeans & Moonbeams
1975 Bongo Fury with Frank Zappa
1978 Shiny Beast Bat Chain Puller
1980 Doc at the Radar Station
1982 Ice Cream for Crow

Eric Clapton

with the Yardbirds

1965 For Your Love
Having a Rave Up

with John Mayall & the Bluesbreakers

1966 Blues Breakers with Eric Clapton

with Cream

1966 Fresh Cream
1967 Disraeli Gears
1968 Wheels of Fire
Goodbye 1969

with Blind Faith

1969 Blind Faith

with Derek and the Dominoes

1970 Layla and Other Assorted Love Songs

Solo

1970 Eric Clapton
1974 461 Ocean Boulevard
1975 There's One in Every Crowd
1976 No Reason to Cry
1977 Slowhand
1978 Backless
1981 Another Ticket
1983 Money and Cigarettes
1985 Behind the Sun
1986 August
1989 Journeyman
1994 From the Cradle
1998 Pilgrim
2001 Reptile
2004 Me and Mr. Johnson
2005 Back Home

The Clash

1977 The Clash
1978 Give 'Em Enough Rope
1979 London Calling
1980 Sandinista!
1982 Combat Rock
1985 Cut the Crap

Alice Cooper

1969 Pretties for You
1970 Easy Action
1971 Love It to Death
Killer
1972 School's Out
1973 Billion Dollar Babies
Muscle of Love
1975 Welcome to My Nightmare
1976 Alice Cooper Goes to Hell
1977 Lace and Whiskey
1978 From the Inside
1980 Flush the Fashion
1981 Special Forces
1982 Zipper Catches Skin
1983 DaDa
1986 Constrictor
1987 Raise Your Fist and Yell
1989 Trash
1991 Hey Stoopid
1994 The Last Temptation
2000 Brutal Planet
2001 Dragontown
2003 The Eyes of Alice Cooper
2005 Dirty Diamonds
2007 Along Came a Spider

Elvis Costello

1977 My Aim Is True
1978 This Year's Model
1979 Armed Forces
1980 Get Happy!!
1981 Trust
Almost Blue
1982 Imperial Bedroom
1983 Punch the Clock
1984 Goodbye Cruel World
1986 King of America
Blood and Chocolate
1989 Spike
1991 Mighty Like a Rose
1993 The Juliet Letters (with the Brodsky Quartet)
1994 Brutal Youth
1995 Kojak Variety
1996 All This Useless Beauty
1998 Painted from Memory (with Burt Bacharach)
2002 When I was Cruel
Cruel Smile
2003 North
2004 The Delivery Man
Il Sogno
2005 Piano Jazz with Marian McPartland
2006 My Flame Burns Blue
2006 The River in Reverse (with Allen Toussaint)

Creedence Clearwater Revival

1968 Creedence Clearwater Revival
1969 Bayou Country
Green River
Willy and the Poor Boys
1970 Cosmo's Factory
1970 Pendulum
1972 Mardi Gras

Crosby Stills and Nash

1969 Crosby Stills and Nash
1970 Déjà Vu (with Neil Young)
1971 Four Way Street (with Neil Young)
1974 So Far (with Neil Young)
1977 CSN 9
1982 Daylight Again Atlantic
1988 American Dream (with Neil Young)
1990 Live It Up
1994 After the Storm
1999 Looking Forward (with Neil Young)

The Cure

1979 Three Imaginary Boys
1980 Seventeen Seconds
1981 Faith
1982 Pornography
1984 The Top
1985 The Head on the Door
1987 Kiss Me, Kiss Me, Kiss Me
1989 Disintegration
1992 Wish
1996 Wild Mood Swings
2000 Bloodflowers
2004 The Cure

Bo Diddley

1958 Bo Diddley
1959 Go Bo Diddley
1960 Have Guitar—Will Travel
Bo Diddley in the Spotlight
Bo Diddley is a Gunslinger
1961 Bo Diddley is a Lover
1962 Bo Diddley's a Twister
Bo Diddley Deagles
Bo Diddley & Company
1963 Surfin' with Bo Diddley
Bo Diddley's Beach Party
1964 Two Great Guitars with Chuck Berry
1965 Hey Good Lookin'
500% More Man
1966 The Originator
1967 Super Blues (with Muddy Waters & Little Walter)
Super Super Blues Band (with Muddy Waters & Howlin' Wolf)
1970 The Black Gladiator
1971 Another Dimension
1972 Where It All Began
Got My Own Bag of Tricks
1973 The London Bo Diddley Sessions
1974 Big Bad Bo
1976 20th Anniversary of Rock & Roll
1977 I'm a Man
1983 Ain't It Good to Be Free
1985 Bo Diddley & Co—Live
1986 Hey . . . Bo Diddley in Concert
1989 Breakin' Through the BS
Living Legend
1991 Rare & Well Done
1992 Live at the Ritz (with Ronnie Wood)
1993 This Should Not Be
1994 Promises
1996 A Man Amongst Men
2002 Moochas Gracias (with Anna Moo)
2003 Dick's Picks #30 1972 5-song Live Session with The Grateful Dead

Donovan

1965 What's Bin Did and What's Bin Hid (UK) Catch the Wind (U.S.)
1965 Fairytale
1966 Sunshine Superman
1967 Mellow Yellow
A Gift From a Flower to a Garden
For Little Ones
1968 The Hurdy Gurdy Man
1969 Barabajagal
1970 Open Road
1971 H.M.S. Donovan
1973 Cosmic Wheels
Essence to Essence
1974 7-Tease
1976 Slow Down World
1977 Donovan
1980 Neutronica
1981 Love is Only Feeling
1984 Lady of the Stars

1993 One Night in Time
1996 Sutras
2002 Pied Piper
2004 Sixty Four
Brother Sun, Sister Moon
Beat Cafe

The Doors

1967 The Doors
Strange Days
1968 Waiting for the Sun
1969 The Soft Parade
1970 Morrison Hotel
1971 L.A. Woman
Other Voices
Full Circle

Bob Dylan

1962 Bob Dylan
1963 The Freewheelin' Bob Dylan
The Times They Are a-Changin'
Another Side of Bob Dylan
1965 Bringing It All Back Home
Highway 61 Revisited
1966 Blonde on Blonde
1967 John Wesley Harding
1969 Nashville Skyline
1970 Self Portrait
New Morning
1973 Pat Garrett & Billy the Kid
Dylan
1974 Planet Waves
Before the Flood
1975 Blood on the Tracks
The Basement Tapes
1976 Desire
1978 Street Legal
1979 Slow Train Coming
1980 Saved
1981 Shot of Love
1983 Infidels
1985 Empire Burlesque
1986 Knocked Out Loaded
1988 Down in the Groove
1989 Oh Mercy
1990 Under the Red Sky
1992 Good as I Been to You
1993 World Gone Wrong
1997 Time Out of Mind
2001 Love and Theft
2006 Modern Times

The Eagles

1972 Eagles
1973 Desperado
1974 On the Border
1975 One of These Nights
1976 Hotel California
Their Greatest Hits 1971–1975
1979 The Long Run

The Faces and Small Faces

Small Faces

1966 Small Faces
1967 From the Beginning
1968 There Are But Four Small Faces
Ogdens' Nut Gone Flake
1969 The Autumn Stone

The Faces

1970 First Step
1971 Long Player
A Nod is as Good as a Wink . . . To a Blind Horse
1973 Ooh La La

Aretha Franklin

1956 The Gospel Soul of Aretha Franklin
1961 Aretha
1962 The Electrifying Aretha Franklin
The Tender, the Moving, the Swinging Aretha Franklin
1963 Laughing on the Outside
1964 Unforgettable: A Tribute to Dinah Washington
Runnin' Out of Fools
1965 Yeah!: Aretha Franklin in Person
1966 Soul Sister
1967 Take It Like You Give It
I Never Loved a Man the Way I Love You
Aretha Arrives
Take a Look
1968 Lady Soul
Aretha Now
Aretha in Paris
1969 Aretha Franklin: Soul '69
Aretha's Gold
1970 This Girl's in Love with You
Spirit in the Dark
1971 Aretha Live at Fillmore West
Young, Gifted and Black
1972 Amazing Grace
1973 Hey Now Hey the Other Side of the Sky
1974 Let Me in Your Life
With Everything I Feel in Me
1975 You
1976 Sparkle
1977 Sweet Passion
1978 Almighty Fire
1979 La Diva
1980 Aretha
Aretha Sings the Blues 1980
1981 Love All the Hurt Away
1982 Jump to It
1983 Get It Right
1985 Who's Zoomin' Who?
1986 Aretha
1987 One Lord One Faith One Baptism
1989 Through the Storm
1991 What You See Is What You Sweat
1996 Aretha Sings Standards
1997 Love Songs
1998 A Rose Is Still a Rose
2003 So Damn Happy
2007 A Woman Falling Out of Love

Grateful Dead

1967 The Grateful Dead
1968 Anthem of the Sun
1969 Aoxomoxoa
Live/Dead
1970 Workingman's Dead
American Beauty

1971 Grateful Dead
1972 Europe '72
1973 History of the Grateful Dead Volume One
Wake of the Flood
1974 Grateful Dead from the Mars Hotel
1975 Blues for Allah
1976 Steal Your Face
1977 Terrapin Station
1978 Shakedown Street
1980 Go to Heaven
1981 Reckoning
Dead Set
1987 In the Dark
1989 Built to Last
1990 Without a Net

Guns N' Roses

1987 Appetite for Destruction
1988 GN'R Lies
1991 Use Your Illusion I
1991 Use Your Illusion II
1993 The Spaghetti Incident?

Jimi Hendrix

1967 Are You Experienced?
Axis: Bold as Love
1968 Electric Ladyland
1970 Band of Gypsys
1971 Cry of Love
1997 First Rays of the New Morning Sun

Buddy Holly

1957 The "Chirping" Crickets
1958 Buddy Holly
That'll Be the Day
1959 The Buddy Holly Story
1960 The Buddy Holly Story, Vol. 2
1963 Reminiscing
1964 Showcase
1966 Holly in the Hills

Jefferson Airplane

1966 Jefferson Airplane Takes Off
1967 Surrealistic Pillow
After Bathing at Baxter's
1968 Crown of Creation
1969 Volunteers
1971 Bark
1972 Long John Silver

Elton John

1969 Empty Sky
1970 Elton John
Tumbleweed Connection
1971 Madman Across the Water
1972 Honky Château
1973 Don't Shoot Me I'm Only the Piano Player
Goodbye Yellow Brick Road
1974 Caribou
1975 Captain Fantastic and the Brown Dirt Cowboy
Rock of the Westies
1976 Blue Moves
1978 A Single Man
1979 Victim of Love
1980 21 at 33
1981 The Fox
1982 Jump Up!
1983 Too Low for Zero
1984 Breaking Hearts
1985 Ice on Fire
1986 Leather Jackets
1988 Reg Strikes Back
1989 Sleeping with the Past
1992 The One
1993 Duets
1995 Made in England
1997 The Big Picture
2001 Songs from the West Coast
2004 Peachtree Road
2006 The Captain & the Kid

Janis Joplin

1967 Big Brother & the Holding Company
1968 Cheap Thrills
1969 I Got Dem Ol' Kozmic Blues Again Mama!
1971 Pearl

Carole King

1970 Writer
1971 Tapestry
1971 Music
1972 Rhymes and Reasons
1973 Fantasy
1974 Wrap Around Joy
1975 Really Rosie
1976 Thoroughbred
1977 Simple Things
1978 Welcome Home
1979 Touch the Sky
1980 Pearls: Songs of Goffin and King
1982 One to One
1983 Speeding Time
1989 City Streets
1993 Color of Your Dreams
1994 Time Gone By
1997 Time Heals All Wounds
1998 Goin' Back
2001 Love Makes the World
2005 The Living Room Tour

The Kinks

1964 The Kinks
1965 Kinda Kinks
1965 The Kink Kontroversey
1966 Face to Face
1967 Something Else by the Kinks
1968 The Kinks are the Village Green Preservation Society
1969 Arthur or the Decline and Fall of the British Empire
1970 Lola versus Powerman and the Moneygoround, Part One
1971 Muswell Hillbillies
1972 Everybody's in Show-Biz
1973 The Great Lost Kinks Album
Preservation: Act 1
1974 Preservation: Act 2
1975 Soap Opera

1976 Schoolboys in Disgrace
1977 Sleepwalker
1978 Misfits
1979 Low Budget
1981 Give the People What They Want
1983 State of Confusion
1984 Word of Mouth
1986 Think Visual
1989 UK Jive
1993 Phobia

Kiss

1974 Kiss
Hotter Than Hell
1975 Dressed to Kill
1976 Destroyer
Rock and Roll Over
1977 Love Gun
1978 Gene Simmons
Ace Frehley
Peter Criss
Paul Stanley
1979 Dynasty
1980 Unmasked
1981 Music from "The Elder"
1982 Creatures of the Night
1983 Lick It Up
1984 Animalize
1985 Asylum
1987 Crazy Nights
1989 Hot in the Shade
1992 Revenge
1997 Carnival of Souls: The Final Sessions
1998 Psycho Circus

Led Zeppelin

1969 Led Zeppelin
Led Zeppelin II
1970 Led Zeppelin III
1971 Led Zeppelin IV Zoso
1973 Houses of the Holy
1975 Physical Graffiti
1976 Presence
1979 In Through the Out Door

Jerry Lee Lewis

1957 Jerry Lee Lewis
1958 Jerry Lee Lewis and His Pumping Piano
1963 Rockin' with Jerry Lee Lewis
1964 The Greatest Live Show On Earth
1965 The Return of Rock
Country Songs for City Folks
1966 Memphis Beat
1969 Another Time, Another Place
She Still Comes Around
1970 She Even Woke Me Up to Say Goodbye
1971 In Loving Memories
1972 Would You Take Another Chance on Me
The Killer Rocks On
Who's Gonna Play This Old Piano?
1973 Sometimes a Memory Ain't Enough
Southern Roots
1974 I-40 Country
1975 Boogie Woogie Country Man
Odd Man In
1976 Country Class
1977 Country Memories
1978 Jerry Lee Keeps Rockin'
1979 Jerry Lee Lewis
1980 Killer Country
When Two Worlds Collide
1982 The Survivors Live with Johnny Cash and Carl Perkins
1983 My Fingers Do The Talking
1984 I Am What I Am
1985 Four Legends (with Webb Pierce, Mel Tillis, and Faron Young)
1986 Class of '55 (with Johnny Cash, Carl Perkins, and Roy Orbison)

1989 Great Balls of Fire
2006 Last Man Standing duets

Little Richard

1957 Here's Little Richard
1958 Little Richard
1959 The Fabulous Little Richard
1960 Clap Your Hands
1960 Pray Along with Little Richard, Vol. 1: A Closer Walk with Thee
Pray Along with Little Richard, Vol. 2: I'm Quitting Show Business
1962 King of the Gospel Singers
1963 Little Richard with Sister Rosetta Tharpe Sings Spirituals
1964 Coming Home
1965 Little Richard is Back
The Wild and Frantic Little Richard
1967 The Explosive Little Richard
Rock N Roll Forever
1969 Good Golly Miss Molly
1970 Little Richard
Rock Hard Rock Heavy
1971 Mr. Big
King of Rock & Roll
The Rill Thing
1972 Friends from the Beginning: Little Richard & Jimi Hendrix
The Second Coming
You Can't Keep a Good Man Down
1973 Right Now
1974 Talkin' 'Bout Soul
1975 Keep a Knockin'
1976 Sings
1979 God's Beautiful City
1986 Lifetime Friend
1992 Shake It All About

The Lovin' Spoonful

1965 Do You Believe in Magic
1966 Daydream
What's Up, Tigerlily?
Hums of the Lovin' Spoonful
1967 You're a Big Boy Now
1968 Everything Playing

1969 Revelation Revolution '69

Lynyrd Skynyrd

1973 pronounced 'leh-'nérd 'skin-'nérd
1974 Second Helping
1975 Nuthin' Fancy
1976 Gimme Back My Bullets
1977 Street Survivors
1991 Lynyrd Skynyrd 1991
1993 The Last Rebel
1994 Endangered Species
1997 Twenty
1999 Edge of Forever
2000 Christmas Time Again
2003 Vicious Cycle

The Mamas and the Papas

1966 If You Can Believe Your Eyes and Ears
The Mamas & the Papas
1967 Deliver
1968 The Papas & the Mamas

Bob Marley

1966 The Wailing Wailers
1970 The Best of the Wailers
Soul Rebels
1971 Soul Revolution
Soul Revolution II
1973 Catch a Fire
African Herbsman
Burnin'
1974 Rasta Revolution
Natty Dread
1976 Rastaman Vibration
1977 Exodus
Kaya
1979 Survival
1980 Uprising
1983 Confrontation

John Cougar Mellencamp

1976 Chestnut Street Incident
1977 The Kid Inside
1978 A Biography
1979 John Cougar
1980 Nothin' Matters and What If It Did
1982 American Fool
1983 Uh-Huh
1985 Scarecrow
1987 The Lonesome Jubilee
1989 Big Daddy
1991 Whenever We Wanted
1993 Human Wheels
1994 Dance Naked
1996 Mr. Happy Go Lucky
1997 The Best That I Could Do
1998 John Mellencamp
1999 Rough Harvest
2001 Cuttin' Heads
2003 Trouble No More
2007 Freedom's Road

Metallica

1983 Kill 'Em All
1984 Ride the Lightning
1986 Master of Puppets
1988 . . . And Justice for All
1991 Metallica The Black Album
1996 Load
1997 ReLoad
1998 Garage, Inc.
1999 S&M
2003 St. Anger

Joni Mitchell

1968 Song to a Seagull aka Joni Mitchell
1969 Clouds
1970 Ladies of the Canyon
1971 Blue
1972 For the Roses
1974 Court and Spark
The Hissing of Summer Lawns
1976 Hejira
1977 Don Juan's Reckless Daughter
1979 Mingus
1982 Wild Things Run Fast
1985 Dog Eat Dog
1988 Chalk Mark in a Rainstorn
1991 Night Ride Home
1994 Turbulent Indigo
1998 Taming the Tiger
2000 Both Sides Now
2002 Travelogue
2007 Shine

Van Morrison

1967 Blowin' Your Mind!
1968 Astral Weeks
1970 Moondance
His Band and the Street Choir
1971 Tupelo Honey
1972 Saint Dominic's Preview
1973 Hard Nose the Highway
1974 It's Too Late to Stop Now
Veedon Fleece
1977 A Period of Transition
1978 Wavelength
1979 Into the Music
1980 Common One
1982 Beautiful Vision
1983 Inarticulate Speech of the Heart
1984 Live at the Grand Opera House, Belfast
1985 A Sense of Wonder
1986 No Guru, No Method, No Teacher
1987 Poetic Champions Compose
1988 Irish Heartbeat (with The Chieftans)
1989 Avalon Sunset
1990 Enlightenment
1991 Hymns to the Silence
1993 Too Long in Exile
1994 A Night in San Francisco
1995 Days Like This
1996 How Long Has This Been Going On (with Georgie Fame)
Tell Me Something: The Songs of Mose Allison
1997 The Healing Game
1999 Back on Top
2000 The Skiffle Sessions—Live In Belfast 1998 (with Lonnie Donegan and Chris Barber)
You Win Again (with Linda Gail Lewis)

2002 Down the Road
2003 What's Wrong with This Picture?
2005 Magic Time
2006 Pay the Devil

New York Dolls
1973 New York Dolls
1974 Too Much Too Soon
1981 Lipstick Killers—The Mercer Street Sessions 1972
1984 Red Patent Leather
1992 Seven Day Weekends
2006 One Day It Will Please Us to Remember Even This

Nine Inch Nails
1989 Pretty Hate Machine
1994 The Downward Spiral
1999 The Fragile
2005 With Teeth
2007 Year Zero

Nirvana
1989 Bleach
1991 Nevermind
1992 Incesticide
1993 In Utero
1994 Unplugged

Parliament-Funkadelic
Parliament
1970 Osmium
1974 Up for the Down Stroke
1975 Chocolate City
1985 Mothership Connection
1977 Get Down & Boogie
1977 Funkentelechy Vs. the Placebo Syndrome
1978 Motor Booty Affair
1979 Gloryhallastoopid
1980 Tombipulation
Funkadelic
1970 Funkadelic
Free Your Mind . . . And Your Ass Will Follow
1971 Maggot Brain
1972 American Eats Its Young
1973 Cosmic Slop
1974 Standing on the Verge of Getting It On
1975 Let's Take It to the Stage
1976 Hardcore Jollies
Tales of Kidd Funkadelic
1978 One Nation Under a Groove
1979 Uncle Jam Wants You
1982 Connections & Disconnections
1981 The Electric Spanking of War Babies
1989 By Way of the Drum

Gram Parsons
with Flying Burrito Brothers
1969 The Gilded Palace of Sin
1970 Burrito Deluxe
solo
1973 GP
1974 Grievous Angel
1982 Live 1973

Pearl Jam
1991 Ten
1993 Vs.
1994 Vitalogy
1996 No Code
1998 Yield
2000 Binaural
2002 Riot Act
2006 Pearl Jam

Tom Petty
1976 Tom Petty & the Heartbreakers
1978 You're Gonna Get It!
1979 Damn the Torpedos
1981 Hard Promises
1982 Long After Dark
1985 Southern Accents
1987 Let Me Up I've Had Enough
1989 Full Moon Fever
1991 Into the Great Wide Open
1994 Wildflowers
1999 Echo
2002 The Last DJ
2006 Highway Companion

Pink Floyd
1967 The Piper at the Gates of Dawn
1968 A Saucerful of Secrets
1969 Music from the Film More
1969 Ummagumma
1970 Atom Heart Mother
1971 Meddle
1972 Obscured by Clouds
1973 The Dark Side of the Moon
1975 Wish You Were Here
1977 Animals
1979 The Wall
1983 The Final Cut
1987 A Momentary Lapse of Reason
1994 The Division Bell

The Pixies
1987 Come on Pilgrim
1988 Surfer Rosa
1989 Doolittle
1990 Bossanova
1991 Trompe Le Monde

The Police
1978 Outlandos d'Amour
1979 Reggatta de Blanc
1980 Zenyatta Mondatta
1981 Ghost in the Machine
1983 Synchronicity

Iggy Pop
with the Stooges
1969 The Stooges
1970 Fun House
1973 Raw Power
1976 Metallic KO
2007 The Weirdness
solo
1977 The Idiot
Lust for Life
Kill City
1979 New Values
1980 Soldier
1981 Party
1982 Zombie Birdhouse
1986 Blah Blah Blah
1988 Instinct

1990 Brick by Brick
1993 American Caesar
1996 Naughty Little Doggie
1999 Avenue B
2001 Beat 'Em Up
2003 Skull Ring

Elvis Presley

1956 Elvis Presley
1956 Elvis
1957 Loving You
Elvis' Christmas Album
1958 King Creole
1959 For LP Fans Only
A Date with Elvis
1960 Elvis is Back!
G.I. Blues His Hand in Mine
1961 Something for Everybody
Blue Hawaii
1962 Pot Luck
1963 It Happened at the World's Fair
Fun in Acapulco
Girls! Girls! Girls!
1964 Kissin' Cousins
Roustabout
1965 Girl Happy
Elvis for Everyone
Harum Scarum
Tickle Me
1966 Frankie and Johnny
Paradie Hawaiian Style
Spinout
1967 How Great Thou Art
Double Trouble
Clambake
1968 Speedway
1969 From Elvis in Memphis
From Memphis to Vegas/ From Vegas to Memphis
1970 Almost in Love
Back in Memphis
1971 Elvis Country I'm 10,000 Years Old
You'll Never Walk Alone
Love Letters from Elvis
Elvis Sings the Wonderful World of Christmas
1972 Elvis Now
He Touched Me
1973 Elvis
Raised on Rock/ For Ol' Times Sakes
1974 Good Times
1975 Promised Land
Today
1976 From Elvis Presley Boulevard, Memphis, Tennessee
1977 Welcome to My World
Moody Blue
1978 Elvis Sings for Children and Grownups Too

The Pretenders

1980 Pretenders
1981 Pretenders II
1984 Learning to Crawl
1986 Get Close
1990 Packed!
1994 Last of the Independents
1999 Viva el Amor
2002 Loose Screw

Prince

1978 For You
1979 Prince
1980 Dirty Mind
1981 Controversy
1982 1999
1984 Purple Rain
1985 Around the World in a Day
1986 Parade
1987 Sign 'O' the Times
1988 Lovesexy
1989 Batman
1990 Graffiti Bridge
1991 Diamonds and Pearls
1992 O+> aka Love Symbol
1994 Come
1994 The Black Album
1995 The Gold Experience
1996 Chaos and Disorder
1996 Emancipation
1998 The Truth
1999 Rave Un2 the Joy Fantastic
2001 The Rainbow Children
2002 One Nite Alone . . .
2004 The Chocolate Invasion
2004 The Slaughterhouse
2004 Musicology
2006 3121

Queen

1973 Queen
1974 Queen II
Sheer Heart Attack
1975 A Night at the Opera
1976 A Day at the Races
1977 News of the World
1978 Jazz
1980 The Game
Flash Gordon
1982 Hot Space
1984 The Works
1986 A Kind of Magic
1989 The Miracle
1991 Innuendo
1995 Made in Heaven

Radiohead

1993 Pablo Honey
1995 The Bends
1997 OK Computer
2000 Kid A
2001 Amnesiac
2003 Hail to the Thief

The Ramones

1976 Ramones
1977 Leave Home
Rocket to Russia
1978 Road to Ruin
1980 End of the Century
1981 Pleasant Dreams
1983 Subterranean Jungle
1984 Too Tough to Die
1986 Animal Boy
1987 Halfway to Sanity
1989 Brain Drain
1992 Mondo Bizarro
1993 Acid Eaters

1995 ¡Adios Amigos!

Red Hot Chili Peppers

1984 The Red Hot Chili Peppers
1985 Freaky Styley
1987 The Uplift Mofo Party Plan
1989 Mother's Milk
1991 Blood Sugar Sex Magik
1995 One Hot Minute
1999 Californication
2002 By the Way
2006 Stadium Arcadium

R.E.M.

1983 Murmur
1984 Reckoning
1985 Fables of the Reconstruction
1986 Life's Rich Pageant
1987 Document
1988 Green
1991 Out of Time
1992 Automatic for the People
1994 Monster
1996 New Adventures in Hi-Fi
1998 Up
2001 Reveal
2004 Around the Sun

The Replacements

1981 Sorry Ma, Forgot to Take Out the Trash
1982 Stink
1983 Hootenanny
1984 Let It Be
1985 The Shit Hits the Fans
1985 Tim
1987 Pleased to Meet Me
1989 Don't Tell a Soul
1990 All Shook Down

Jonathan Richman and the Modern Lovers

1976 Modern Lovers
1977 Jonathan Richman and the Modern Lovers
Rock 'n' Roll with the Modern Lovers
1978 Modern Lovers Live
1979 Back in Your Life
1983 Jonathan Sings!
1985 Rockin' and Romance
1986 It's Time for Jonathan Richman and the Modern Lovers
1988 Modern Lovers 88
1989 Jonathan Richman
1990 Jonathan Goes Country
1991 Having a Party with Jonathan Richman
1992 I, Jonathan
1993 Jonathan, Te Vas a Emocionar!
1995 You Must Ask the Heart
1996 Surrender to Jonathan
1998 I'm So Confused
2001 Her Mystery Not of High Heels and Eye Shadow
2004 Not So Much to be Loved as to Love

The Rolling Stones

1964 England's Newest Hitmakers
1965 The Rolling Stones, Now!
Out of Our Heads
December's Children and Everybody's
1966 Aftermath
1967 Between the Buttons
1967 Flowers
Their Satanic Majesties Request
1968 Beggars Banquet
1969 Let It Bleed
1971 Sticky Fingers
1972 Exile on Main Street
1973 Goats Head Soup
1974 It's Only Rock 'n' Roll
1976 Black and Blue
1978 Some Girls
1980 Emotional Rescue
1981 Tattoo You
1983 Undercover
1986 Dirty Work
1989 Steel Wheels
1994 Voodoo Lounge
1997 Bridges to Babylon
2005 A Bigger Bang

The Ronettes

1964 Present the Fabulous Ronettes Featuring Veronica
1965 The Ronettes

Roxy Music

1972 Roxy Music
1973 For Your Pleasure
Stranded
1974 Country Life
1975 Siren
1979 Manifesto
1980 Flesh and Blood
1982 Avalon

Santana

1969 Santana
1970 Abraxas
1971 Santana III
1972 Caravanserai
1973 Welcome
1974 Borboletta
1974 Greatest Hits
1975 Lotus
1976 Amigos
Festival
1977 Moonflower
1978 Inner Secrets
1979 Marathon
1981 Zebop!
1982 Shangó
1985 Beyond Appearances
1987 Freedom
1990 Spirits Dancing in the Flesh
1992 Milagro
1993 Sacred Fire: Live in South America
1994 Brothers
1999 Supernatural
2002 Shaman
2005 All That I Am

The Sex Pistols

1977 Never Mind the Bollocks, Here's the Sex Pistols

1980 The Great Rock 'n' Roll Swindle

The Shangri-Las

1964 Leader of the Pack
1965 Shangri-Las-65

Simon and Garfunkel

1964 Wednesday Morning: 3 A.M.
1966 Sounds of Silence
1966 Parsley, Sage, Rosemary and Thyme
1967 The Graduate Original Soundtrack
1968 Bookends
1970 Bridge over Troubled Water

Sly and the Family Stone

1967 A Whole New Thing
1968 Dance to the Music
1968 Life
1969 Stand!
1971 There's a Riot Goin' On
1973 Fresh
1974 Small Talk
1975 High on You
1976 Heard Ya Missed Me, Well I'm Back
1979 Back on the Right Track
1983 Ain't But the One Way
2003 Live at the Fillmore East 1968

Patti Smith

1975 Horses
1976 Radio Ethiopia
1978 Easter
1979 Wave
1988 Dream of Life
1996 Gone Again
1997 Peace and Noise
2000 Gung Ho
2004 Trampin'
2007 Twelve

The Smiths

1984 The Smiths
1985 Meat is Murder
1986 The Queen is Dead
1987 Strangeways, Here We Come

Bruce Springsteen

1973 Greetings from Asbury Park, N.J.
1973 The Wild, the Innocent and the E Street Shuffle
1975 Born to Run
1978 Darkness on the Edge of Town
1980 The River
1982 Nebraska
1984 Born in the U.S.A.
1987 Tunnel of Love
1992 Human Touch
1992 Lucky Town
1995 The Ghost of Tom Joad
2002 The Rising
2005 Devils & Dust
2006 We Shall Overcome: The Seeger Sessions

Steely Dan

1972 Can't Buy a Thrill
1973 Countdown to Ecstasy
1974 Pretzel Logic
1975 Katy Lied
1976 The Royal Scam
1977 Aja
1980 Gaucho
2000 Two Against Nature
2003 Everything Must Go

Steve Miller Band

1968 Children of the Future
1968 Sailor
1969 Brave New World
1970 Your Saving Grace
Number 5
1971 Rock Love
1972 Recall the Beginning . . . A Journey from Eden
Anthology
1973 The Joker
Living in the U.S.A.
1976 Fly Like an Eagle
1977 Book of Dreams
1981 Circle of Love
1982 Abracadabra
1984 Italian X-Rays
1986 Living in the 20th Century
1988 Born 2B Blue– solo
1993 Wide River

T. Rex

As Tyrannosaurus Rex

1968 My People Were Fair and Had Sky in Their Hair . . . but Now They're Content to Wear Stars on Their Brows
1968 Prophets, Seers & Sages – The Angels of the Ages
1969 Unicorn
1970 A Beard of Stars

As T. Rex

1970 T. Rex
1971 Electric Warrior
1972 Bolan Boogie
The Slider
1973 Tanx
1974 Zinc Allow and the Hidden Riders of Tomorrow
Light of Love
1975 Bolan's Zip Gun
1976 Futuristic Dragon
1977 Dandy in the Underworld

Talking Heads

1977 Taking Heads: 77
1978 More Songs About Buildings and Food
1979 Fear of Music
1980 Remain in Light
1982 The Name of This Band is Talking Heads
1983 Speaking in Tongues
1984 Stop Making Sense
1985 Little Creatures
1986 True Stories
1988 Naked

Television

1977 Marquee Moon
1978 Adventure
1982 The Blow-up, recorded live
1992 Television

Traffic

1967 Mr. Fantasy
1968 Traffic
1969 Last Exit
1970 John Barleycorn Must Die
1971 The Low Spark of High Heeled Boys
1973 Shoot Out at the Fantasy Factory
1974 When the Eagle Flies
1994 Far From Home

Ike and Tina Turner

1960 The Soul of Ike and Tina Turner
1961 The Sound of Ike and Tina Turner
1962 Dance with Ike & Tina Turner & Their Kings of Rhythm Band
1963 Don't Play Me
Cheap Dynamite
It's Gonna Work Out Fine
Please Please Please
1965 Ohh Poo Pah Doo
1966 River Deep – Mountain High
1966 Ike & Tina Turner and The Raelettes
1969 Outta Season
1969 Fantastic
Get It Together
Her Man His Woman
The Hunter
1970 On Stage
1971 Workin' Together
'Nuff Said
Something's Got a Hold on Me
Funkier Than a Mosquitos Tweeter
1972 Feel Good
1973 Let Me Touch Your Mind
Nutbush City Limits
1974 Strange Fruit
Sweet Rhode Island Red
The Gospel According to Ike and Tina
The Great Album
1977 Delilah's Power
1979 Airwaves

U2

1980 Boy
1981 October
1983 War
1984 The Unforgettable Fire
1987 The Joshua Tree
1988 Rattle and Hum
1991 Achtung Baby
1993 Zooropa
1997 Pop
2000 All That You Can't Leave Behind
2004 How to Dismantle an Atomic Bomb

Van Halen

1978 Van Halen
1979 Van Halen II
1980 Women and Children First
1981 Fair Warning
1982 Diver Down
1984 1984
1986 5150
1988 OU812
1991 For Unlawful Carnal Knowledge
1991 Balance 1995
1998 Van Halen III

The Velvet Underground

1967 The Velvet Underground and Nico
1968 White Light/White Hear
1969 The Velvet Underground
1970 Loaded

Tom Waits

1973 Closing Time
1974 Heart of Saturday Night
1975 Nighthawks at the Diner
1976 Small Change
1977 Foreigh Affairs
1978 Blue Valentine
1980 Heartattack and Vine
1982 One From the Heart
1983 Swordfishtrombones
1985 Rain Dogs
1987 Franks Wild Years
1988 Big Time
1992 Night on Earth
1992 Bone Machine
1993 The Black Rider
1999 Mule Variations
2002 Blood Money
Alice
2004 Real Gone
2006 Orphans: Brawlers, Bawlers & Bastards

Weezer

1994 Weezer
1996 Pinkerton
2001 Weezer
2002 Maladroit
2005 Make Believe

The White Stripes

1999 The White Stripes
2000 De Stijl
2001 White Blood Cells
2003 Elephant
2005 Get Behind Me Satan
2007 Icky Thump

The Who

1965 The Who Sings My Generation
1966 Happy Jack
1967 The Who Sell Out
1969 Tommy
1970 Live at Leeds
1971 Who's Next
1973 Quadrophenia
1975 The Who By Numbers
1978 Who Are You
1981 Face Dances
1982 It's Hard
2006 Endless Wire

Wilco

1995 A.M.
1996 Being There
1998 Mermaid Avenue (with Billy Bragg)
1999 Summerteeth
2000 Mermaid Avenue II (with Billy Bragg)
2002 Yankee Hotel Foxtrot
2003 Down with Wilco with the Minus Five
2004 A Ghost Is Born
2007 Sky Blue Sky

Stevie Wonder

1962 The Jazz Soul of Little Stevie Wonder
1963 Recorded Live: The 12 Year Old Genius
1965 Up-Tight
1966 Down to Earth
1967 I Was Made to Love Her
1968 Someday at Christmas
Eivets Rednow
For Once in My Life
1969 My Cherie Amour
1970 Signed, Sealed, and Delivered
1971 Where I'm Coming From
1972 Music of My Mind
Talking Book
1973 Innervisions
1974 Fulfillingness' First Finale
1976 Songs in the Key of Life
1979 Journey Through the Secret Life of Plants
1980 Hotter than July
1982 Stevie Wonder's Original Musiquarium
1984 The Woman in Red Soundtrack
1985 In Square Circle
1987 Characters
1991 Jungle Fever
1995 Conversation Peace
Natural Wonder
2005 A Time to Love

Neil Young

with Buffalo Springfield

1966 Buffalo Springfield
1967 Buffalo Springfield Again
1968 Last Time Around

with Crosby, Stills, Nash and Young

1970 Déjà Vu
1971 Four Way Street
1988 American Dream reunion album

solo

1968 Neil Young
1969 Everybody Knows This is Nowhere (with Crazy Horse)
1970 After the Gold Rush
1972 Harvest
1973 Time Fades Away
1974 On the Beach
1975 Tonight's the Night
Zuma with Crazy Horse
1977 American Stars 'N Bars
1978 Comes a Time
1979 Rust Never Sleeps (with Crazy Horse)
1980 Hawks & Doves
1981 Re-ac-tor (with Crazy Horse)
1982 Trans
1983 Everybody's Rockin' (with the Shocking Pinks)
1985 Old Ways
1986 Landing on Water
1987 Life with Crazy Horse
1988 This Note's for You (with the Bluenotes)
1989 Freedom
1990 Ragged Glory (with Crazy Horse)
1992 Harvest Moon
1994 Sleeps with Angels (with Crazy Horse)
1995 Mirror Ball (with Pearl Jam)
1996 Broken Arrow (with Crazy Horse)
2000 Silver & Gold
2002 Are You Passionate? (with Booker T. & the M.G.'s)
2003 Greendale (with Crazy Horse)
2005 Prairie Wind
2006 Living with War

Frank Zappa

1966 Freak Out!
1967 Absolutely Free 1967
1968 We're Only in It for the Money
1968 Lumpy Gravy
Cruising with Ruben & the Jets
1969 Uncle Meat
Hot Rats
1970 Burnt Weeny Sandwich
Weasels Ripped My Flesh
Chunga's Revenge
1971 Fillmore East—June 1971
200 Motels
1972 Just Another Band from L.A.
Waka/Jawaka
The Grand Wazoo
1973 Over-Nite Sensation
1974 Apostrophe '
Roxy & Elsewhere
1975 One Size Fits All
Bongo Fury
1976 Zoot Allures
1978 Zappa in New York
Studio Tan
1979 Sleep Dirt
Sheik Yerbouti
Orchestral Favorites
Joe's Garage
1981 Tinsel Town Rebellion
Shut Up 'n Play Yer Guitar
You Are What You Is
1982 Ship Arriving Too Late to Save a Drowning Witch
1983 The Man from Utopia
Baby Snakes
London Symphony Orchestra, Vol. 1
1984 Boulez Conducts Zappa: The Perfect Stranger
Them or Us October 18,1984
Thing-Fish
Francesco Zappa
1985 Frank Zappa Meets the Mothers of Prevention

Bibliography

1986	Does Humor Belong in Music?
	Jazz from Hell
1987	London Symphony Orchestra, Vol. 2
1988	Guitar
	Broadway the Hard Way
1991	The Best Band You Never Heard in Your Life
	Make a Jazz Noise Here
	Beat the Boots
1992	Beat the Boots II
	Playground Psychotics
1993	Ahead of Their Time
1993	The Yellow Shark with Ensemble Modern

ZZ Top

1971	ZZ Top's First Album
1972	Rio Grande Mud
1973	Tres Hombres
1975	Fandango!
1977	Tejas
1979	Degüello
1981	El Loco
1983	Eliminator
1985	Afterburner
1990	Recycler
1994	Antenna
1996	Rhythmeen
1999	XXX
2003	Mescalero

Books

Azerrad, Michael. *Our Band Could Be Your Life: Scenes from the American Indie Underground 1981–1991*. New York: Little Brown, 2001.

———. *Come As You Are: The Story of Nirvana*. London: Virgin Books, reissue paperback, 1993.

Bangs, Lester. *Psychotic Reactions and Carberator Dung*. New York: Knopf, 1987.

Bockris, Victor. *Patti Smith: An Unauthorized Biography*. New York: Simon & Schuster, 1999.

Booth, Stanley. *The True Adventures of the Rolling Stones*. New York: Vintage Books, 1985.

Cooper, Kim, and David Smay, eds. *Lost in the Grooves: Scram's Capricious Guide to the Music You Missed*. New York: Routledge, 2004.

Des Barres, Pamela. *I'm With the Band: Confessions of a Groupie*. Chicago: Chicago Review Press, 2005.

Eisen, Jonathan, ed. *Twenty Minute Fandangos and Forever Changes: A Rock Bazaar*. New York: Vintage Books, reissue paperback, 1971.

Frith, Simon. *Sound Effects: Youth, Leisure, and the Politics of Rock 'n' Roll*. New York: Pantheon Books, 1982.

George, Nelson. *The Death of Rhythm & Blues*. New York: Random House, 1988.

Gimarc, George. *Punk Diary 1970–1979*. New York: St. Martin's Press, 1994.

Hammond, John. *John Hammond on Record: An Autobiography*. New York: Penguin, 1981.

Klosterman, Chuck. *Killing Yourself to Live: 85% of a True Story*. New York: Scribner, 2006.

Marcus, Greil. *Mystery Train: Images of America in Rock 'n' Roll Music*. New York: Dutton, reissue paperback, 1982.

McKeen, William. *Rock and Roll Is Here to Stay: An Anthology*. New York: W.W. Norton & Company, 2000.

The New Rolling Stone Encyclopedia of Rock & Roll. New York: Rolling Stone Press, updated 2001.

Presley, Priscilla Beaulieu, and Sandra Harmon. *Elvis and Me*. New York: Putnam, 1985.

Priore, Domenic. *Look! Listen! Vibrate! Smile!* San Francisco: First Last Gasp Printing, 1995.

Ramone, Dee Dee. *Lobotomy: Surviving the Ramones*. New York: Thundermouth Press, 1997.

Ribowsky, Mark. *He's a Rebel: Phil Spector, Rock and Roll's Legendary Producer*. Cambridge, MA: Da Capo Press, 2007.

Russell, Ethan A. *Dear Mr. Fantasy: Diary of a Decade*. New York: Houghton Mifflin, 1985.

Sheffield, Rob. *Love Is a Mix Tape: Life and Loss, One Song at a Time*. New York: Crown, 2007.

Spitz, Robert Stephen. *The Making of Superstars: Artists and Executives of the Rock Business*. New York: Anchor Press/Doubleday, 1978.

Spungen, Deborah. *And I Don't Want to Live This Life: A Mother's Story of Her Daughter's Murder*. New York: Ballantine Books, 1996.

Tosches, Nick. *Unsung Heroes of Rock 'n' Roll: The Birth of Rock in the Wild Years Before Elvis*. Da Capo, 2005.

Willis, Ellen. *Beginning to See the Light: Pieces of a Decade*. New York: Knopf, 1967.

Films

The Devil and Daniel Johnston. Sony Pictures.

Bob Dylan—Don't Look Back. New Video Group.

Festival Express. New Line Home Video.

The Last Waltz. MGM.

Monterey Pop. Criterion.

Woodstock—3 Days of Peace & Music (The Director's Cut). Warner Home Video.

Web Sites

All Music Guide
www.allmusicguide.com

Recording Industry Association of America
www.riaa.com

Rock and Roll Hall of Fame
www.rockhall.com

Rock's Backpages Library
www.rocksbackpages.com

Trouser Press Guide
www.trouserpress.com

ACKNOWLEDGMENTS

Thanks to Ward Calhoun, an excellent editor who inspired us to write at a brisk pace. Thanks for contributions from Lisa Purcell, Suzanne Lander and everyone else at Hylas. Special shoutouts to Chris Carroll, David Marshall, Kristine McKenna, Jon Vesey, Ken Beck, Mark Lipsitz, Jeff Calder, John Flansburgh, Andy Krikun, Melanie Rock and Ike Kitman. Thanks also to Ellie Kitman, for her patience, and to Gail, Jeff, and Chris—the members of Updike—for rock and roll inspiration.

Picture Credits

The following abbreviation is used: RF—Redferns

7 PB/RF **8** Mick Hutson/RF **9** Mick Hutson/RF **10** GAB Archives/RF **11** RB/RF **12** GAB Archives/RF **13** RB/RF **13** Gems/RF **14-15** Tom Hanley/RF **16** Fiona Adams/RF **17** Cummings Archives/RF **18** Rob Verhorst/RF **19** Petra Niemeier/RF **20** GAB Archives/RF **21** Richard Upper/RF **21** Donna Santisi/RF **22** Phil Dent/RF **23** Debi Doss/RF **24** David Redfern/RF **24** Paul Bergen/RF **25** Harry Goodwin/RF **26** Cyrus Andrews/RF **27** RB/RF **28** Vitaliano Napolitano/RF **29** GAB Archives/RF **29** GAB Archives/RF **30** Ebet Roberts/RF **31** Ilpo Musto/RF **32** Richard E Aaron/RF **33** Bob King/RF **33** Chris Gabrin/RF **34** GAB Archives/RF **35** Ebet Roberts/RF **36** Mike Hutson/RF **37** David Redfern/RF **37** Ebet Roberts/RF **38** Jan Persson/RF **39** Gunter Zint/RF **40** Val Wilmel/RF **41** Ebet Roberts/RF **42** Fiona Adams/RF **43** Ebet Roberts/RF **44** RB/RF **45** David Redfern/RF **46** RB/RF **47** Clayton Call/RF **48** Mick Hutson/RF **49** GAB Archives/RF **50** Barry Levine/RF **50** GAB Archives/RF **51** Robert Knight/RF **52** GAB Archives/RF **53** John Rodgers/RF **54** GAB Archives/RF **55** Robert Knight/RF **56** Ebet Roberts/RF **56** Gna/RF **57** GAB Archives/RF **58** RB/RF **59** Richard E Aaron/RF **60** GAB Archives/RF **61** Paul Bergen/RF **61** David Redfern/RF **62** Fin Costello/RF **63** GAB Archives/RF **63** Dick Barnatt/RF **64** Ian Dickson/RF **65** Richi Howell/RF **66** Gems/RF **67** RB/RF **68** Gems/RF **69** GAB Archives/RF **70** GAB Archives/RF **71** GAB Archives/RF **72** Fin Costello/RF **73** Tony Russell/RF **74** GAB Archives/RF **75** David Warner Ellis Photography/RF **76** Gems/RF **77** Gunter Zint/RF **78** Christina Radish/RF **79** Mick Hutson/RF **80** Nicky J. Sims/RF **80** Paul Bergen/RF **81** Robert Knight/RF **82** GAB Archives/RF **83** Ebet Roberts/RF **84** Robert Knight/RF **85** John Rodgers/RF **86** Clayton Call/RF **87** GAB Archives/RF **88** GAB Archives/RF **89** RB/RF **90** GAB Archives/RF **91** GAB Archives/RF **92** GAB Archives/RF **92** GAB Archives/RF **93** Fin Costello/RF **94** Richard E Aaron/RF **95** Mick Hutson/RF **95** Peter Pakvis/RF **96** Richard E Aaron/RF **97** Carey Brandon/RF **98** Gai Terrell/RF **99** Richard E Aaron/RF **99** Richard E Aaron/RF **100** Ebet Roberts/RF **101** Ebet Roberts/RF **102** Ebet Roberts/RF **103** GAB Archives/RF **104** Jon Hopkins/RF **105** Paul Bergen/RF **105** David Redfern/RF **106** Robert Vincett/RF **107** Jorgen Angel/RF **108** Peter Pakvis/RF **109** Richard E Aaron/RF **110** Gems/RF **111** David Redfern/RF **112** RB/RF **112** Tabatha Fireman/RF **113** GAB Archives/RF **114** Mick Gold/RF **115** Stephen Wright/RF **116** Richard E Aaron/RF **117** Fin Costello/RF **118** GAB Archives/RF **119** Jim Sharpe/RF **120** David Warner Ellis Photography/RF **121** Jan Persson/RF **122** Keith Morris/RF **123** GAB Archives/RF **124** Ebet Roberts/RF **124** Ebet Roberts/RF **125** Richard E Aaron/RF **126** Petra Niemeier/RF **127** GAB Archives/RF **128** George Chin/RF **129** Paul Bergen/RF **130** Ebet Roberts/RF **131** GAB Archives/RF **132** Ebet Roberts/RF **132** Ebet Roberts/RF **133** Paul Bergen/RF **134** Ebet Roberts/RF **135** Paul Bergen/RF **136** GAB Archives/RF **137** Chris Morphet/RF **137** David Warner Ellis Photography/RF **138** Patrick Ford/RF **139** Phil Dent/RF **140** Lorne Resnick/RF **141** GAB Archives/RF **141** Gems/RF **142** RB/RF **143** Robert Knight/RF